ELIZABETH RUSCH

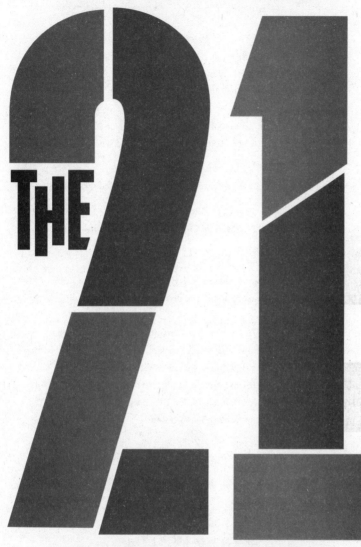

THE 21

THE TRUE STORY OF THE YOUTH WHO SUED THE U. S. GOVERNMENT OVER CLIMATE CHANGE

GREENWILLOW BOOKS

An Imprint of HarperCollins *Publishers*

Library of Congress Cataloging-in-Publication Data is available.
ISBN 978-0-06-322085-0 (hardcover)
23 24 25 26 27 LBC 5 4 3 2 1
First Edition

Greenwillow Books

For the 21
and all young climate warriors

There is no better gift a society can give children
than the opportunity to grow up safe and free,
[with] the chance to pursue whatever dreams they may have.
Our Constitution guarantees that freedom.
—U.S. Supreme Court Chief Justice John Roberts

THE 21 YOUTH PLAINTIFFS IN *JULIANA V. UNITED STATES*

(In order of appearance. Age and hometown at the time the case was filed.)

Jayden Foytlin, 12, Rayne, Louisiana, whose home flooded.

Xiuhtezcatl (pronounced shu-TEZ-caht) Martinez, 15, Boulder, Colorado, who is an Indigenous anti-fracking activist and hip-hop musician. Also lead plaintiff in the Colorado state case.

Jaime Butler, 14, Flagstaff, Arizona, who was driven off her Navajo Reservation by lack of water from drought. Also lead plaintiff in the Arizona state case.

Kelsey Juliana, 19, Eugene, Oregon, the oldest and first-named plaintiff, who mentors younger activists. Also, a plaintiff in the Oregon state case.

Zealand Bell, 11, Eugene, Oregon, whose sports participation is threatened by heat and whose mother's ski resort job is threatened by lack of snow.

Hazel van Ummersen, 11, Eugene, Oregon, who suffered two bouts of heat exhaustion due to extreme temperatures.

Avery McRae, 10, Eugene, Oregon, animal lover and swimmer whose favorite rivers and lakes are drying up.

Sahara (pronounced sa-HAIR-a) **Valentine**, 11, Eugene, Oregon, who is shy and athletic and suffers from asthma.

Nathan Baring, 15, Fairbanks, Alaska, a Quaker who fears the chaos climate change has brought to Alaska and will bring to the world.

Sharon Baring, Nathan's mom

Levi Draheim, 8, Satellite Beach, Florida, youngest plaintiff, whose home island will likely be submerged by rising seas in his lifetime.

Leigh-Ann Draheim, Levi's mom

Isaac Vergun, 13, Beaverton, Oregon, an outgoing, optimistic advocate for people of color, who is also an athlete suffering from asthma.

Miko (pronounced me-ko) **Vergun**, 14, Beaverton, Oregon, was born in the Marshall Islands, which will be lost to sea-level rise. She and Isaac were adopted by American parents.

Jacob Lebel, 18, Roseburg, Oregon, whose family farm is threatened by drought, heat, and wildfires.

Alex Loznak, 18, Kellogg, Oregon, is a member of the seventh generation to grow up on his family farm. He's interested in a law career.

Miriam Oommen, 18, Eugene, Oregon, writes music and participates in direct actions to slow fossil fuel development.

Tia Hatton, 18, Bend, Oregon, who is a competitive Nordic skier facing dwindling snowpack and asthma.

Journey Zephier, 15, Kauai, Hawaii, is a descendant of Indigenous chiefs and is threatened by sea-level rise, food insecurity, and severe flooding.

Nic Venner, 14, Lakewood, Colorado, is a neurodivergent outdoor enthusiast who sees their beloved forests destroyed by drought, insect infestations, and wildfires.

Vic Barrett, 16, White Plains, New York, who is threatened by weather disasters and rising seas.

Sophie Kivlehan, 16, Allentown, Pennsylvania, who has missed school due to severe weather events. She is also the granddaughter of former NASA climate scientist James Hansen.

Aji Piper, 15, Seattle, Washington, who is a songwriter exposed to wildfire smoke, toxins in local seafood, and severe climate stress.

LAWYERS FOR THE YOUTH PLAINTIFFS

(in order of appearance)
Julia Olson, Our Children's Trust
Andrea Rodgers, Our Children's Trust
Philip Gregory, pro bono private attorney working with Our Children's Trust

THE DEFENDANTS AND THEIR LAWYERS

President Barack Obama and his administration
Sean Duffy, U.S. Department of Justice attorney
Fossil fuel industry representatives (intervenors)
Quin Sorenson, private attorney
(And five other private attorneys)

President Donald Trump and his administration

Sean Duffy, U.S. Department of Justice attorney

Eric Grant, Deputy Assistant Attorney General, U.S. Department of Justice

Jeffrey Clark, Assistant Attorney General, U.S. Department of Justice

(And fourteen more U.S. Department of Justice attorneys)

President Joseph Biden and his administration

Sean Duffy, U.S. Department of Justice attorney

Attorney General Merrick Garland

Solicitor General Elizabeth Prelogar

(A number of other U.S. Department of Justice attorneys have also been involved.)

THE FEDERAL JUDGES AND JUSTICES

U.S. District Court

Eugene, Oregon

Thomas Coffin

Ann Aiken

U.S. Ninth Circuit Court of Appeals

San Francisco, California, panel

Sidney Thomas

Marsha Berzon

Alex Kozinski

Michelle Friedland

U.S. Ninth Circuit Court of Appeals

Portland, Oregon, panel

Mary Murguia

Andrew Hurwitz

Josephine Staton, sitting by designation

U.S. Supreme Court Justices

Anthony Kennedy

John Roberts

Elena Kagan

CONTENTS

PART II

Will the Youth Get a Trial?

PART III

Can the Youth Resurrect Their Case—and Save the Planet?

PART IV

Do Young People Have a Constitutional Right to a Stable Climate?

PART I

Can a Lawsuit Alter the Course of Climate Change?

August 2016

At 5:00 a.m. on August 13, 2016, 13-year-old Jayden Foytlin of Rayne, Louisiana, bolted upright in her bed.

Bam. Bam. "Wake up! WAKE UP!"

Jayden had been deep asleep when her sisters Erin and Grace banged on her bedroom door.

"It's coming from your room!" they yelled.

Jayden spun around to get up, and when she put her feet down, she found herself ankle-deep in water. Shocked, she rushed to the door and flung it open. Water gushed out.

The small, mostly flat, coastal-prairie town of Rayne lies about fifty miles from the Gulf of Mexico. Lush and green, the area's natural ponds and waterlogged rice and crawfish fields dotted the landscape. But Jayden's neighborhood of quiet streets had never flooded before.

Now water spread throughout the house, surrounding furniture. Toys floated around. "It's like a pool in here, Jayden!" her little brother cried.

The siblings called their mom in a panic.

More than twenty inches of rain had fallen on southern Louisiana in just forty-eight hours. Because their town had never flooded before, Jayden's mom had thought it was safe to go to a neighboring town to help pile sandbags around friends' and families' houses. Now she didn't know how or when she would get home. Rushing water covered the roads, stranding cars and trucks.

Jayden's mom told the kids to shove everything they could find—towels, pillowcases, boards—under the doors leading to the outside. Jayden and her siblings rushed around in soggy socks, but the floodwaters kept oozing in and seeping up through the foundation and carpet. Fearing electrocution, the kids ran around unplugging electronics.

Then the toilets, sinks, and bathtubs began overflowing with sewage. The smelly, orangish brown sludge flowed down the hallway to the bedrooms, drenched the living room, and coated the kitchen floor. Jayden was terrified.

Southern Louisiana had been hit by a thousand-year flood—a massive flood predicted to happen only once every thousand years. But something awful was going on. In the last two years, the United States had suffered *eight* five-hundred-year floods and *five* additional thousand-year floods. And now this.

The U.S. government knew such disasters would happen. They knew that the planet was warming from the burning of fossil fuels, whose emissions trapped heat like a greenhouse. They knew that rising ocean and air temperatures increased evaporation. They knew that at warmer temperatures, air and clouds held more moisture, triggering heavier and longer deluges of rain.

Despite this knowledge, the government did nothing to stop these heat-trapping emissions. Even worse, they actively supported the dangerous fossil fuel energy system. In fact, as Jayden and the people of Southern Louisiana suffered, President Barack Obama's administration held an auction in New Orleans to lease a section of the Gulf of Mexico roughly the size of Virginia for more oil and gas drilling.

Jayden's mom made it home that night, but the rain continued for days and the flooding for weeks. With floodwaters surrounding Jayden's house and no shelters available, the family huddled in the drenched living room. They tore out the saturated carpet, but mold crawled up the walls around them.

In the next few days, Jayden's whole family fell ill. Burning with fever, Jayden lay on a mattress on the bare concrete of their living room floor, her head pounding and her stomach roiling.

One thought helped her hold on. Her misery could be powerful evidence in the lawsuit she and twenty other young people had filed a year earlier against the U.S. government to end the climate crisis.

Would her suffering and the suffering of the other young plaintiffs convince the courts to stop the federal government from endangering their lives?

A Lawsuit Is Born
2006, Ten Years Earlier

August 2006 was sweltering in usually temperate Eugene, Oregon. Environmental lawyer Julia Olson, 35 years old and eight months pregnant, slipped into a movie theater to escape the heat. Slim and strong but with a bulging belly, she relaxed into her seat in the dark, cool theater and began to watch *An Inconvenient Truth*.

As the documentary laid out in stark detail how the burning of fossil fuels imperiled our planet, she felt a deep pit forming in her stomach and thought: *Why aren't we doing more about this?* The impacts—wildfires, droughts, rising seas—flashed before her. She pressed her palm onto her belly and began to cry. "It just hit me like a rock that we were doing something to our planet that my children and all children would have to live with and suffer through," she said.

Growing up in Colorado Springs, Colorado, Julia loved reading thrillers and fantasized about being an undercover agent with a mission to save the planet. Her family climbed 14,000-foot peaks together, and Julia always felt most alive in nature. Many in her family had careers in medicine, and Julia assumed she'd be a doctor when she grew up.

That began to change when she was 17 years old. That's when a man she didn't even know pointed an AR-15 semiautomatic weapon at a car she was sitting in and fired. Shrapnel tore through her left arm and chest, collapsing her lung. But it wasn't the week in the hospital that changed things.

Still sore and numb from surgery, Julia who was still just a teen, had to speak in court at the shooter's sentencing hearing. She was scared, vulnerable, and unprepared. "There are moments that give moral clarity to your life," she said. "That experience made me question the criminal justice and incarceration system and gun control but also got me really intrigued by the legal process. I was more interested in healing people and the planet than just sending people to prison."

Eventually, Julia turned this new interest in the law and her passion for the natural world into a career as a public interest environmental lawyer, representing nonprofits such as the Sierra Club, Wilderness Watch, and Santa Monica Baykeeper. But even though she won most cases, this piece-by-piece approach felt like playing a game of Whac-A-Mole.

Watching the devastation and chaos on the large movie screen, Julia realized she would never beat something as enormous as climate change if she didn't change her approach. She knew that "until we can have the federal government stop pushing fossil fuel energy down all of our throats and really switch us to a clean energy system, the problem is going to perpetuate."

But how could she make that happen? Was there any way to take down the whole fossil fuel energy system and address climate change quickly and all at once?

An Audacious Plan
2010-2011

Julia considered this question, brainstorming ideas with other lawyers and University of Oregon law professor Mary Wood. Professor Wood had an idea to apply a tested legal strategy to combat climate change. U.S. citizens are protected by powerful legal doctrine called the public trust, which requires that governments preserve natural resources for public use. Since the 1800s, courts have ruled that governments can't sell off or harm resources that we need to live and thrive.

Professor Wood thought the public trust doctrine could be applied to protect the atmosphere and put the brakes on fossil fuel emissions and other pollution. But she was a professor with a theory, not a lawyer who brought cases to trial.

When she and Julia met, sparks flew. Professor Wood's idea fit well with a wide-reaching approach Julia wanted to pursue. Collaborating with other lawyers, Julia wanted to prepare as many as fifty legal actions on climate change to file on the same day in states all across the country. Her team would also take on the federal government over climate change. The strategy could even go global.

All the petitions and lawsuits would represent the rights of youth. Because of their developing minds and bodies, kids were most harmed by the climate crisis. With their long lives ahead of them, they had the most to lose. They couldn't vote, so they had no power in the political system. They needed the courts to stand up for them and their right to a healthy atmosphere and stable climate.

In April 2010, Julia and her closest female friends climbed to the summit of Spencer Butte, a rocky knoll with views of the rolling coast range, the green Willamette Valley, and the snowy peaks of Mount Jefferson and the Three Sisters. As the sun softened pale gold and pink over the scene, she breathed her intention aloud.

"We're going to file cases everywhere . . ."

Julia created a nonprofit called Our Children's Trust, with three other women attorneys offering guidance as her board of directors.

One important task was identifying young people who were being affected by the climate crisis and who were passionate about making change. Julia asked for ideas from Kids Versus Global Warming, an organization founded by Alec Loorz when he was 12. How about 10-year-old Xiuhtezcatl (pronounced shu-TEZ-caht) Martinez who was fighting fracking in Boulder, Colorado? they suggested. Or Jaime Butler, age 10, who lived on a Navajo Reservation where climate-change-induced drought forced her mom to drive more than fifty miles to buy water?

Local environmental activists connected Julia with 15-year-old Kelsey Juliana of Eugene. "There's this amazing girl," they told her. "She really, really cares about the issue of climate change and does all kinds of activism."

Julia met with the interested youth, asking if they would be willing to be plaintiffs, the people who officially brought the cases, against their governments. Our Children's Trust would provide legal representation free of charge.

"Yes, I want to do that," Kelsey said. She joined 10-year-old Olivia Chernaik to sue the State of Oregon. Jaime wanted to take on Arizona, and Xiuhtezcatl signed on to be the lead plaintiff in Colorado. Kids eagerly lined up all across the country: 17-year-old Akilah Sanders-Reed of New Mexico, 18-year-old Bo Dossett of Tennessee, 13-year-old Glori Dei Filippone of Iowa, and many, many more.

At the beginning, the operation was scrappy, with law students doing the brunt of the legal work. But Julia needed big hitters, as well. The group didn't have much money—Julia wasn't even paying herself for the first six months—so she had to find lawyers who would work for free. She called every lawyer she knew and asked for volunteers. "I didn't just want environmental lawyers," she said. "I wanted trial lawyers. I wanted constitutional lawyers, people who could think outside the box."

Julia met with trial lawyer Phil Gregory when he was in town from California visiting his youngest son at the University of Oregon. He hadn't thought much about climate change, but Julia began sending him things to read and asked him about how to present the ideas in court. "She looks you in the eye and she's a force of nature," Phil said. Fascinated by the legal approach and impressed with Julia's passion, he signed on to help with the effort—for free.

Even with the most skilled attorneys and committed youth plaintiffs, the legal actions faced an uphill battle. Julia and the kids were blazing new legal ground against immensely powerful defendants. Could they prevail?

First Attempts
2011-2014

Around Mother's Day 2011, with the help of Our Children's Trust, young people from all fifty states filed petitions and complaints against their state governments. The cases asked the courts to declare that the atmosphere was a public trust resource and to order state governments to protect it from the ravages of climate change, using the best available science.

At the same time, a group of five teens led by 16-year-old Alec Loorz filed the suit *Alec L. v. McCarthy* against the federal government in federal court, with Julia and Phil representing them. The federal case made a similar public trust argument but asked the federal government in Washington, D.C., to protect the atmosphere from climate change. "Young people will be affected most by climate change and by our government's inaction," Alec told the press. "We can't vote, and we don't have money to compete with lobbyists. We do, however, have the moral authority and the legal right to insist that our future be protected."

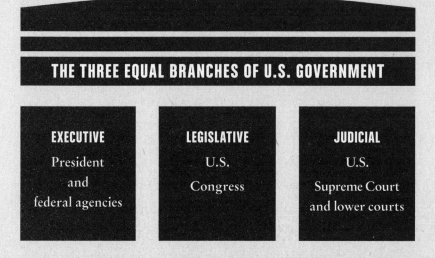

THE THREE EQUAL BRANCHES OF U.S. GOVERNMENT

EXECUTIVE	LEGISLATIVE	JUDICIAL
President and federal agencies	U.S. Congress	U.S. Supreme Court and lower courts

U.S. FEDERAL AND STATE COURT SYSTEMS

State courts handle lawsuits related to state law, and the federal courts handle issues related to federal laws, the U.S. Constitution, and disputes among states. Federal lawsuits are filed in district courts, the lowest of the three levels, also known as the trial courts. District court judges first consider whether a lawsuit is strong enough to go to trial. If it is, the district court holds a trial to decide the facts in the case and apply the law. The losing side can ask the appeals court to review district court rulings. Disagreements over the appeals court rulings are resolved in the U.S. Supreme Court. State cases can also move through lower state courts to state appellate courts to state supreme courts and ultimately the U.S. Supreme Court.

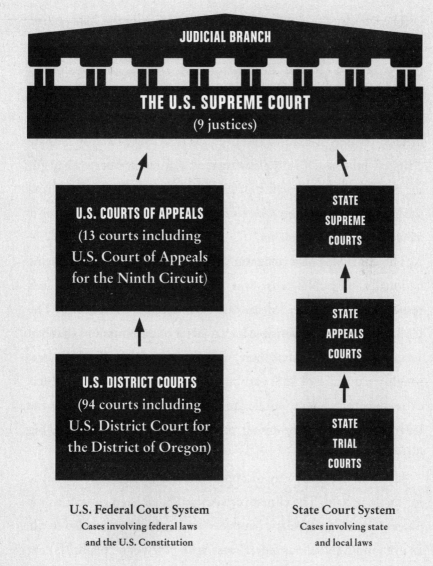

U.S. Federal Court System
Cases involving federal laws
and the U.S. Constitution

State Court System
Cases involving state
and local laws

The wheels of justice moved painfully slowly in the state courts, with cases wallowing in pretrial debates. In federal court, in 2014, they ground to a halt. A Washington, D.C., federal court dismissed the case. It was a gut punch.

"The courts didn't like the argument that the federal government, a trustee of natural resources, was *failing to act* on climate change," Julia said. "In the law there is a difference between arguing that your government has *failed to do something* and arguing the government *is doing something* unconstitutional." The latter is a much easier case to make.

The court was also reluctant to apply the public trust doctrine nationally, as public trust was more often considered a state's responsibility. But the federal case was incredibly important. The United States was responsible for a quarter of the emissions that had accumulated in the atmosphere, warming the planet. Furthermore, roughly a quarter of U.S. carbon emissions came from fossil fuels extracted from federal public lands, which were controlled by the federal government. Stopping these emissions could make a big difference.

Julia and her team were disappointed but were also in this battle for the long haul. The climate crisis would just keep getting worse unless something dramatic happened to stop it. They decided to file an even more audacious federal case with new young plaintiffs that would address both of the federal court's issues.

In the new case, they would argue that the federal government was *actively* and *knowingly* causing climate change. And they would point directly to the most important law of the land: The U.S. Constitution. The Fifth Amendment to the Constitution states that "no person shall . . . be deprived of life, liberty, or property without due process of law." Over time, this has come to mean that some rights—such as life, liberty, property—are so important that the government cannot take them away without an extremely good reason.

The government's active support of the fossil fuel system— granting permits for the drilling of gas and oil and the mining of coal and subsidizing fossil fuels for example—deprived kids of all three fundamental Constitutional rights. "In order to protect life, we need to protect . . . our children's health and welfare," Julia said. "It's about the integrity of their bodies, it's about the security of their homes and schools, [it's about] stable shorelines and the very air they breathe."

To make such a bold claim, Julia had to find young plaintiffs whose experiences demonstrated that their life, liberty, and property were threatened by climate change. The team had to find kids who would be willing to take on the president, the most powerful person in the country, as well as the whole federal government.

Julia had some ideas on where to turn first.

Life
2015

Xiuhtezcatl Martinez, the anti-fracking hip-hop warrior and lead plaintiff in the Colorado case, had attended one of the first hearings of the federal case in Washington, D.C. He was fascinated and inspired. Ultimately, his state case was dismissed, but he told Julia: "I want to be part of the next federal case." At 15, he was the first youth to sign on.

Julia had been immensely impressed and moved by other youth plaintiffs in the state cases, as well. Jaime Butler, now 14, whose family had been forced to move off their Navajo Reservation because of drought, also joined the new federal case.

Julia had come to know and deeply respect Kelsey Juliana, now 18, one of the youth plaintiffs in the ongoing lawsuit against the state of Oregon. Kelsey, who had long straight shiny brown hair and bright blue eyes, bubbled with enthusiasm and ended up doing so much more than being a plaintiff in the Oregon case. She helped Our Children's Trust organize a camp for young kids in Eugene who wanted to work on climate change. "I was so impressed by Kelsey's pure enthusiasm and her care for the younger students and her wanting to support young people," Julia said. When Julia invited her to the new federal case, Kelsey was all in.

Kelsey and Julia also reached out to some of the kids from the camp who were eager to do more: Zealand Bell, age 11, and Avery McRae, Hazel van Ummersen, and Sahara Valentine, age 10.

In some ways fifth-grader Sahara seemed an unlikely candidate to become a plaintiff in such a massive, momentous lawsuit. Slim with long brown hair, fair skin, and braces, Sahara was a shy kid, often afraid to talk to people one-on-one. "I didn't want there to be, like, an awkward silence," said Sahara. "I was really scared of awkward silences." Sahara felt better in group settings because they didn't have to talk and could rely on other people to keep the conversation going. But climate change was endangering their life and they couldn't keep quiet about it.

Sahara suffered from asthma. A few times a month, Sahara's throat closed up, making it hard to breathe. Once in the middle of the night, they woke up in the dark of their own room, unable to inhale. A great pressure, like someone was sitting on their chest, kept Sahara from breathing in. Wheezing, coughing and feeling lightheaded, they were terrified that the next breath would be their last.

They ran to their parents' room but couldn't take in enough air to tell them about the asthma attack. Sahara bumped the bed in a panic.

Their parents awoke. "Sahara, what is it? Are you okay?"

Sahara clutched their throat and their heart.

Their parents pulled them to the car. "We're going to the emergency room!"

As they stepped outside, cool, fresh air hit Sahara's face. They sucked in a deep breath. Healing air slipped into their lungs and their breathing settled down.

Whenever Sahara had an asthma attack, the best treatment was fresh, clean air. But, more frequently, fresh air was not something anyone could depend on. Summers in Oregon used to be mild. But now, 100-degree Fahrenheit heat waves and droughts were common. Pollen seasons started earlier, lasted longer, and filled the air with irritants. Worse, more-frequent and more-massive wildfires polluted the air with smoke. "I should be in control of how much I can breathe," Sahara said, "but I'm not in control, not at all."

Sahara was deeply worried about what might happen next. "My future is not guaranteed, and future generations' lives are not guaranteed." Sahara would do anything to fight climate change—even face the fear of being the center of attention.

That's why when they got an email from Julia Olson about suing the federal government over climate change, Sahara was intrigued. "I read it and understood it to some degree," they said. They asked their parents what a plaintiff was and what a lawsuit meant. "It felt like a super-cool opportunity," Sahara said. "Just what I was looking for."

Sahara knew that Avery McRae, a fourth grader from school, would be joining the suit. Avery rode horses, took care of chickens she'd named after flowers, and ran fundraisers for snow leopards, wolves, and salmon. Avery joined the suit to protect the creatures she loved and her own future.

One of Sahara's friends had already signed up. Sahara and Hazel van Ummersen were born just a day apart and their families had been close since then. "I completely trusted Hazel and Julia and knew they would have my best interests at heart," Sahara said.

Even with supportive friends, supportive family, and a supportive community, Sahara felt intimidated. "I'm just this little kid and the government is so big," Sahara said. "The whole thing felt really huge."

Liberty
2015

Julia wanted the lawsuit to reflect the "beautiful diversity of our country" and the "geography of America the beautiful," so Our Children's Trust cast its net for potential youth plaintiffs even wider.

When Nathan Baring of Fairbanks Alaska was 15, his mom Sharon got an unexpected call. Someone from the Alaska Center for the Environment told her that some kids were suing the federal government over climate change. They had read about Nathan's environmental work and wondered if he might be interested in joining as a plaintiff.

The call caught Sharon off guard. "Who are you?" she asked. "What are you talking about?"

They told her about a group called Our Children's Trust, which was organizing youth-led lawsuits to combat climate change. "I am not interested in offering up our child, our son, for somebody's else agenda," Sharon said.

As a little kid, Nathan was pale with a bowl haircut. A sensitive kid, he wasn't much good at school at first. As he got older, he started doing better academically. He also skied and was a defender for two competitive soccer clubs in Fairbanks. School and sports were helping him find his place in the world.

But Nathan, a third-generation Alaskan, was also beginning to think that his world was not stable. He had heard a University of Alaska-Fairbanks scientist talking about climate change. Alaska, he learned, was warming twice as fast as the rest of the country. Ice that used to reflect the sun's heat was melting, and the land and water left behind absorbed more heat, heating things up even more. This rapid climate change was triggering warmer, wetter winters, earlier and bigger pollen blooms, and wildfires.

As Nathan thought about how winters had changed from when he was little, he began to connect the dots. The usual cold, mostly dry winters had become much more erratic. Temperatures swung from 10 degrees Fahrenheit below zero to 35 degrees above and rainy—then plummeted again, causing freezing.

Nathan also noticed other odd things going on around him. Sinkholes—strange, dark, liquidy pits—opened up on the nearby tundra. Roads and highways slumped, buckled, and caved in. Mud underground created bulges that slid down hillsides, sometimes bursting and threatening buildings, roads, and bridges. "If you have eyes and you walk out your back door, you can see the changes that have taken place over only my short childhood," Nathan said.

The phenomena Nathan witnessed was due to melting permafrost. Permafrost is soil, rock, and sand held together by ice that stays frozen all year long. Officially, an area must stay frozen for two years to qualify as permafrost. But the permafrost underlying *85 percent of Alaska* had been frozen harder than concrete for thousands of years. Because of climate change, 40 percent of the world's permafrost could thaw by the end of the century.

The more Nathan learned about climate change, the more worried he became. And not just about his hometown. Wildfires in the western region of the United States were getting bigger and lasting longer. Drought was drying up huge areas. Lack of snow in the Rockies threatened the Colorado River, which provided water for sixty million people. The ocean was becoming more acidic. Ocean acidification endangered marine species, which provided food for more than a billion people. Warming waters also threatened fish, especially in Alaska, which was home to one of the last major wild fisheries on earth. Other food supplies could be massively disrupted, too. "People become crazy and do desperate things when they don't have basic things like food and water," Nathan said. "It feels like we're all stuck in a simulated game right now, and everything points to this game not ending well." When chaos became the norm, Nathan wondered, what does that do to your options in life?

Nathan's mom knew how much Nathan worried about his future. She also knew that he had been trying to speak out about it, testifying to the city council and meeting with state legislators. People listened but their responses were patronizing. "It had that pat, pat, pat on the head quality, like 'I'm glad you're learning about the legislative process. Now go back to school,'" she said.

That's why she didn't immediately hang up on the call about the lawsuit.

The caller told her about Our Children's Trust's state lawsuits. Then it clicked. Sharon had recently watched Bill Moyers interview an 18-year-old named Kelsey Juliana about a lawsuit she brought in Oregon. Sharon remembered thinking, "My gosh, this is exciting, this is so hopeful."

She did some research and noticed that Our Children's Trust's focus was not on personal gain. "There seemed to be a selfless component to it," she observed.

Still, Nathan's mother struggled over whether to mention it to Nathan. For one thing, they were Quakers, and Quakers don't look to the court system to resolve conflict—they depend on sharing and deep listening. Plus, "You don't just sue the federal government without consequences." She worried about how it would affect his life and by association their family's life. Could it affect their jobs? Could it impact his sister?

When she finally told Nathan about the federal lawsuit, he was ready to jump right in. "I am tired of people disregarding what I have to say when they are not going to live with the consequences," he told her.

And he thought the courts were a good way to go. The Constitution protected liberty, which meant having some control over your destiny. How could it be legal for the federal government to take that away by contributing to climate change? Trying to appeal to public opinion or the legislature wasn't working. Climate change cut too deep and was too uncomfortable for too many people.

If you do this, his mom told him, you will need to be all in, and be all in for the right reasons.

In Alaska, so many people's livelihoods depended on fossil fuels. Nathan's dad was a teacher, and his mom was a nurse. Taxes that paid their salaries came partially from oil production.

At least a quarter of the state's jobs were in the oil industry. One of Nathan's neighbors worked at Alyeska Pipeline. Another worked as a construction manager for a refinery. Nathan knew many people employed by petroleum, mining, and oil companies and by British Petroleum.

Some of Nathan's closest friends did not believe in climate

change. In the cafeteria, Nathan tried debating with them. He told them that almost all scientists—99 percent—agree that the burning of fossil fuels increases the amount of carbon in our atmosphere, which acts like a blanket heating the planet.

"It's a hoax," they said, or, "Oh, that is fabricated data."

He couldn't blame them. "When the only real economy we've had up here since the 1970s is oil, it's not really a matter of 'Can the data prove that climate change is real?' It's, 'Who is going to be here for us when oil is gone? What are we going to do? How are we going to live?'"

Still, when his mom talked to him about the lawsuit, he was excited. He was going to sue the federal government! This was the way to make sure everyone took young people's futures seriously.

His mom wanted him to slow down, to really think it through. She suggested he meet with a Clearness Committee. In this Quaker tradition, the group of younger and older adults from the community would gather to ask Nathan questions, to make sure he was clear about what suing the federal government meant, how long it might take, and how long it could affect his life.

When the group met, Nathan told them about the suit. The members could see he was excited.

"Where is this fire coming from?" one asked.

"I've marched, I've lobbied in the state capitol, I've written letters to the editor," Nathan said. "I've done pretty much everything that is available to a young person who can't vote."

The committee members nodded. They knew of his work.

"There is no incentive whatsoever for policymakers to care what young people think because we have no political power," Nathan continued.

No one could argue with that.

Nathan was getting charged up. "We are seen as parodies of our parents, like we don't have our own independent voice. And it's time. It's time to give young people a seat at the table where these energy decisions are being made especially when they're just throwing away our future."

"What values ground you in this decision?" someone asked.

Nathan had to think about that one. Stewardship, certainly. He felt called to care for the environment.

But also, community, not just in Fairbanks but the whole global community.

And justice. The people most vulnerable to the dangers of climate change often had no voice.

"How long might the lawsuit take?" someone asked.

"Umhm, maybe a year," he answered. "I guess it could be more."

"And how might it affect your life?"

He thought for a moment, taking in the curious faces around him. He considered the gravity of deciding to sue the federal government. "I guess it could change the course of my life . . ."

Life, Liberty, Property
2015

Seven-year-old Levi Draheim, an energetic kid with a springy bleached afro and lively green eyes, thought his home on a barrier island in Florida was paradise. On the east side, he had the Atlantic Ocean, white sandy beaches, and sparkling waves where he played, swam, and surfed. He even watched sea turtles laying eggs on the beach in the middle of the night. On the west side of the barrier island, on the Indian River Lagoon, Levi splashed around, paddled in a kayak, and watched wildlife with his friends.

But his home was slipping away before his eyes. The sea was rising, eroding and swallowing up the beaches around him. Even worse, he'd seen maps of the future impacts of climate change on his neighborhood. The ocean would reach his house in a few decades and would submerge it in seawater by the end of the century.

What would happen to his family and his friends? Would he ever be able to show his own kids the awesome place he grew up? Maybe, he thought, they could take a boat out and dive down to it like visiting a shipwreck.

All this haunted Levi at night. In his dreams, "the barrier island and beaches are destroyed, and I can't figure out where I am or where I should go. It's dark, and there are piles of leaves, sticks, and broken cars. I'm on the beach, and there's nobody around me. I see rubble and wonder where my family and everyone else is."

But the reality of climate change was more than just a bad dream. "I know that there is a small amount of time left to act to protect our barrier island and my home . . ." he said. "Without changes, I'm afraid I will lose my home and that my nightmares will become real."

Though only 7 years old, Levi Draheim worked on behalf of the planet and all its living creatures as if his own life depended on it. He helped sea turtles, cleaned up trash, and planted sea oats to help stabilize eroding dunes. His energy and his commitment to doing something seemed unstoppable.

One day after church, Levi's mom Leigh-Ann was talking about Levi's passion for the environment with their minister. He mentioned that Our Children's Trust was looking for kids to do some really interesting climate work.

On the phone, Julia told Leigh-Ann about their plans to sue President Obama and the federal government for their contributions to climate change. Because kids couldn't vote and because they were going to live with the impacts of climate change much longer than adults, they made especially powerful plaintiffs for the case. Would Levi be interested in joining?

Leigh-Ann had loads of questions: "What happens if we lose? What happens if we win? Would this have any impact on his permanent record, legally?" Levi was only seven, and his mother needed to know that this was legit and that he wouldn't be hurt by being involved.

Julia explained that Levi would have to make a statement about how climate change affected him. They'd file the lawsuit, have pre-trial hearings, and hopefully go to trial. If he was willing, Levi might have his deposition taken by the government and share his story on the stand. If he was interested, he could do a media interview here or there. That's about it.

Levi thought it sounded cool. "How long will it take?" he asked.

Julia and her team hoped to be ready for trial in a year.

To Levi, a year felt like "absolutely the longest time ever."

But he was over the moon about the idea. He loved talking about the environment and getting other people to care. He loved that people in court might listen and actually fix things. "I wanted to be able to tell my children, if I had children, and siblings, if I had siblings, that I did everything I could to fight for our future, that I took action in the biggest way I could."

But later that night Levi had doubts. We were just a bunch of kids, he thought. "Would people take us seriously? Would they take climate change seriously?"

His mom continued to have some concerns, too. How could this lawsuit affect Levi's childhood? How might it affect their lives? "We expected it to be just one more thing we did to help the environment like a beach cleanup or planting sea oats," said Levi's mom. "It became way, way, way, way bigger than that."

Oregon Youth Plaintiffs Meet
Spring 2015

Julia originally wanted no more than fifteen youth plaintiffs. Managing communications with clients could be difficult and time-consuming. But more kids kept stepping up. "When we got to twenty-one, I'm like, okay, that's all."

To begin developing the case, Julia invited the young plaintiffs who lived in Oregon to gather in Eugene. Siblings Isaac, 13, and Miko Vergun, 14, from Beaverton, Oregon, a suburb of Portland, wondered what it would be like to meet Julia and some of their fellow climate warriors.

For years, Isaac and Miko had been speaking at climate change events and were often the youngest ones there and often the only people of color. Both adopted at a young age by white parents, Isaac and Miko had different reasons for joining the case. Miko feared for the country where she was born, the Marshall Islands, whose five islands and twenty-nine atolls averaged just six feet above sea level. Rising seas had already toppled sea walls and flooded the capital and could swallow up whole islands by 2035. "That'd be super devastating because our people, our hearts, our soul, our being lies with the land," Miko said.

Like Sahara, Isaac suffered from asthma. It got in the way of everything he loved, running track, playing basketball, even hanging outside with his friends. Being Black made his struggles to breathe potentially more dangerous. In addition to health care inequities, African Americans suffered from worse airway inflammation and weakened responses to medicine. While an average of eleven people died of asthma every day in the United States, as a Black person, Isaac was three times more likely to die from asthma than a white teen.

"For a while, I was confused as to why I didn't see a lot more Black and brown people out being climate activists," Isaac said. After all, people of color, often denied loans to buy homes in attractive neighborhoods, were more likely to live near coal plants and be exposed to poor air quality. Then he realized that he was lucky to have the time to work on climate injustice. "Many Black and brown communities have a lot of other things to worry about like job security, violence, and over-policing," he said. "So, I try to take it upon myself to bring a Black voice to the climate movement."

Isaac and Miko traveled the two hours down to Eugene to meet up with the rest of the Oregon crew at the Friendly Street Market, a little mom-and-pop grocery. Julia brought her two kids, both younger than Isaac and Miko.

They all grabbed snacks and a table on the outdoor patio. Miko was pretty quiet but Isaac, a total extrovert, was in heaven. He chatted with upbeat Kelsey, sweet Hazel, shy Sahara, and animal-lover Avery. He asked 18-year-olds Jacob Lebel and Alex Loznak about what it was like to live on family farms. He connected with Miriam Oommen, 18, who was South Asian and had a cool folk-punk look, about music. He talked sports with Tia Hatton, 18, who was a competitive Nordic skier in Bend, and Zealand, 11, who played basketball just like he did.

It was the first time Isaac had been with a bunch of kids his own age all working on the climate crisis. For the first time, he felt a deep sense of community and belonging in the movement.

When Julia started talking about the case, her energy filled the patio. She laid out her thinking clearly and with utter respect for the kids. "A lot of times, being in middle school, I'd get treated like I didn't know anything," Isaac said. Julia was different. "She knew that we knew what we were doing, what we were signing up for. She treated us like we had the cognitive ability to think about the issues deeply but also that we weren't lawyers, we hadn't gone to law school, so she broke down all the legal jargon to make it more digestible."

She also made it clear that they all had work to do.

Building a Case
Spring and Summer 2015

Julia explained to the young activists that to have any chance of winning the lawsuit, the team had to build a really compelling case. The complaint they filed to start the lawsuit needed to grab the judges' attention. "Good lawyers are good storytellers," Julia said. "And our stories come from you, the plaintiffs."

That spring and summer, the legal team worked with all 21 young people to write up their claims. Many of the kids wanted to tell the judges how climate change affected their health. Sahara and Isaac had asthma, which endangered their lives. Miriam, Nathan, and others suffered allergies that were worsening from earlier and thicker pollen blooms. Hazel wrote about two bouts of heat exhaustion brought on by extreme temperatures.

Julia knew that as the lawsuit moved through the courts, a number of judges would read the complaint and that different stories would capture the interest of different judges. Some judges might be troubled by how drought had driven Jaime Butler off the Navajo Nation, interfering with her ability to practice her Indigenous traditions. Xiuhtezcatl and 15-year-old Hawaiian Journey Zephier were also Indigenous youth hurt personally and culturally by climate change.

Outdoor-enthusiast judges might identify with the loss of

31

backpacking opportunities suffered by 14-year-old Nic Venner in Colorado; the loss of Nordic ski opportunities for Nathan and Tia; the loss of clean and full rivers and lakes for Avery, who loved to swim. Judges who had themselves endured a weather disaster might identify with Vic Barrett, 16, of New York; Jayden Foytlin, 12, of Louisiana; or Sophie Kivlehan, 16, of Pennsylvania, who had to cope with destructive hurricanes, floods, hailstorms, and tornadoes. Seafood lovers might share the worries of Kelsey and Aji Piper, 15, of Seattle, who could no longer eat or even touch shellfish from the Puget Sound when the warming waters triggered toxic algae blooms. Judges with business interests or connections to farming might relate to how climate change threatened the livelihoods of Zealand's mom who worked at a ski resort, or Jacob's and Alex's parents who struggled to eke out a living from family farms amid lengthening droughts and wildfire seasons.

And what judge could turn away from the reality of Levi's home going underwater? Or Miko losing her homeland forever?

Over the next few months, Julia and her team of lawyers worked hard to focus and sharpen the kids' stories. "We all had to become experts in bringing constitutional claims," said co-counsel Phil Gregory. "We had to understand our plaintiffs' experiences, position them at a constitutional level related to life, liberty, and property."

Prominent climate scientist James Hansen, who was Sophie's grandfather, signed on as a plaintiff-guardian for his granddaughter and for future generations. With his expertise he could speak to how climate change would affect young people of the future.

The team also had to present evidence that the federal government was to blame. After all, most people held the gas, coal, or oil industries responsible for emitting carbon. Julia and her team needed to show that the president and his administration controlled the nation's energy supply. They controlled permits to drill and mine and to ship fossil fuels in and out of the country. They granted permits to release gases, such as carbon dioxide, and even granted subsidies to the fossil fuel industry.

The young people were particularly outraged by the government's approval of pipelines that ran through farms, ranches, and native lands. So, the lawyers included the construction of pipelines in their descriptions of government actions causing climate change.

When the lawyers shared the draft complaint with the young plaintiffs, Nathan read the document carefully, so he would know what they were arguing and so he would be able to follow what happened next. Four key arguments resonated with him.

One: The government through its support of fossil fuels knowingly put the kids in harm's way and threatened their "personal security." Nathan's sense of security was certainly being eroded by the disruptions in winter weather, especially the bizarre ice storms that knocked out power, closed roads, felled trees and burst pipes.

Two: The government's actions promoting climate change endangered fundamental rights granted to the kids by the U.S. Constitution: life, liberty, and property. Levi, so vulnerable to climate change on his barrier island, was the perfect example, Nathan thought. Jacob and Alex had so much to lose on their family farms, too. Every plaintiff felt the erosion of these essential rights.

Three: The government was discriminating against the kids by valuing adults and the current economic benefits of burning fossil fuels more highly than the kids' lives and well-being. Clearly, investment in oil and gas projects meant more to the government than saving the forests, snow, ice, water, and permafrost Nathan and other young Americans needed to survive and thrive.

Four: The government had an obligation to protect shared resources—such as land, water, and air—now and for the future. This was the public trust claim. Yes, thought Nathan, shouldn't the government be working to protect the nation's natural resources for him and for future generations?

The lawsuit asked the court for two kinds of help, called relief. One, they wanted declaratory relief, in which a judge would declare the kids' constitutional right to a stable climate. The young people also requested injunctive relief, in which the judge would require the federal government to create a plan aimed at lowering carbon dioxide in the atmosphere to 350 parts per million, the level that science showed would stabilize the climate.

The complaint seemed exactly right to Nathan. "We are having our security and our future thrown away in front of our eyes by power-makers who are going to be dead before anything really significant happens," he said.

But he and the other youth wondered: Could this lawsuit really change the country's course on climate change?

Case Filed

August 12, 2015

On International Youth Day, August 12, 2015, Julia was ready to file the ninety-five page complaint that would kick off the new federal lawsuit. With Kelsey Juliana as the lead plaintiff, the case would be known as *Juliana v. United States.* Julia and her colleagues would represent the 21 youth from Alaska, Arizona, Colorado, Florida, Hawaii, Louisiana, Pennsylvania, New York, Oregon, and Washington State. The suit named President Barack Obama and federal agencies such as the Environmental Protection Agency and Departments of Energy and Transportation as defendants.

On filing day, some of the Oregon plaintiffs—Kelsey, Hazel, and Avery from Eugene, Alex from Kellogg, and Isaac and Miko Vergun from Beaverton—gathered in the offices of Our Children's Trust, a blue house with beige trim and lots of bike storage. The offices had a sunny, homey feel, with golden hardwood floors and a sign in the bathroom stating: "Please recycle toilet paper rolls."

Isaac couldn't help but think how unusual it was for young people to be in such a potentially powerful position. "I feel like as youth, we're never asked: What do we want or need from our government? We're always just told to do stuff and it's just like, oh, that's just how it is, you know?"

This felt so different. "This would be a big moment," he said. "We're like, no, we're not settling for 'This is just how it is.' We're going to fix it because it's going to affect us, we have a stake in it, and no one is doing anything about it. It's up to us ultimately to protect our future—now."

The kids and lawyers assembled in the conference room where a large strip of white paper taped to the walls encircled the room. There, staff had tracked with red, green, blue, and purple markers the timeline of what the government knew about climate change. Isaac walked around the room, like it was an art gallery, reading the timeline. "It gave me goosebumps," he said. "It was a combination of empowering and inspiring. It was like, 'How can we lose?' All this evidence was wrapped around us, and there were hundreds of binders of papers and articles and research. When we have this much evidence, how could we lose?"

To electronically file the complaint, the young people and their lawyers huddled around a laptop. Kelsey held Hazel on her hip so she could see as Julia set up the complaint to submit to the U.S. District Court in Eugene. They all watched intently as Julia read aloud: "Warning: Clicking the next button on the next screen commits to this transaction. You will have no further opportunity to modify the submission if you continue." She paused. "Does someone want to push the button?"

Hazel's hand shot into the air. "I do!" she called out, just as Avery said: "Yes!"

"Together?" Julia suggested.

Hazel and Avery hovered over the button, grinning.

Everyone huddled closer.

The girls clicked the button.

Everyone cheered and clapped. The girls jumped up and down and hugged.

The staff printed out the complaint and placed it into a black binder labeled "Judge's Copy." They all piled in cars and drove to the Wayne L. Morse Courthouse. Gleaming silver in the sunlight like a giant space station, the glass and steel courthouse loomed six stories high above a railway track that carried fossil fuels through town. The young people and their lawyer clambered up two concrete flights of stairs, past a large mural of the preamble of the Constitution. They made their way through security like they were in an airport and walked through the vast modern hallway with its dark-gray slate floors, their sneakers squeaking. Isaac looked around in awe, wondering if and when they would be back here for a trial.

The group strode past the offices of their U.S. senators and U.S. representatives toward the District Clerk, whose office had reception windows like some doctors' offices. Surrounded by the kids, Julia handed the binder to the clerk.

Then, they hustled out the building, grinning and barely able to believe what they had done. They huddled to take a photo on the courthouse steps. "One, two, three!" they yelled, and jumped into the air.

"I was just super elated and happy the whole entire day," Isaac said.

While the filing was a big deal to Isaac, the lawsuit didn't register much with his school and sports friends. They were more interested in the next basketball game, the release of a new sneaker, or when they were going to the mall.

Sahara didn't think much about the filing either. It was just two days after their eleventh birthday. "It passed over my head a bit," they said.

In Florida, Levi bolted off to tell his friends. "Me being a super-hyperactive kid, I was just like: Oh my gosh, this is the best thing ever, going on and on about it. Yada, yada, yada, this is so exciting, just really, really exciting."

His friends listened and nodded, not really sure what Levi was talking about.

Nathan, who was in Alaska, was all fired up, too. Soon after the filing, when CNN requested an interview, Nathan agreed to do it. "I was like, 'Oh, shit.'" But he was excited, too. "It was like, 'Oh my god, I have this crazy platform to be heard.' One minute no one wants to listen to a fifteen-year-old talk, and then next we're talking to national news outlets."

Other national media took note. Legal Planet called the lawsuit "provocative." MSNBC described it as the "first-of-its-kind." CounterPunch dubbed it "a landmark."

A Slate reporter wrote: "At first glance, the circumstances surrounding this lawsuit read like a storyline straight out of a Disney movie: On one side, a group of energetic kids, joined by a wise and genial grandfather [climate scientist James Hansen] who is fond of fedoras. On the other side, the president of the United States. Will the kids save the world?"

People wondered how far the lawsuit would get. Even the Slate reporter tempered his enthusiasm: "Whether this case gains significant traction—and more importantly, how many years it takes for this case or one like it to succeed—may well decide Americans' quality of life for generations. But just as the struggle for same-sex marriage felt hopeless until it succeeded, right now, for these kids at least, it's a long shot."

Environmental law professors across the country were even more skeptical. "I thought it was not only a little crazy but also counterproductive," said Lisa Heinzerling, professor of law at Georgetown University. "I even thought that using children as plaintiffs was gimmicky, a sort of PR stunt. And I didn't think much more about it."

Julia followed the media coverage but was more concerned about the powerful defendants. The 21 youth were represented by Our Children's Trust, which now had an annual budget of only $350,000, mostly from private donations and small grants. Their tiny team of lawyers would be up against the U.S. Department of Justice, which had almost ten thousand lawyers and budget of $27 billion.

"When you sue a government," said Phil, "it's not like they're gonna say, 'Oh my gosh, you're absolutely right! All the science is saying climate change is destroying your future, so we better do something about it.' No, they are going to assemble a lot of resources to oppose the case, to try to kick it out."

Is that what President Obama and his federal government would do?

Strange Bedfellows
2015-2016

Some observers were surprised that President Barack Obama, a Democrat, was the first named defendant in *Juliana v. United States*. Surely, people thought, he and his administration were headed in the right direction on climate change. Just weeks earlier, Obama announced his Clean Power Plan to cut carbon dioxide emissions from power plants by 32 percent by 2030. He called the effort "the biggest, most important step we've ever taken to combat climate change." And he banned offshore drilling in the Arctic.

But in his 2012 State of Union Address, Obama, who had received $2.5 million in campaign contributions from the energy sector that year, bragged about his support of fossil fuels, saying: "We've opened millions of new acres for oil and gas exploration, and tonight, I'm directing my administration to open more than 75 percent of our potential offshore oil and gas resources." True to his word, gas and oil production grew by more than 60 percent in the next few years. And by 2016, his administration had spent more than $33 billion on fossil fuel projects around the world.

This flip-flopping on climate change was a big reason the kids needed court intervention, according to climate scientist James Hansen. His declaration submitted to the court said: "In my opinion, this lawsuit is made necessary by the at-best schizophrenic, if not suicidal, nature of U.S. climate and energy policy . . . The federal government continues to permit and otherwise support industry's efforts to exploit fully our reserves of gas, coal, and oil, even in the face of increasing overwhelming evidence that our continued fossil fuel dependency . . . constitutes one of the greatest threats to our nation, human civilization and nature alike."

The government saw things differently. Jeffrey H. Wood, an attorney with the Justice Department, which would handle *Juliana*, told the *New York Times* that "this lawsuit is an unconstitutional attempt to use a single Oregon court to control the entire nation's energy and climate policy." Indeed, the government soon filed a motion to dismiss the case.

People told Julia it was hopeless and that the kids would never win.

And then, three industry groups representing hundreds of fossil fuel companies such as BP, Chevron, ExxonMobil, and Shell joined the case as intervenors. That meant that while not named as defendants, this powerful industry felt they had a stake in the outcome and wanted to join the defense. The industry groups, or intervenors, called the suit "a direct threat" to their members' businesses. They wanted to prevent "massive changes" and an "unprecedented restructuring of the economy" that could result if the 21 won.

Miko, the plaintiff fighting for the survival of the Marshall Islands, thought the intervenors might help the kids make their case. "It was really weird because on one side you'd have the government and the fossil fuel industry and on the other side you'd have us, some kids," she said. "We just had to sit back and be like, 'This is exactly what we are talking about!'"

Sharon Baring, Nathan's mom, was surprised and worried when the huge energy companies got involved. "I started realizing, holy crap. This is big. This is really, really big and they are scared," she said. "And when people are scared, they do really damaging things." She was up all night, thinking about the people who had gotten hurt while following their conscience, while working to do what is right. She realized she didn't care about their house or their land or their stuff. But would there be threats to their safety? Would there be threats to Nathan and to her daughter, who wasn't even involved in the case?

As the young people and their lawyers waited for a hearing on the motion to dismiss, the Obama administration continued to send wildly mixed signals on climate change. On December 12, 2015, the President committed the U.S. to the Paris Agreement, an international treaty on climate change that included 196 countries, nearly every nation on the planet.

But joining the Paris Agreement, while a historic move, would not likely make much of a dent in climate change. The agreement allowed the planet to warm a total of 1.5 to 2 degrees Celsius, temperature increases that scientists say are dangerous for kids and humanity. Scientists calculated that even if the world met the terms of the agreement, the planet would warm 2.7 degrees Celsius, which is 5 degrees Fahrenheit. Furthermore, the limits set for each country were just pledges those countries would try to hit. There was nothing to ensure that anyone would actually attain them. The United States had no legal obligation to comply.

Days later, President Obama signed a bill ending a forty-plus-year-old ban on crude (unrefined) oil exports. The American fossil fuel industry, which lobbied heavily for the measure, could now ramp up oil production and lay pipelines and railroad tracks to move it and sell it overseas.

The impact of this change was stunning. It was the carbon equivalent of opening forty-two coal burning plants at a time when climate scientists said that much of the world's oil needed to stay buried if we had any hope of saving the planet.

All this made Julia and the kids even more eager to move past the initial pleadings and motion stages and get to trial. "We'll have the best facts and the best experts testifying in a court of law about what is really happening and what is, as we currently understand it, the maximum level of CO_2 we should have in order to preserve our fundamental rights," Julia said. "It'll be huge."

But they faced a long road to trial. *Juliana v. United States* was currently in the district court in Eugene, Oregon, where Magistrate Judge Thomas Coffin would rule on pretrial motions like this motion to dismiss. District Court Judge Ann Aiken would likely need to approve his ruling. Even if the judges did not dismiss *Juliana*, the kids faced a long process called "discovery," where both sides had to share information about witnesses and evidence they wanted to present at trial.

What would happen with the case, no one could guess. Creative lawyering had triumphed in landmark cases like *Brown v. Board of Education,* which desegregated schools, and *Obergefell v. Hodges,* which established the right to same-sex marriage. "Cases like this are brave attempts to reform or extend the legal system into new areas, so it's innovative and risky at the same time," said Jonathan Cannon, a professor at the University of Virginia School of Law.

But the stakes were high. University of Oregon professor Mary Wood put it this way: "The planet is on the docket."

Meet the Plaintiffs
March 2016

The first hearing, on the government's motion to dismiss *Juliana*, was nearing. It would be the first time all 21 young plaintiffs gathered with their lawyers in court.

Nathan's mom drove him to the Fairbanks airport for his trip to Eugene, Oregon. She couldn't help but think how strange it was that her 16-year-old son was involved in a lawsuit against the federal government. She realized: "I'm trusting these people that I've never met. I'm trusting that he'll be cared for."

When she got home, she headed out for a walk. Their neighborhood was near the airport so she could hear the roar of Nathan's plane taking off. "There he goes." Her heart ached. "He's so beyond my wingspan. He is entering into a world I will never know."

Our Children's Trust promised to cover the plaintiffs' expenses, but with their tight budget, it was a stretch to pay for the travel and lodgings. So, they found local plaintiff families to host the out-of-town youth.

All 21 youth plaintiffs would meet for the first time at a local pizza joint. With a group this big, this diverse, and from so many parts of the country, everyone wondered what the dynamics would be like.

When the 21 began to arrive, it was awkward. The youth and

some of their parents stood around not sure what to do. Oregon was a culture shock for Jayden, a Louisianian who loved sweet tea and Cajun and creole food. She worried: "What if the other plaintiffs don't like me?"

Sahara stuck close to Hazel and Avery. They chatted with Jayden a bit, and Sahara thought she was "super-duper sweet, just a kind, kind person."

Kelsey arrived like a ray of sunshine. Nathan was wowed by her radiant smile, her radiant energy. *She's so awesome,* Nathan thought. "We're fighting the government, and this is going to be such an uphill battle but she's so happy and dancing and saying 'Hi' to everyone. To be honest, I was starstruck."

Then Isaac arrived wearing his tracksuit and charming smile. "He's younger than me but I was like, oh, man, that kid is cool," Nathan said.

When Levi arrived, with his bleached afro, sharp green eyes, and wide smile, he flew toward Nathan, a bundle of energy, and jumped into his lap.

Hand raised, palm out, he said. "Hi! I'm Levi!"

Nathan laughed. "I'm Nathan."

Levi ran off to greet someone else. The youngest and the smallest, Levi spent a lot of time off the ground. The young plaintiffs hoisted him onto their shoulders, spun him around, or chucked him into the air and caught him.

Isaac and Zealand, who already felt like friends from the first meeting, called Levi over and reached out and grabbed each other's wrists, so their arms formed a chair for Levi to settle into.

"One," they dropped their arms.

"Two," they dropped them again.

"Three!" They tossed Levi into the air. Again and again and again.

"Best thing EVER!" Levi said.

Julia asked the restaurant to put on some music. She loved campfire sing-alongs and played a bit of ukulele. Music always lifted her spirit and brought people together. Mumford & Sons' song "I Will Wait" blasted out. Julia started dancing.

"It's just really, really fun to have somebody who acts sort of like a kid but is super-duper intelligent. Probably one of the smartest people I know," said Levi. "Besides my mom."

Levi chowed some vegan pizza with this "really, really great cheese" and pineapple. "It was AMAZING!" he said. After scarfing down their food, the kids sat in a circle and talked about their environmental work, how Levi planted sea oats on the dunes to prevent erosion, how Isaac and Miko were on a mission with Plant-for-the-Planet to add a trillion trees to forests across the globe.

When the older kids talked, Nathan felt like an imposter, nowhere near as experienced in his climate activism. Xiuhtezcatl talked about how he spoke in front of the United Nations when he was 6 years old and how his family founded Earth Guardians, which trains other kids to be environmental activists. Kelsey was already suing the state of Oregon over climate change. Aji was a plaintiff in a different case suing Washington State.

Isaac was energized by the group. "Hearing their stories, what they had to say, their own actions and how they got involved in the lawsuit was super, super awesome," he said. But he was equally thrilled to just hang out with kids from all over the country. He'd never known anyone from Hawaii before meeting Journey. He'd never known anyone from Florida, and now he knew Levi. He never imagined meeting anyone from Alaska, and now he was friends with Nathan.

Later, when Levi calmed down a bit, he started to feel chilly. For a kid from Florida, Oregon was like the Arctic. Xiuhtezcatl noticed, took off his jacket, and placed it over Levi's shoulders.

Already, the 21 felt like family.

The day of the hearing, March 9, 2016, dawned gray and drizzly, typical spring weather in Oregon. Julia downed her favorite morning drink, a mate latte. The nonprofit newsroom Common Dreams ran an article with the headline: "All Eyes on Oregon Courtroom Where It's 'Small Children vs. Big Oil.'" It quoted climate activist Naomi Klein as saying this was, "the most important case on the planet right now."

The plaintiffs knew they had to be really professional during the hearing. They had all gotten an email saying to dress nicely, no jeans or big hoodies. They all tried to get a good night's sleep so they would be alert and respectful.

Sahara worried about what to wear. Their black Patagonia puffy coat was like a comfort blanket. They decided to wear a dress with the coat over it. Levi picked out gray pants and a gray vest with a bright blue shirt. Nathan, who had a suitcase full of plaid flannels, opted for a solid button down.

Avery, who was staying at home with her family, spent the morning drawing horses and singing along to musicals. When it was time to go, she put on her lucky golden slippers.

Dressed in their finest, the kids headed to the courthouse. Supporters, reporters, and TV crews filled the block in front of the building. Some people carried a twenty-five-foot-long banner that read, "Kids suing to save the climate!" Supporters yelled: "What do we want? Climate justice! When do we want it? NOW!"

"I thought I was prepared," Isaac said. "But I was very overwhelmed, like, Oh, my gosh, this is so many people, thank the Lord I'm not a testifier, that I'm not speaking on our behalf."

So many of the supporters were young people, students from middle and high schools from Eugene, Portland, central Oregon—all over the state—who road-tripped to cheer the climate kids on. "You couldn't tell who was a plaintiff and who wasn't because we all look like we belonged there," Isaac said. Reporters from every publication and TV station Isaac could think of had come. Wow, he thought, this is kind of a big deal.

Miriam was also startled by the attention. "That's when I realized, Okay, this isn't about me," they said. "It's not even about us. This is a step we're taking to represent, really, our larger community."

Julia and the 21 young plaintiffs pushed through the tall glass doors. They showed their IDs and walked through metal detectors and up a flight of slate gray stairs to the third floor, which held courtrooms one through eight. The hallway, stark white and gray with a view of a patio with a massive metal sculpture, felt a bit like a modern art gallery. A sign above two tall smoky-gray doors spelled out COURTROOM FOUR in 3D capital letters. A side door marked the witness waiting room, which was empty. The hearing would include the young plaintiffs and their lawyers, the government and oil industry lawyers, and the interested public. A stern sign warned: Turn off cell phones, not just set to mute or vibrate.

Inside, the courtroom was all wood: tall wooden benches under a circular opening with light wood panels drawing eyes toward the judge's bench. It was just like Isaac had seen on the TV show *Law & Order*.

The 21 filed into two benches on one side. Parents and other supporters filed in behind them until the courtroom was jam-packed. Julia and her colleague Philip Gregory set up at one table in front of the judge while the three lawyers representing the fossil fuel industries set up at the other. Sean Duffy, the lawyer representing the U.S. government, had not arrived yet.

Julia scooted out to use the restroom. The marble hallway was empty then, quiet and a little solemn. Then she heard echoing footsteps and saw a man with short-cropped hair, a subdued blue suit, walking toward her. He was carrying a briefcase and looked pale.

"Sean Duffy?" Julia asked, reaching her hand out to him. "I'm Julia Olson."

He shook her hand but looked nervous like he had seen something unsettling. "You have quite a crowd here," he said.

Julia smiled. "Yeah, it's exciting. It's a big case."

"I've never seen anything like it," he said.

Back in the courtroom, Sahara and Avery sat next to each other holding hands for support. Kelsey scooted in next to Levi. Levi was a very active kid, constantly moving, even shifting around and wiggling while seated. Knowing he was going to have to sit still for an extended period of time terrified him.

To Isaac, the room felt hot, humid, and stuffy. He started sweating. He was getting nervous. Not because he was going to be speaking or anything. He felt nervous for Julia, who had returned to her desk. Would the judge ask a question she couldn't answer? Would he try to trip her up?

He and the other plaintiffs waited quietly. In his coverage for

CNN, reporter John D. Sutter described the scene this way: "[The kids] wore nose rings and braces. Suits too big in the shoulders . . . The backs of some heads barely peeked above the courtroom's wooden benches. But these plaintiffs, however young and small, united behind a massive cause that should inspire any of us old folk: They're suing the U.S. government—and President Barack Obama—for failing to act rapidly to stop climate change."

"It's the future suing the present. The climate kids versus the feds."

The lawyers were ready at long tables facing the judge's bench.

"All rise . . ."

All Rise

March 9, 2016

Shuffling, squeaks, and bumps filled the courtroom as the kids scrambled to their feet, smoothing their clothes, standing as straight as they could.

Judge Thomas Coffin, an elderly white man in black robes, gazed down at them. The courtroom was rather dark, with recessed lights glowing from the ceiling. The warm wood walls on both sides narrowed as they approached the judge's bench, drawing all attention to him.

Judge Coffin's job here was not to decide whether the plaintiffs proved their case or not—that was the purpose of a trial. In this pretrial hearing, he just had to figure out whether the plaintiffs had a true beef with the government that the courts could resolve. If not, he would dismiss the case.

"All right. Good morning, everyone."

As the hearing began, the room fell quiet.

The soft click, click, click of the court reporter typing every word served as a steady backdrop to the voices of the judge and the lawyers.

Sean Duffy, the lawyer for the government who had filed the motion to dismiss, began his argument from the desk. "Your Honor, our Constitution vests responsibility for addressing important

51

issues of public interest such as climate change with our democratically elected representatives.

"The plaintiffs in this case have brought a broad and sweeping challenge seeking to have the federal court take over from the political branches the difficult role of determining how to address climate change. The court should decline plaintiffs' request to shortcut the political process."

Nathan listened intently, his hair neatly smoothed back and his hands clasped, nervous that the judge might agree that their case was too broad and sweeping.

The lawyer listed ways that the kids were asking the court to go further than they ever had before. "Plaintiffs ask the court to exercise jurisdiction over and determine the rights that are owed to future generations, persons who are not alive today. No court has done so."

"They ask the court to find that the federal government has atmospheric trust obligations. No court has so found.

"Plaintiffs ask the court to find a substantive due process right to be free from climate change. No court has done so . . ."

He argued that this type of problem is designed to be resolved by two of the three political branches—the executive and legislative branches—not the courts.

When Sahara and Avery heard something that made them mad, they couldn't whisper to each other, so they squeezed hands. The political branches *were* the problem, they thought. Squeeze.

The judge and the lawyer got into a debate about whether the Constitution required the federal government to protect the nation's air, water, and land for the public trust.

Julia listened intently.

Judge Coffin asked Sean Duffy a question about the territorial waters of the United States, the zone of ocean from the shore to twelve nautical miles out: "If Congress were to sell the territorial waters to Exxon, for example, could Exxon then exclude the public from surfing, fishing, boating, and swimming in the Pacific Ocean unless they paid a fee to Exxon? Say $10,000 a year to enjoy the waters? Would there not be some sort of constitutional issue raised over the alienation of something that clearly belongs to the nation?"

What a profound question, Julia thought. It got to the heart of why protection of the public trust was so important. There's often a moment during oral arguments when she gets an inkling of whether or not the judge really understands her case. He seemed to get it.

But how would the government lawyer address the issue?

Sean Duffy gave a long and complicated answer that boiled down to this: The federal government had no constitutional obligation to protect any natural resource for the public trust.

Judge Coffin seemed shocked. Julia was, too. *How could anyone suggest that the government could sell the Pacific Ocean and allow a private company to block all access to it?*

The judge had more questions about the public trust doctrine and whether it applied to the atmosphere. To the government lawyer, he said: "I understand it's your position as well that the Public Trust Doctrine has only been applied to waters and submerged lands under the water. It's never been applied to the atmosphere; is that correct?"

The lawyer agreed.

The judge pressed on: "What is the distinction, in your view, between water and the atmosphere in terms of whether or not a Public Trust Doctrine would apply to one but not the other?"

Sean Duffy paused. "[The] land itself is more or less fixed; whereas with respect to the atmosphere the same cannot be said. The atmosphere is not fixed."

"But both resources are vital to life," the judge added.

The lawyer paused again. "Both resources are vital to life," he acknowledged.

Nathan thought this was a win for their side. The judge seemed to get why the atmosphere should be considered a public trust resource.

Next Sean Duffy introduced the idea of standing, an issue the lawyers would contest hotly in this pretrial stage of the case. Julia knew this would happen. The Department of Justice's standard approach to environmental and constitutional cases was to keep the courthouse doors closed. They did this by fighting on the grounds of standing.

To bring any case to trial, the party bringing the suit, in this case the 21, must prove to the court that they have a right to sue. In federal court, that meant showing three things: that they have been injured, that the defendants at least partially caused the injury, and that the court can do something to fix it, at least partially.

The government's motion to dismiss argued that so many parties contributed to climate change that it would be impossible to prove that the government had caused the kids' harms. Furthermore, the courts had no right to tell the other branches of government, the executive and legislative branches, what to do about climate change. So, the courts could not provide a remedy. And that meant the kids had no right to even be in court. They had no standing.

To Nathan, it felt like a battle between good and evil. He wondered if Sean Duffy really believed what he was saying. Did he really believe that the kids didn't have a claim? That the government played no part in the crisis? That the kids were trying to destroy the separation of powers? "I was like, 'Do you hear yourself, man?'"

Isaac was also shaken by the idea that they might not have standing to sue. They were citizens. They were under eighteen. They couldn't vote or run for Congress. With no representation in the legislative and executive branches, courts offered the only way to get their voices heard.

Judge Coffin took the government's concerns seriously: "There is no question that the remedies aspect of the plaintiffs' complaint is troublesome because it does ask the court to assume jurisdiction over a baker's dozen federal agencies," he said. "And I am a little bit perplexed at how this court sitting out here in the District of Oregon would have jurisdiction over a lot of these agencies that are basically headquartered in Washington, D.C."

The government lawyer seemed pleased and then outlined another reason that the kids had no right to be in court. They had no constitutional claim. "There is simply no constitutional right to a pollution-free environment," he said.

Sahara gave Avery's hand a tight squeeze. This is so dumb, Sahara thought. Obviously, we have a right to a healthy and stable atmosphere and future!

The judge pushed back a bit. "They said it's their right to be free from climate change that will be deleterious and severely injurious to their health and well-being, not just climate change, but climate change that goes beyond the pale."

The kids nodded silently in agreement, holding on to hope.

Next the fossil fuel industry lawyers presented their case. Nathan was curious about the industry lawyers Julia would be facing, so he had looked them up. He found that one had defended Exxon when its tanker *Exxon Valdez* spilled eleven million gallons of oil into Alaska's Prince William Sound. Another was one of the ten highest-paid lawyers in the world.

All Isaac knew is that one of them looked like Hank Hill, the character from the animated series *King of the Hill*.

Industry attorney Quin Sorenson approached the podium. He was fair and tall, wearing what looked like an expensive suit. He spoke with a deep, commanding voice. "I'd like to start off by addressing what I see as a fundamental defect in the claims . . ." he said. "It is an issue of government action versus inaction."

Quin Sorenson seemed calm and confident.

"It was very obvious that he had done this type of thing many times," said Nathan. "We were not his first rodeo."

The lawyer argued that the kids had no case because they were not asking the courts to stop government action. "Rather, what they allege is that government must do more."

What about the federal government issuing permits to drill?" the judge mused. "Isn't [granting a permit] *action* as opposed to *inaction*?

"It is not," the lawyer replied. "What they are alleging is government must do more . . ."

"But isn't that two sides of the same coin?"

"I don't believe so, Your Honor."

The industry lawyer spoke at length about many different court cases and many legal principles. The formality of the presentation surprised Nathan. "I'm like, 'Where is the passion?' The industry lawyer seemed like he was just collecting a paycheck."

Julia had given all the kids notepads for times like this. Some

drew the lawyers and others sketched mythical creatures like drag-
ons. Some older kids took notes. Like most of the younger plaintiffs, Sahara's notebook was mostly blank. They'd never heard
many of the terms and found much of the discussion confusing.

Miriam was so bored, they dozed off. "Which is embarrassing.
But to be honest, as a teen who had not really thought much about
the law beforehand, it's this cold, sterile environment where you
have to wear fancy clothes and stand up and sit down."

To deal with having to sit still for so long, Levi shifted his
weight. He fiddled with his pencil. He bent down to tie his shoe,
even though it didn't need tying.

Then the judge turned to Julia. It was her turn to talk.

Levi and the other young plaintiffs were all ears.

Wearing a crisp black pantsuit, her wavy hair pinned back, Julia
made eye contact with the judge. "You could see in her face and
hear in her voice that she had a stake in this," Isaac said. "You could
tell she was just waiting for this moment."

She rested both hands on her notes. With a serious and focused
expression, she began: "Your Honor, these twenty-one young people filed their complaint with this court in order to seek an order to
prevent these federal defendants from continuing to put plaintiffs
and their vital natural systems in danger and at catastrophic risk
from greenhouse gas emissions and climate destabilization. At its
core, this case is about *survival* and whether the federal defendants
can continue to threaten it."

Julia was eloquent, her voice clear and emphatic with no ums or
ands or buts. No filler words. No long pauses except for dramatic
effect.

"Defendants continue to mischaracterize plaintiffs' case as seeking a right to be free from all carbon dioxide emissions or all climate change, and I think Your Honor has questioned them about that. And, indeed, that is not plaintiffs' claim. Instead, plaintiffs claim the right to be free from government acts that threaten their personal security and the allegations of harm to their lives and their liberties and their property. And they seek that same equal protection of the law for posterity [future generations]."

Glancing just momentarily at her notes, she counted down the main reasons the court should let this case go to trial. Judge Coffin leaned forward.

"First . . . the federal defendants are causing extraordinary substantial harm such that these plaintiffs' rights to life and survival are actually threatened.

"Second, the constitutional violations and the plaintiffs' injuries are occurring today, even though the full deprivation and the full harms won't happen until the future.

"Third, the infringement is not just catastrophic in nature, it's actually irreversible, which is a really important point in this case.

"Fourth, the young people, as well as our country's posterity, are the politically powerless minority that the Constitution was set up to protect . . .

She took a deep breath. "For all of these reasons, the plaintiffs are here because they are in need of extraordinary protection from this court, and because of the urgency, this may be their last resort for a meaningful remedy."

In other words, these kids had nowhere else to turn. They need the court to step in.

Wow, Isaac thought. You go. "Julia knew what she was doing," he said. "And no one was going to stop her."

Julia then displayed graphics that showed that the government has known for more than fifty years that burning fossil fuels would cause irreversible damage, damage that would be "apocalyptic," and that government agencies continued to support fossil fuels even as carbon emissions continued to climb.

Because this was a constitutional case, Julia argued, the court could issue a nationwide remedy, like it did in *Brown v. Board of Education*, the case that desegregated schools. "The full harm that is being locked in place today needs to be addressed today by the court," she said.

She closed with: "There is no more time to waste. We are dealing here with the rights of these children to be secure and the government's significant role in destroying that security. And our nation will be properly served when this court exercises its constitutional duty and hears this case. The remedies requested will preserve plaintiffs' rights to life, to liberty, to property, and secure our nation for our posterity.

"Thus, these motions to dismiss must be denied.

"Thank you, Your Honor."

The 21 young people wanted to stand up and cheer.

The fossil fuel industry lawyer rebutted by repeating the arguments he made before.

Then court was adjourned.

The kids tumbled out of the courtroom and down the steps to face a shining sun and a cheering crowd.

The Court of Public Opinion
March 2016

Julia hoped the American public would take note of what was happening. "People should be enraged," she said. "This is the part of democracy that people don't see, but when you watch government lawyers, side by side with industry lawyers, stand up in front of a judge and say these kids don't have a right to be protected against catastrophic climate change and the U.S. Constitution doesn't protect that right, that's powerful."

Our Children's Trust and the 21 wanted to raise awareness of their government's role in climate change. So, they held a press conference on the courthouse steps.

The lead plaintiff, Kelsey Juliana, took the microphone. "We unite as a team of courageous, brave, actively hopeful youth warriors, who are engaging and advocating for our constitutional rights," she shouted as if leading a rally. "Government? Who do you work for? The interests of corporate industry? Or the interests of the people and of your children and your great-grandchildren?"

Alex Loznak took the mic and told the crowd that he grew up on a farm settled by his great-great-great-great-grandmother after journeying on the Oregon Trail in 1868 and how droughts and fires brought on by climate change have endangered that farm.

"Politicians have failed to stem the tide of global warming," he said. "Now it is up to the courts to pick up the slack."

Journey Zephier, of the Yankton Sioux Nation, who wore the beaded jewelry of his people, said: "We are in the fight of our lives and future lives, and we fight out of love and respect for all on Mother Earth."

Vic Barrett, a New Yorker who had already been clobbered by climate disasters such as Superstorm Sandy, held the mic to his round deep-brown smiling face and said: "I am young, I'm a teenager, and I want to have fun and be creative and hang out with my friends. I want to do what I love and live a life full of opportunities. I want the generation that follows to have the same opportunities as I have." While the modest but enthusiastic crowd of supporters cheered, Levi tried to whistle his support for the speakers.

At the end, Julia took the microphone, and everyone could see this was not just a job for her. "I want everyone to remember for a moment that there was a time in this nation when we had founders. And James Madison said, many hundreds of years ago, that the courts needed to be independent tribunals of justice, to stand as an impenetrable bulwark against abuses of power by government—in order to protect individual liberties: lives, rights, property, things that we hold fundamental. That was the purpose of founding this country. It was the purpose of the U.S. Constitution and the Declaration of Independence. And they did it because they *knew* that there would be abuses of power in government, and that the courts needed to act as a check on those abuses of power."

She raised her hand and voice.

"What we have today is not just a failure to act! The government is not just sitting by and doing nothing! They are doing *everything* to cause this problem. They are permitting extraction. Thirty percent of our fossil fuels come from federal public lands. They permit every refinery, every power plant. Every source of enormous pollution in our country is operating under a permit issued by the U.S. government. Every transport of fossil fuels across state lines and internationally, imports and exports, every single bit of that is permitted and authorized and subsidized and funded by the U.S. federal government.

"They are not just standing by doing nothing, they are doing everything to cause the infringement of these plaintiffs' constitutional rights to personal security, to life"—she glanced at Levi—"to Levi's property. And this court must be that impenetrable bulwark against those infringements of constitutional rights, if our Constitution means anything."

The crowd cheered.

She paused and spoke slowly and emphatically. "I want everyone to know that we are not just in a climate crisis. We will have a significant constitutional crisis and a crisis in our democracy if this doesn't work."

"That's right!" yelled a woman from the audience.

"And I just want to remind everyone that when we march in the streets and when we lobby Congress and when we do acts of civil disobedience and everything else, those are democratic acts. But *this* is also what democracy looks like."

The crowd went wild.

As they cheered, Julia embraced the kids around her. "You could feel this emotion wash over her and wash over us like we just did this big thing, together," Nathan said.

• • •

During the question-and-answer period of the press conference, one of the reporters asked the kids if they'd missed school for the hearing. Many yelled out, "Yes," and some put their thumbs up. Hazel took the mic and said: "Yeah, we're missing school. You know, it was a little bit boring to sit in that place for two hours. We are spending our time doing this while our government and adults aren't doing anything. They're just standing by!"

She passed the mic to Alex who said: "I told my professors that I had to miss school to appear in court today and they asked me: 'Did you commit a crime?'" He paused. "No, no, the federal government did."

Some people laughed and clapped but many of the kids looked sober.

When the Q&A ended, the kids hustled down the steps, and reporters mobbed them, hoping to grab a quick interview. Sahara slipped away. "A lot of the plaintiffs are super comfortable with doing interviews and speeches and public speaking, just speaking off the cuff," they said. "But it was super-duper scary for me. I was super shy and worried I would fumble or get embarrassed, so I just stayed clear of the reporters."

The next day, an article about the hearing appeared in the publication *Inside EPA*. It began: "Federal Court Judge Thomas Coffin appeared skeptical of novel claims brought by youth plaintiffs in a high-profile climate change case . . ."

The article highlighted the part of *Juliana* that the judge had called "troublesome," where the suit "asks the court to assume jurisdiction over a bakers' dozen of government agencies and raises balance of power concerns." It also quoted an unnamed legal expert who said the case has a "low probability of success."

The 21 prayed they could beat the odds.

But would their case be over before it ever really began?

Youth: 1, Government/Oil Companies: 0
April 2016

About a month later, on April 8, 2016, Julia was in California with her husband. They were about to head to a Mexican restaurant to celebrate her recent birthday when she received an email saying Judge Coffin had ruled: He denied the motion to dismiss!

She ran to her computer to let the plaintiffs know and to set up a conference call with them.

They were all ecstatic.

"This decision marks a tipping point on the scales of justice," Kelsey told the press exuberantly.

"Judge Coffin in effect declares [that] the voice of children and future generations, supported by the relevant science, must be heard," James Hansen announced in the press release.

Xiuhtezcatl and Vic posted a video on social media, filmed inside a car, talking over each other. The beginning went something like this:

Xiuhtezcatl: Okay, so, we've been in this frickin' crazy lawsuit. We sued the government. All the kids at my school were like "Oh my gosh, Xiuhtezcatl, you sued the president," and I'm like YEAH!

Vic: We did. We actually did it . . .

Xiuhtezcatl: Judge Coffin RULED in our favor . . . he ruled in favor of the young people rather than with big money and the government . . . Oh my god! Holy!

Vic: I was like screaming! I was flipping out!

Xiuhtezcatl: If there is ever a chance for us to get federal regulations on carbon dioxide, like this is it, like this is IT!

They riffed for a while on the possible implications of the win, and they ended on:

Xiuhtezcatl: We need people to know that we are winning, to not give up hope, to not lose faith, like, we are freaking killing it.

Vic: We're building the future right now.

Xiuhtezcatl: Hell yeah, change the world and chill.

Judge Coffin called the lawsuit "unprecedented." His ruling was unprecedented, too.

The youth's right to be heard in court, called "standing," had three requirements—and the 21 met them all.

Injury: Did the kids allege specific injuries personal to them?

Judge Coffin said yes, they asserted "injuries that are personal in nature." He listed "jeopardy to family farms," "increased temperatures and wildfires," "lost recreation opportunities," and "harm to family dwellings from superstorms."

Causation: Did the kids show a connection between government actions and their injuries?

Judge Coffin said yes, there was "an alleged strong link" between the government's actions and the production of carbon dioxide, which contributed to climate change, which caused their injuries.

Redressibility: Was it likely that the courts could do something to address the harm?

Judge Coffin said yes, that "regulation by this country, in combination with regulation already being undertaken by other countries, may very well have sufficient impact to redress the alleged harm."

Standing had been a stumbling block for many climate-change cases in the past. With a problem so big and so unwieldy, it had been tough to prove individual harm and point to the party responsible. To the surprise of many observers, this court ruled that the 21 had a chance at proving individual harm caused by government conduct and that courts could provide a remedy.

Forbes magazine described the ruling as legalese for "global warming may eventually hurt all of us, but it will hurt our children and grandchildren the most, so they have the right to sue."

CNN's headline said: "Major Victory for Kids Suing Obama." The columnist, John Sutter, marveled at how the "profoundly smart" case shifted his thinking. "To me, part of that victory is getting all of us to look at climate change differently," he wrote. "The climate kids' argument is multifaceted and nuanced, bringing in concepts of public trust doctrine as well as constitutional rights to life, liberty, and property. But one of the oh-wow points they're making is this: Young people and unborn generations are being discriminated against when it comes to the U.S. propagation of climate change.

"They will live through an era of rising seas, heat waves, droughts, floods, and extinctions that are without precedent. Yet they have little or no voice in the political system that, despite some bold steps in the right direction, continues to lease federal property for fossil fuel extraction and continues to subsidize pollution."

The ruling did not yet mean that the kids would get a trial. Indeed, the government and fossil fuel company representatives immediately asked trial Judge Ann Aiken to review the ruling. Her decision could either move *Juliana* along or stop it in its tracks.

She scheduled oral arguments for September, six months later.

But a lot happened with two of the plaintiffs, first Miriam and then Jayden, in the meantime.

On the Other Side of the Law
May 13-15, 2016

In May 2016, plaintiff Miriam Oommen opened an email from their lawyers advising the plaintiffs to avoid putting themselves in a position of being arrested for acts of civil disobedience. Miriam knew what that was about.

Born of an immigrant from India and a white rural Midwesterner, Miriam grew up in Eugene running around barefoot in the woods, making forts, and sleeping under the stars.

Miriam heard about climate change at a pretty young age and was terrified. "It's a mental and emotional stressor growing up into an apocalypse," said Miriam. "This existential threat felt overwhelming and at times I couldn't really think about anything else."

In high school, Miriam joined a forest defense group that took "direct action," like sitting on a platform high in a tree to stop logging of old-growth forests. When Kelsey first approached them about the lawsuit, Miriam wasn't sure if they wanted to focus more on civil disobedience or to work through lawful, legal means. "Frankly, I hadn't made up my mind, but I figured if the situation was really as dire as I understood it to be, we needed to try different tactics."

Miriam didn't exactly consult their parents on the decision to join the case. A self-described angsty metalhead teenager,

Miriam had given them cause for concern at times. When Miriam told them about the lawsuit, "they probably thought it was a safer and better thing than some of the other things I could get into," Miriam said.

But for Miriam, being part of the lawsuit was not enough. "I didn't want to be just a pretty face, and I didn't want to just sit around waiting," said Miriam. "I needed to *do* something." So, they did.

Now a first-year student at Seattle University, Miriam got wind of a worldwide effort to "Break Free" from fossil fuels. They and some other students decided to join a direct action in Anacortes, a coastal town about sixty miles from campus. A Shell oil refinery planned an expansion and was going to add rail lines, which meant more oil and more oil trains. "Oil trains are very dangerous, like bombs going through neighborhoods," Miriam said.

Almost a hundred activists would spend the weekend camped out on the tracks. Miriam was surprised at how orchestrated every detail was. The group, Break Free PNW, called the train station to warn that there would be people on the tracks. They found a nearby farm to use as a staging ground. Organizers asked: If the police showed up, or rather *when* the police showed up, who was willing to stand their ground and risk arrest?

Miriam knew that for better or for worse, the 21 young plaintiffs were the face of *Juliana v. United States* and that while some people would be supportive of direct-action work, some wouldn't. But it was also possible that Miriam's connection to the case could bring needed attention to the protest.

So Miriam and six others volunteered to stand their ground. All seven donned white coveralls with a big green X on the back, so everyone—the protesters and the police—could identify the die-hards. Miriam and the others wrote the phone number of Break Free's legal team on their arms in marker.

On the evening of Friday, May 13, the activists rushed onto the tracks. Dusty flat farmland surrounded them with rolling hills off in the distance. Thick clouds puffed out of the nearby refinery's smokestacks. Activists raised tents, signs, and artwork. Wind whipped at a green and yellow banner that spanned the track: "Coal, oil, gas, NONE shall pass!"

Miriam and the others dressed in white sat in a circle on the tracks and bound themselves together with rope, chicken wire, and duct tape. This "tactical lockbox" would delay police who tried to arrest them.

Before long, a line of police cars pulled up on the road near the tracks.

Miriam eyed them warily.

At first, nothing happened. The officers leaned on their cars, chatting with each other, watching and waiting.

Miriam was nervous, but that night and the next day passed peacefully, with the activists talking, singing, eating, and sleeping while bound together on the tracks.

Then at 5:30 a.m. on Sunday, May 15, just as the sun was rising, the police moved in. Boots stomped and police radios blared. Clad in riot gear and holding batons and guns, officers surrounded the activists, yelling, "Hands up!" and "Don't move!"

They ordered the crowd to disperse. Many of the activists did. The seven students on the tracks remained seated and began singing, "We Shall Overcome." Miriam was terrified.

Officers grabbed them and sawed through the rope, chicken wire, and duct tape.

In addition to the handful of students, police detained dozens of older protesters and led them to the back of police vans. At the station, they were all charged with criminal trespassing.

"It was a bit controversial," Miriam said. "The lawyers try to paint a very specific picture of who we are, law-abiding citizens who are trying to make change inside the system. Direct action, civil disobedience, especially getting arrested, pushes the boundaries outside the system."

Julia shared her thinking with the plaintiffs: "There's a very important place for peaceful, nonviolent acts of disobedience, and I totally understand why people feel compelled to do everything in their power about climate change," she said. She explained that there were a lot of people willing to engage in those peaceful demonstrations, but only 21 people who could be plaintiffs in *Juliana v. U.S.*

"Breaking the law is generally seen as a bad thing," Miriam admitted. "But sometimes the negative consequences of not breaking the law are worse. That's when it gets confusing, and in my opinion, more interesting."

Miriam didn't want to jeopardize the lawsuit, but they didn't want to forgo other methods of making change either. They would keep open all their options.

Climate change would not wait for the lawsuit to make its way through the courts. And meanwhile, all the young people on the planet were still in danger.

A Thousand-Year Flood
August 2016

It was early in the morning of August 13, 2016, when 13-year-old Jayden Foytlin of Rayne, Louisiana, was awakened by banging on her bedroom door. She spun around to get up, but when she put her feet down, she found herself ankle-deep in climate change.

Jayden's home, which was never expected to flood, was deluged with rain, stranding her and her siblings with water rising around them and inside the house.

One of Julia's staff alerted her to Jayden's plight. Julia, upset, sad, and worried, sent an email to the other plaintiffs to let them know what was happening. Sahara remembered how much they had liked Jayden and was really concerned about her. "I was like 'Can this really be real? Is this actually happening?'" Sahara said. "It was hard to fathom. It sounded really scary and honestly really stressful. I would have no idea what to do in that situation. It was just heartbreaking."

While Louisiana flooded, the federal government offered up a section of the Gulf of Mexico the size of Virginia to lease for oil and gas exploration. The contrast between the injury Jayden suffered and the government's support of the fossil fuel system was stark. Once things settled down, Julia asked Jayden if she was willing to share her story for the court.

Listening to Jayden share details was an emotional experience for Julia. A strong advocate who is also empathetic, she deeply felt Jayden's pain and loss. But she also knew her story would be a powerful, visceral way to bring the harms the plaintiffs had suffered, and continued to suffer, to life for Judge Aiken.

Less than a week before the September hearing on the motion to dismiss, the team filed Jayden's written statement, called a declaration, with the court. In it, she described Rayne: "In our town, about 80 percent of the residents live below the poverty line. Like most others in our town, our family did not buy flood insurance because we supposedly live outside of the floodplain. We have never had a problem with flooding in our neighborhood."

When the flooding started, she wrote: "I was scared and did not know what to do. We called our mom and told her what was happening. Mom told us that she was trying to get home to us, but that she did not know when she could get there. The roads were flooding, with cars floating down highways. It took her all day to get home to us. Her car was swept up in the flood. On her way home, my mom had to walk through floodwater up to her thighs."

Jayden described sewage pouring into her home and how the rain and flooding continued for two weeks. "We had nowhere to go. We could not go outside because of all the rain and floodwaters. There were no shelters. All of the grocery stores were closed. We were basically stranded. So, we kept sleeping in our house that was full of sewage and floodwater damage."

Jayden described the destruction of their furniture and mattresses, how sewage soaked their carpets, floors and walls and how the storm damaged the ceiling and roof. Most of her little brother's toys were destroyed.

A quarter of Jayden's town was underwater. Pets drowned. "We have had all types of creatures coming into our home: a snake, colonies of ants trying to escape the water, and spiders. Horses of nearby neighbors had chemical burns up to their stomachs from touching the polluted floodwater."

In the days after the flood, her family got "real sick," Jayden wrote. "Everyone in my family had flu-like symptoms with fevers and sore throats, as well as stomach pain and diarrhea. My whole body felt hot, and my hands were very cold. I had bad headaches, a sore throat, and an upset stomach."

She mentioned the Obama administration's huge oil leasing auction held right after the flood, which would only worsen climate change, and concluded: "Unless they are ordered to stop, these Federal Defendants will continue to cause destabilization of our climate, and more and more storms and floods will threaten my personal security, my life, my liberties, my property, and that of my family. I think these Federal Defendants should be required to go to a trial where they will have to explain in court why they say they are doing so much to address climate change, but plan to keep fossil fuel production and consumption and pollution increasing for decades . . ."

Jayden's experience and all the climate devastation Julia knew about in detail weighed on her. As the hearing neared, she granted an interview with CNN reporter John Sutter. Filmmakers working on a documentary about *Juliana* were also present. John asked Julia how much her own kids, 12-year-old Tayo and 9-year-old Bay, who she was pregnant with when this all began, knew about the lawsuit.

She explained that the boys understood her work, and at the

same time she tried to shield them from the horrors of climate change as much as possible. She hadn't let them watch the climate change documentary *An Inconvenient Truth,* and if they asked about climate change, she reassured them: "I'm taking care of this; I'm going to fix this."

That's a huge burden to shoulder. John asked: "What does it feel like to say that?"

Julia's eyes welled. "I have to cry . . . or I'm going to cry in court," she said. "It's when I talk about my kids and being a mom that I just lose it."

Near the end of the interview, Julia shared her fears about the planet young people will inherit if governments don't turn things around in time. As she painted a picture of kids dealing with the catastrophes sure to come, she teared up again.

Then she looked at John and the film crew around her.

"How come the rest of you aren't crying?"

Julia doubled down on her preparation for the hearing. She reread everything, all of the briefs and legal arguments that had been filed with the court, including all her team's filings and the filings from the defendants. She also reviewed relevant rulings from past cases. She rewrote her opening and closing arguments, edited them, and tweaked them. She practiced in her office, rehearsed in the shower, even reviewed arguments out loud as she hiked up to the top of Spencer Butte, the scenic knoll near her home.

She and her team set up moot courts, where her colleagues pretended to be judges, asking her the hardest questions they could think of. She tried her best to answer them, stopping when she got stuck, restarting, clarifying, and sharpening her responses as she went. She covered all the possible questions once, then again, and again.

As she perfected her presentation, she stood in front of the mirror focusing on her facial expressions, on how she would deliver her key points. She saw before her a mom and an experienced lawyer, solid in her convictions and knowledge of the law, who had to nail her arguments for the good of the plaintiffs and her own children. She went back and forth between feeling confident in her capacity to be an effective advocate and feeling insecure about shouldering the weight of this ambitious endeavor.

She tried to eat well—lots of veggies—and exercise to help prepare and settle her body for the big day. But the most important moment of preparation was her final meeting with the plaintiffs. Julia was an officer of the court, the one permitted to stand up and speak to the judge. But really the whole case was about the 21.

17
All Together Now
September 2016

For this hearing, Our Children's Trust had scraped together enough money to rent a huge house in Eugene for the out-of-town plaintiffs.

When the house filled up, the kids blasted loud music. They wrestled. They kicked a soccer ball around. They huddled in the bathroom doing hair and make-up. And all day long, they ate. Chips, string cheese, seltzers. Levi, now age 9, tried his first jojos. "They're seasoned potato wedges, super salty," he said. "Best thing ever!"

Levi, who had lived in Florida his whole life, got excited about all the hills in Eugene and borrowed a scooter for a ride. With no idea of what he was doing, he zoomed down a hill, skidded and crashed. "I was having so much fun that I didn't really think about it until I was bleeding all over the place."

Kelsey and his mom helped him clean up, so he'd be presentable at court.

The evening before the hearing, all 21 plaintiffs gathered at a long picnic table in the backyard of the plaintiff house.

While the kids devoured pizza and Pepsi, Julia stood at the head of the table. "A couple quick reminders," she called out. They quieted down. "Cell phones have to be off in the courtroom. You're

77

all going to look sharp, I know, because you looked awesome last time."

Nic Venner, now 15, a plaintiff from Colorado who is neurodivergent asked: "Um, can we bring any other pieces of paper or information into the room? So, if we get really bored, we could stuff some math homework into our pockets?"

Julia laughed. "If you are bored to tears, please do math." Everyone cracked up, made more jokes, and then settled down again.

Julia reviewed where the case stood, how they overcame the first huge hurdle with Judge Coffin's ruling in their favor and how the government was on the defensive. The next step was convincing Judge Ann Aiken to turn down the defendants' motion to dismiss the case. They needed Judge Aiken's support to move to a full trial.

Julia acknowledged that it wouldn't be easy. "She may ask me really hard questions tomorrow," she said. "That's her job."

"No, she WILL!" Nic blurted out.

Julia smiled. "She *will* ask me some really hard questions and that's okay. We're going to be ready."

The kids broke into applause and hooted and hollered.

Sixteen-year-old Aji Piper of Seattle had prepared something special for Julia. He stood up and the kids egged him on. "Aji! Aji!"

Aji, with his light brown skin, dark eyebrows, and a fluffy halo of curly black hair, gave a wry, shy smile. The afternoon sun glowed behind him as he began to sing a slow, mournful tune.

I want to be free, so free, like a flower and a bee
Like a bird up in the tree, like a dolphin in the sea.
I wanna fly high, so high, like an eagle in the sky
And when my time is come, I'm gonna lay down and die.

Nathan watched Julia closely. She was in the moment, taking power from Aji's song, from all the plaintiffs gathered around her. The beauty of the song, the connection he felt to Julia and all the kids hit Nathan hard and he teared up.

Julia's eyes glistened as she nodded and bit her lip. She loved these kids like her own. She would fight for them like they were her own.

Second Hearing
September 13, 2016

The next morning dawned under bright skies.

Julia opened her eyes and felt immediately anxious. In the shower that morning, she ran through key arguments. Dressed in her usual crisp dark pantsuit and white blouse, she headed to the kitchen. Her kids were there having a bite before meeting her at the courthouse. After they ate, right before Julia headed out the door, she did one thing to get pumped up. She turned on some music—loud. "Speak for the Trees," a hip-hop song Colorado plaintiff Xiuhtezcatl recorded with his siblings, filled the room. Julia's family danced and bounced around the kitchen, singing the lyrics.

We slash and we burn, but will we ever learn?
The forest catches fire, a small part of us will burn.
I'm not the Lorax, but I still speak for the trees.
The survival of our forest depends on you and me . . .

After one more song by Mumford & Sons that Julia danced to with her colleagues before every oral argument, she felt fully present, blood pumping, and heart soaring. She was ready to face the federal government, the fossil fuel industry, and the judge.

At the plaintiff house, Levi's mom and the other chaperones shooed the kids out the door. Did everyone use the bathroom?

Did kids have their rain gear? Did they have their water bottles? A granola bar?

The youth and their lawyers once again hustled up the steps to the shiny glass-and-steel Wayne Morse Courthouse with supporters cheering them on. "All right, here we go!" Kelsey yelled.

Levi's mom brought a backpack, and the kids stuffed things in and handed her some jackets, which she tied around her waist. "They are still teenagers, still kids, even though they are out there saving the world," she said.

Again, Kelsey slid in next to Levi in the front row. Levi wore what he called "a bow tie that strangles, long pants that are way too wide, and a shirt that is too tight in the armpits." He swung his feet, which didn't even touch the floor. Jayden, still reeling from the flood just a month earlier, also took a seat in the front, wearing her signature choker necklace and black-rimmed Weezer glasses. The other plaintiffs filled the rows behind Julia and her two colleagues.

Local support was growing, and the audience filled overflow rooms. People also overflowed courtrooms in Portland and other cities along the West Coast to watch the hearing.

Judge Ann Aiken, black-robed with close-cropped brown hair, pale skin, and a broad smile, banged her gavel and began with a quick lesson on court etiquette, perhaps for the benefit of the kids: "For those who have never been here, please do not in any way display any feelings one way or the other. We are here to listen, all of us . . .

"Today is the day to hear arguments from everyone to supplement the written documents that they have provided and to do what lawyers do best, and that is address issues that they feel they need to underscore for the millionth time."

Then she addressed the lawyers on both sides. "Please don't be repetitive."

The federal government lawyer Sean Duffy, again clad in a suit and tie, was the first to approach the podium. He began with a stunning admission: "We do not question the science. Climate change threatens our environment and our ecosystems. It alters our climate systems, and it will only worsen over time. It is the result of man-made emissions."

Yes! the kids thought to themselves. Julia knew Sean Duffy was a dad with young kids. He might not have known much about climate change before taking this case, but perhaps he appreciated the dangers now. But she also knew that lawyers like to win, and that they can get entrenched in the positions they take. The admissions did not mean the government was willing to let them get to trial.

Indeed, he argued that the judge should dismiss *Juliana* for two main reasons: First, Congress and the executive branch should address climate change, not the courts; and second, the government was already working to address the problem.

Really? Jayden thought. Her house flooded because of climate change and was still a complete mess, with torn-up carpets and mold growing on the damp walls. She was afraid every time it rained. And what was the government doing? Permitting more drilling.

Judge Aiken questioned Sean Duffy about the proper role of the courts and pace of the government's climate change work: "Doesn't the court have a role as the third branch of government to assist you?" she asked. Couldn't the court give the government reason to address the climate crisis with "all deliberate speed"?

But Sean Duffy once again took issue with the kids' claim that a stable climate was a fundamental right. It was not listed in the U.S. Constitution and the courts had never found a fundamental right to a stable climate system before. Without a stable climate as a fundamental right, he argued, the kids had no due process claim, meaning they had no case.

How can you argue that as we're all sitting right here, very vulnerable, in front of you? Sahara thought.

Next up was Quin Sorenson, the corporate, impeccably suited lawyer representing the fossil fuel companies.

In his polished presentation, he made the same argument that he did before, that the judge should dismiss *Juliana* because someone can only be sued if their *actions* caused injury. Failure to act to prevent injury was not enough. "The government is not alleged to have created climate change," he said. "They are alleged to have allowed climate change to be created by not restricting the emissions of other parties . . ."

Jayden knew well that this was not true. Even as her home flooded, the federal government kept actively contributing to climate change by leasing Gulf waters for drilling.

The industry lawyer also argued that because climate change was widespread, it was impossible to place the blame anywhere specifically. Isaac thought that was ridiculous. Everyone knew that the United States was one of the biggest contributors to climate change. Reducing emissions in the U.S. could make a huge difference. He hoped Julia would make that point.

Finally, it was Julia's turn. She approached the podium, her wavy hair loose at her shoulders. "Good morning, Your Honor. May it please the court, I am Julia Olson here on behalf of the plaintiffs. I would like to acknowledge their presence in the courtroom today."

She gazed back at the 21, and they nodded at her, the bond between them visible.

She launched in. "Your Honor, this case is about government-imposed danger and harm over at least five decades that shocks the conscience and rises to the level of infringement of these young plaintiffs' inalienable constitutional rights to their personal security, to life, liberties, and property, as well as public trust resources."

"Just last week, after the hottest summer on record, President Obama said to the *New York Times* that the reports he gets from his top science advisor on climate change are, quote, 'terrifying.'"

Julia told Jayden's story, about the flood waters seeping in from everywhere, sewage flowing like a river through her home. Jayden flinched. It was hard to relive that experience.

Julia spoke clearly, crisply, and with passion. She pointed out that a report released by the government just the previous week stated that the increased frequency and severity of these storms and floods were directly attributable to climate change. "The question is whether defendants' conduct has contributed to that monumental threat and if it rises to the level of a constitutional violation," she said.

She blasted the defendants' argument that courts cannot review the federal government's behavior. "It is inconceivable in our democracy and under our U.S. Constitution that when our federal government has acted for decades knowingly, affirmatively, and deliberately . . . that their actions would be insulated from judicial review."

The defendants, she said, have totally mischaracterized the case. "I want to be very clear that this case is not about a federal government sitting passively . . . Instead, these federal defendants have been active perpetrators of constitutional infringements over decades . . ." she said, referring to thousands of permits and authorizations for drilling, mining, and pipelines.

"The United States not only controls the makeup of our energy system, which has been dominated and remains dominated by fossil fuels, it controls the energy supply, and it controls the pollution that comes out of that energy system at the end of the day."

Julia had to educate each judge along the way about the evidence in the case, so again, she pulled up slides of the timeline that showed how long the government had known about the harm climate change causes.

Isaac was relieved when she pointed out that the United States was responsible historically for a quarter of global emissions. Reducing U.S. emissions could really help stabilize the climate of the whole planet.

Julia closed by pointing out that the government had yet to address the most important question before the court: Can liberty and justice exist if the climate system that supports all life is destroyed?

She acknowledged the "enormous magnitude" of the case and asked that the judge provide a "constitutional check on the other branches of government" before it's too late.

"Thank you, Your Honor," she said.

Before ending the hearing, Judge Aiken told the kids, who looked hopeful and worried in equal measure, what would come next. "So, for purposes of your education, the court takes these matters under advisement [and we] generally have an obligation to try and get a ruling out in sixty days. I will do my best to get that out on or before that date. But I am not going to promise any particular timeline. All right?"

But Julia and the kids felt the clock ticking. Every month that went by was another month of emissions building up and locking in more heat. "I don't want to see another family go through what we are experiencing," Jayden told CNN and other reporters after the hearing. "Thirteen people died in the flood . . . Nobody should have to bury their loved ones simply because the government wants to bury their heads from the truth or because oil companies want to bury themselves in money."

At a press conference on the courthouse steps, Vic, in pants and a maroon button-down, stepped up to the mic. "At first, I was going to talk to you guys about really big stuff like sustainable development and how many people there are on earth and how important climate change is. But I really wanna talk to you about how happy I am." Everyone laughed.

"Basically, I'm happy because I'm here." He gestured to the kids surrounding him. "I'm happy to be with my friends again. And I'm happy to be suing the U.S. federal government." Everyone laughed and clapped.

"There's a lot going on right now that would suggest that I have no reason to be happy." He got more serious. "The sea levels are rising, and the earth, which so gracefully houses us, has been betrayed by our dependence on fossil fuels. The United States federal government and the biggest coalition of fossil fuels in the world just sat [a few] feet away from me and tried to deny their responsibility for climate change—also known as the biggest threat to my future." Vic stood taller and smiled. "But I don't really care because they don't have that power over me. The most power that exists in this space is standing behind me." He looked back at his new group of friends. "And all these people supporting this lawsuit. I know that we're really powerful and we're making a huge change."

Julia felt such unadulterated joy and hope at that moment. She thought the oral argument went really well, that Judge Aiken got it. And now standing in the sunshine with these young people and all their supporters "excited and jazzed and playful and uplifted," the moment felt so full of possibility.

The 21 returned home to wait. Would Judge Aiken accept Judge Coffin's ruling that the youth had standing and could proceed? Or would she modify or even reject it? Sixty days felt like a lifetime.

Would Judge Aiken allow them to go to trial?

They Knew
2016-2017

The 21's legal team knew that if they got to trial, to have any chance of success, they would need to present evidence to prove that the federal government *knew* that its support of fossil fuels endangered citizens. For this, co-counsel Phil Gregory was inspired, in part, by lawsuits lung cancer victims brought against tobacco companies. Their success hinged on uncovering documents showing that tobacco company executives knew that cigarettes were addictive and caused cancer.

So, while dealing with these pretrial motions, Our Children's Trust also sent out a small team of staff and volunteer investigators to search for hard evidence that the government had long known about climate change and the threat it posed to people.

Much of the material they needed was created before the internet, so they relied on old-fashioned detective legwork, conducting interviews, following leads, scanning bookshelves, and digging through papers.

One of the plaintiffs, Alex Loznak, who was raised on a farm that had been in his family for seven generations, wanted to be a lawyer when he grew up. He volunteered to join the hunt for proof. He traveled to Abilene, Kansas, to the imposing white stone Dwight D. Eisenhower Presidential Library, where he combed through letters, memos, and reports. At the Harry S. Truman Presidential Library in Independence, Missouri, he sifted through piles of presidential papers, looking for any mention of fossil fuels or global warming.

He also dug deep into the archives of the John F. Kennedy Presidential Library in Boston, which held twenty-four million pages of correspondence, staff notes, and personal papers. The regal cream-colored building overlooked Dorchester Bay, adjacent to Boston Harbor. Inside the hushed research room, Alex requested box after box of documents and thumbed through the materials carefully.

Then something caught his eye: An exchange of letters between President Kennedy's assistant and Senator Clinton Anderson from New Mexico. The senator had urged the president to read an article published in *Fortune* magazine in 1955. In it, a scientist predicted that carbon dioxide emissions were going to warm the planet, melt glaciers, and cause 15 feet of sea-level rise, endangering coastal towns and cities. Kennedy's assistant responded, thanking the senator for the letter and article. Alex rechecked the date. The correspondence was from sixty years ago. He had found the first known mention of the perils of global warming in official White House documents.

In the search for evidence, the team also tracked down former science experts for past presidents of the United States and visited them in their homes, digging through bookshelves and boxes of reports and notes from dusty attics and damp basements.

The team uncovered a 1965 report from President Lyndon Johnson's scientific advisors warning that the accumulation of greenhouse gases like carbon dioxide from the burning of fossil fuels threatened "the health, longevity, livelihood, recreation, cleanliness and happiness of citizens who have no direct stake in their production but cannot escape their influence."

A 1969 memo to President Nixon's White House counsel John Ehrlichman warned that the burning of fossil fuels could cause "apocalyptic change" from sea-level rise, endangering New York City and Washington, D.C.

The legal team amassed more than 36,000 pages of evidence into thick white binders that filled walls of shelves in Our Children's Trust's office. "Every president [since Kennedy] knew that burning fossil fuels was causing climate change," Julia said. "Our government, at the highest levels, knew and was briefed on it regularly by the national security community and the scientific community. They have known for a very long time that it was a big threat."

Notably, most of the evidence came from government reports. "We have them with their own words," Julia said. "It's really the clearest, most compelling evidence I've ever had in any case I've litigated in over twenty years."

But would they ever get to present this evidence in court? And if they did, would it be enough?

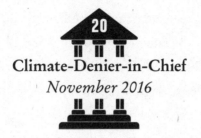

Climate-Denier-in-Chief
November 2016

As Julia and the youth were getting ready for their court battle, the country was battling over which candidate should be the next president. Democrats fielded Hillary Clinton, who campaigned to keep and improve on Obama's climate policies and work for the United States to meet the targets they promised in the Paris Agreement. She talked about installing half a billion solar panels and cutting oil consumption by a third.

Republicans settled on Donald Trump who posted more than a hundred tweets calling climate change a hoax and attacking wind and solar power. Many tweets revealed a deep misunderstanding of global climate change, which leads to extreme weather events across the weather spectrum, both hot and cold. He also repeatedly confused the difference between local weather and global climate.

On December 6, 2013, he tweeted: "Ice storm rolls from Texas to Tennessee—I'm in Los Angeles and it's freezing. Global warming is a total, and very expensive, hoax!"

On February 15, 2015, he wrote: "Wow, 25 degrees below zero, record cold and snow spell. Global warming anyone?"

On October 19, 2015, he tweeted: "It's really cold outside, they are calling it a major freeze, weeks ahead of normal. Man, we could use a big fat dose of global warming!"

On the campaign trail, Trump promised to pull the United States from the Paris Agreement and undo Obama's climate regulations.

Knowing that the fate of the lawsuit was still very much up in the air, the plaintiffs watched the results trickle in on election night, November 8, 2016, with growing alarm.

They were shocked when Trump won.

Oh my god, Isaac thought, the second this guy gets wind of our case, he's going to get the whole thing thrown out. He was scared for Julia's sake, thinking about what she was going to be up against. "I was very confused and anxious because I knew that in a blink of an eye, the Trump administration could change things. They could be relentless and overwhelming and overbearing to an extent that would exhaust us all and exhaust all our resources," he said.

After the election, the kids had a conference call with Julia and her team. Many of the plaintiffs were disheartened and a few shed tears. They had heard Trump and his supporters deny climate science and minimize youth voices. They worried that a Trump administration would further bolster fossil fuels and further imperil their futures.

Isaac dug deep to find a bright side. "Getting a person completely against everything you are standing up for makes your stuff seem a lot more legitimate," he said.

Trump as the opponent in the lawsuit might make more sense to some people, Miriam thought, but only to people who were not looking closely. "The Obama administration said, 'Climate change is bad, and we have to do something about it,' but behind the scenes, they opened up oil wells and permitted new fossil fuel infrastructure," Miriam pointed out. "Trump said, 'Climate change is a hoax, and I don't care at all and I'm going to do as much extraction as possible.'" The reality was that climate change was so much less partisan than it seemed. "It's not Democrat versus Republican," Miriam said. "No one is doing nearly enough."

Julia couldn't disagree. Trump would be the newest executive in a long line of presidents neglecting to protect the country against the perils of climate change. The actions of Presidents Kennedy, Johnson, Nixon, Ford, Carter, Reagan, Clinton, the Bushes, and Obama contributed to the current crisis. "Every president that preceded did something that made climate change worse," she said.

Julia and the other lawyers tried to stay positive—it was still the same case, and it was still going to move forward with the Trump administration as the defendants. But honestly, no one knew what Trump and his people would do. And they still didn't know how Judge Aiken would rule. All they knew for sure was that with a climate-denier as president, the case mattered more now than ever.

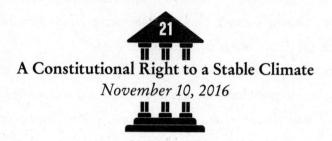

A Constitutional Right to a Stable Climate
November 10, 2016

Just two days after the election, Sahara was asked to step outside of their humanities class. They were worried. "When you hear someone asking you to step out of the classroom, you think. 'Oh, is something wrong?'"

Then Sahara saw Julia and Avery waiting for her in the courtyard. Julia was grinning. "I've got news," she said.

The students stared at her wide-eyed.

"Ready?" Julia said. Then she started to read from Judge Ann Aiken's fifty-four-page opinion: "Exercising my 'reasoned judgment,' I have no doubt that the right to a climate system capable of sustaining human life is fundamental to a free and ordered society . . ."

Avery and Sahara grabbed each other's hands and squeezed.

"It's a favorable ruling!" Julia said. "Judge Aiken denied the motion to dismiss!"

"We're going to trial!" Avery yelled.

"Thank you, Judge Aiken!" Sahara cheered.

Julia was moved by the eloquence and beauty of the opinion and read a bit more: "A stable climate system is quite literally the foundation of society, without which there would be neither civilization nor progress."

Julia stretched out her arms to the kids. They embraced.

"So, the case moves ahead?" Sahara asked.

Julia nodded. "We still have a long way to go."

Isaac's mom picked him up from school that day.

"I have news," she said, holding up a phone to his face.

Isaac tried to wave the phone away. "Okay, why are you recording?" He was annoyed at how parents always seemed to want to record everything for Facebook.

"We heard from the court today."

She started to read an excerpt of the ruling.

"I ADOPT Judge Coffin's Findings and Recommendation, as elaborated in this opinion. Defendants' Motion to Dismiss and Intervenors' Motion to Dismiss are DENIED."

Isaac whooped, overwhelmed and overjoyed.

That night after dinner, Levi's mom told him about the ruling. Screaming and laughing, he ran around the house yelling. "It was like being allowed to live at Disney World or something like that!" he said.

The 21 were flying high. They had a giddy conference call, laughing and chattering and cheering.

Then they had to get busy. Dozens of media outlets wanted interviews, so they talked about what they wanted to say and divided up the list. "After about ten seconds of being excited, we had to focus," said Nathan. "We still had a lot of work to do."

Time magazine reported that the kids won "a notable battle," setting the stage for a "landmark decision on climate change." *Teen Vogue* declared: "This is huge."

Jeffrey Sachs, director of Columbia University's Earth Institute, called it "a remarkable opinion." Slate called it "an unprecedented move in the American legal system." The article quoted Michael Burger, executive director of the Sabin Center for Climate Change Law at Columbia University. "There is no question that this decision, in both its eloquence and its bold declaration of a new constitutional right, breaks new ground," he said. "In the context of Tuesday's election and the threat of a Trump administration that may well be steadfastly opposed to any climate action whatsoever, this provides some hope that our courts will step forward and protect the health and well-being of current and future generations."

University of San Francisco law professor Alice Kaswan called the opinion brave. "Most courts are terrified of this kind of litigation," she said. "It's raising issues they're afraid are very political and [puts them] in the role of trying to decide who's responsible or forcing people to act. But this court is saying, 'We've been too shy.' I think she believes the judiciary can't sit by."

Others in the legal community admitted to being surprised. "I think the fact that the plaintiffs have survived a motion to dismiss means that it's got to be taken somewhat seriously," Daniel Etsy, an expert in environmental law and policy at Yale University, told the *Washington Post.*

"I will confess, that like virtually every other environmental law professor in the country, when this case was first filed, there was a lot of skepticism. This is big and bold and new and really uncharted territory," said Ann Carlson, professor of environmental law at UCLA School of Law. "[Then] they won in district court, much to the shock of many, many observers. It's remarkable to read the papers in this case," she said. "It's compelling."

The kids' confidence in the case also bloomed. "It felt like it would be smooth sailing from here," Isaac said. "Maybe there would be a few hiccups along the way and going through the courts could take a while, but it seemed like nothing could destroy or derail our case."

But that was far from true.

PART II
Will the Youth Get a Trial?

Obama Responds
November 2016-January 2017

Judge Aiken's historic decision gave the kids and their lawyers two promising ways forward. One, the team could try to convince President Obama to settle *Juliana* before Trump took office. A settlement is a legally binding agreement between opposing parties that resolves the dispute and ends the lawsuit. In this case, the settlement might include acknowledgment of a right to a stable climate as well as concrete actions such as ending fossil fuel extraction on public land.

Plaintiff Alex Loznak, who grew up on his family's farm, loved the settlement option. "I'd very much like to sit down with President Obama," he said. "We have two months left." The rest of the 21 agreed.

So, Our Children's Trust approached the Justice Department about settlement and reached out to their network to encourage the White House to come to the table to negotiate. But they got nowhere.

Jeffrey Sachs, director of Columbia University's Earth Institute, implored the Obama administration to do what it could to support the kids' case before leaving office. "Settle this lawsuit," he told the press. "It's the last opportunity for the Obama administration to get this right—and if they continue to challenge this suit in their last days, shame on them." But Obama wouldn't settle.

Then, just a week before Donald Trump's inauguration, Obama's legal team made a surprising move. On January 13, 2017, they filed a seventy-page answer to the kids' complaint conceding on the record much of the kids' case.

This was a big step. For the first time in history, the federal government admitted to a court of law that, among other things:

- Carbon dioxide emissions were currently altering the atmosphere and would continue to alter Earth's climate for thousands of years.

- The Earth had already warmed about 0.9° Celsius (1.5° Fahrenheit) since massive burning of fossil fuels began in the mid-1700s and if left unchecked would increase more than 6° C (11° F) by 2100.

- Human activities, including the burning of fossil fuels, were changing the global climate at a pace and in a way that threatened human health and welfare now and in the future.

- Climate change was associated with an increase in allergies, asthma, cancer, cardiovascular disease, stroke, heat-related deaths, food-borne diseases, injuries, toxic exposures, mental health and stress disorders, and neurological diseases and disorders.

- The United States alone contributed more than *25 percent* of cumulative global CO_2 emissions from 1850 to 2012.

In other words, the federal government admitted that climate change was real, it was caused by human activity including the burning of fossil fuels, it harmed people, and the harms would worsen over time.

Julia and her team compared the complaint they filed to start the lawsuit side-by-side with the Obama administration's answer, highlighting in color the facts the government admitted. As the rainbow unfolded before them, the kids' lawyers realized that huge parts of the lawsuit would not be contested at trial. "The Obama administration's answer could be a rock for us going forward," said Phil. "The fundamental science facts were there for the judge to build her opinion on."

Still, no one knew how the fossil fuel industry and the Trump administration would respond. Would they deny these admissions? Would they throw up more roadblocks to stop the case from going to trial?

The Changing of the Guard
January–March 2017

Donald Trump was inaugurated on January 20, 2017. Almost immediately, the administration removed all mention of global warming and climate change from the White House website. The new president began systematically overturning Obama's Clean Power Plan and reducing staffing in the Environmental Protection Agency. With the Trump administration taking a sharp turn away from respect for science and acknowledgment of the climate crisis, Julia worried that they would try to walk back the science facts their predecessors had admitted on the record.

Julia and her team reached out to officials at the newly reorganized Justice Department to ask about the lawsuit. No one returned their calls or emails.

She also worried that they would delete or destroy government letters, emails, or documents on climate change she needed as evidence for the case. She submitted a letter requesting the court to ensure that the government didn't destroy records related to climate change. The government balked.

Judge Coffin, who would handle scheduling and all pretrial motions and matters, called a case-management conference between the two parties.

Julia advocated hard for a speedy trial. "I think we all are aware that time is really the enemy of these plaintiffs right now, and the status quo is the enemy of the plaintiffs," she said.

Then she brought up the issue of the defendants preserving documents relevant to the case. The government lawyer, still Sean Duffy, protested.

Judge Coffin said: "They are just asking you, if I understand it correctly, not to destroy any evidence, any of this material that you take down from the website but to preserve and archive it . . . Do you have any objection to doing that?"

But the government did not want to change its ordinary processes of archiving, destroying emails, and writing over tapes. "It's actually a very onerous process for the agencies to redo their recordkeeping practices," Sean Duffy said.

Julia tried a different tactic, offering to move quickly on discovery. In discovery, both parties submit lists of witnesses and requests for the opposing side to produce specific documents that could become evidence at trial. Lawyers on both sides can examine the evidence and depose (or interview under oath) the witnesses. That gives each side the information they need to make their best case. Judge Coffin agreed and tried to set a timeline.

The government objected: "The notion that we can, in under seventy days, do this massive amount of depositions is just unfathomable and divorced from reality based on my experience," Sean Duffy said.

Judge Coffin interjected: "Okay. Everybody is starting to use phraseology that, to me, is somewhat overstated: Unimaginable, unfathomable, immense, impossible, *et cetera*."

The judge floated the idea of conducting the trial in phases, with the first phase addressing the science of climate change, the harms to the kids, and whether the government was liable for those harms. If the government was found liable, the second phase would cover redress, or what the government should do about it.

They discussed the number of expert witnesses Julia's team would need. To Judge Coffin, the fifteen or twenty Julia wanted seemed excessive, and he asked her to whittle down the list. She said she would try.

The government lawyer said he might need an equal number of experts to rebut her witnesses. "Well, that's fine," the judge said, "but I get the impression that . . . the plaintiffs' experts take their information from government findings and science and a lot of your experts agree with their assessment. So . . . don't fight just for the sake of fighting. If there's things you agree on."

Phil and Julia were surprised that the Trump administration did nothing to walk back all the science that had been conceded by the Obama administration. But they weren't in the clear there yet. Unsurprisingly, the fossil fuel industry intervenors denied or refused to admit the science facts admitted by the Obama administration. That meant the youth's team would have to prove it all with evidence at trial regardless.

Judge Coffin warned the intervenors that their position meant that the kids' lawyers could request all kinds of documents about the fossil fuel industry's knowledge of climate change. The unspoken message was: Would you really want that information revealed?

The meeting ended on a disturbing note.

"Your Honor, we have one additional point, and it's not directly related to what we are discussing today," Sean Duffy said. "But I just want to raise it in full candor."

Here we go, Julia thought.

Then the government lawyer dropped a bomb. His superiors at the Justice Department were considering a rare "interlocutory appeal." The normal process in a lawsuit was that the district court judge would handle all pretrial motions, hold a trial, and make a ruling. After the trial and ruling, the losing side could appeal to the higher court, in this case the Ninth Circuit Court of Appeals.

Interlocutory appeal would allow the Ninth Circuit to review what the district court was doing before there was a trial record, before the youth and the experts ever had a chance to testify in court. On what basis could the government do that? Julia wondered.

She worried, too, that early review could jeopardize their case. The higher court's job was not to look closely at the evidence, and the evidence was vital to winning.

Julia and her team had no choice but to wait and see whether the government would pursue this strategy. In the meantime, they turned up the heat on the fossil fuel industry representatives who had joined the case. Our Children's Trust submitted a document request for correspondences from the last fifty years between members of the oil, gas, and coal industries and the government about climate change. Establishing the role the fossil fuel companies played in government decisions would help make the case. But it was also a bold, up-the-stakes move. The documents could uncover early knowledge of the research on the dangers of climate change that these powerful companies would rather the public not know. It could reveal company efforts to sow doubt about the dangers of climate change. And the federal government might not like what the documents revealed about how much influence industry lobbying had on government policies and actions.

Such details could cause public outcry. Just a few years back, a *Los Angeles Times* investigation had uncovered proof that ExxonMobil knew the risks of climate change in the 1970s but downplayed the risk to shareholders for decades. Discovery for this trial could uncover similar damaging documents. Lawyers around the country were excited that this information might become public. Everyone wondered: Would the fossil fuel intervenors turn over the documents or back out of the lawsuit?

The federal government followed through on their threat for an early appeal. On March 7, 2017, they filed a motion asking Judge Aiken to allow an interlocutory appeal to the Ninth Circuit Court of Appeals. They also asked that she stay proceedings, meaning all preparations for the trial would halt.

The government argued that Judge Aiken made clear errors in her interpretation of the law in her historic ruling and that discovery for the trial would be too onerous for the government. They wanted *Juliana* dismissed.

Bloomberg Law called it "a rare move" to ask the court to "go over the head of the district court judge in Oregon hearing the case and kill the lawsuit outright."

While Julia and her team worked to keep the trial on track, the kids themselves were facing their own challenges.

Three Plaintiffs Struggle
April 2017

Jayden Foytlin, the plaintiff whose house flooded in Louisiana, was excited to celebrate her fourteenth birthday in April by going roller skating. Top of her invite list was her best friend and cousin Madison. Most weekends, the girls hung out shooting hoops in the driveway or playing video games on the couch.

Growing up in oil country as a kid who cared about the environment, Jayden felt pretty isolated. The oil and gas industries were Louisiana's largest industries. In her town, many people worked on oil rigs in the Gulf of Mexico—including, for a time, her dad. In the recent election, nearly 60 percent of Louisiana's vote went to Trump. At school, kids teased her. Around town, people gossiped about her. "You're being brainwashed," they told her. "What is wrong with you?" they asked.

"It's really hard to make friends because people have a different mindset than I do," she said.

And then, as Jayden's birthday approached, something odd happened. Madison's mother wouldn't answer texts about the birthday party.

On the day of the party, Jayden bustled around her home, which still had bare cement floors and damaged walls from the flood. She hoped that Madison could join them at the last minute.

As the family climbed into the car to head to the rink, Jayden's mom's phone chirped. It was Madison's mom. Madison would not be coming. Not only that, but because of the lawsuit, she would not allow Madison to hang out with Jayden anymore. "I don't want nothing to do with children being in adult situations nor will any of our children," Madison's mom texted. "I think it's pathetic that a young girl is even involved in something like this."

Sitting in the car in the driveway, staring at the basketball hoop, Jayden realized she might never get to hang out with her best friend again. A painful emptiness welled up inside her.

Though it would surely be easier and less lonely, Jayden couldn't give up on the lawsuit. She had seen with her own eyes how the rising seas were carving out the coast, how hurricanes and floods were battering her town and her whole state. She had read the science about how bad things could get. If anything, whether she ended up friendless or not, she wanted to do more about climate change, to speak up about it even more loudly.

She wasn't the only plaintiff feeling compelled to do more.

That spring, Miriam, now a sophomore at Seattle University, wanted to become more of a spokesperson for the lawsuit. While the media focus earlier had been on a few of the more well-known plaintiffs—such as Kelsey Juliana who was the lead plaintiff and Xiuhtezcatl who already had a following for his rap music—media interest had increased, and the team needed to spread the responsibilities. But talking to reporters and being quotable didn't come naturally to Miriam. "I was nervous and spent a lot of time talking in long, run-on sentences that never appeared in any article," they said.

Our Children's Trust offered the youth various opportunities for media training, explaining how to preserve privacy and empowering them not to answer questions they didn't want to answer or that were outside their expertise. Rather than scripting what to say, the training encouraged the 21 to use their own authentic voices and stories.

For Miriam, this was easier said than done. "I'd talk to a reporter, then read the article and see what they quoted, and what they don't quote, which is most everything. Then I'd talk to another reporter, read the article, and notice that they liked shorter sentences. So, I tried to say more, with fewer words." One day, Miriam, who was a resident advisor for their dorm, had to leave an RA meeting to talk to a reporter from *National Geographic*. "My coworkers were like, 'Wait, there's a *National Geographic* reporter in our dormitory?'" It was exciting but nerve-wracking.

Around the same time, 9-year-old Levi began giving speeches about climate change and the lawsuit. His first one was April 19, 2017. Barely four feet tall, he was dressed in shorts, sandals, and a bright blue T-shirt that read: "Climate Change is Real." Standing in front of about a hundred Florida citizens, he held a mic in one hand and note cards in the other.

"Hi. My name is Levi, and I'm an environmentalist." He gave the crowd a small, slightly nervous smile.

He looked down at his note cards. "You may have heard that I'm part of a court case suing the U.S. government for not doing enough to help prevent climate change . . ."

He tried to flip to the next note card but had trouble while holding the mic. He bumbled through some details about the suit, shifting his weight back and forth, struggling to find his place. "If climate change continues, sea level rise will happen. And then,

Florida will be underwater, and my home will be underwater. And that's scary."

His note cards fluttered to the floor. He scrambled to pick them up and continued, adding more details about the lawsuit. But he got tripped up again. So, he concluded. "Thank you for your time. If you have any questions, I will be honored to answer them." He was momentarily embarrassed, but soon off playing with kids from the audience.

He practiced some more and a week later, at a March for Science rally, Levi gave it another try. Wearing a bright blue T-shirt and bright blue pants, he stood before a crowd with the bright blue sky behind him, wind whipping through his hair. He grabbed the mic confidently.

"My name is Levi, and I'm a nine-year-old environmentalist. I live in Satellite Beach. I am here today to tell you that science shows that climate change is real, and I am doing something about it." His face registered determination. "I am one of 21 youth plaintiffs suing the U.S. government and the fossil fuel industries who are not doing enough to combat climate change." The crowd clapped and Levi stood straighter. "They're not listening to the scientists. We want the U.S. government to follow the laws that are already in place, and to listen to scientists, so that they can protect my future and future generations. Scientists have told the government about climate change for over fifty years. And the government has done nothing about it. Now us kids have to do something about preventing climate change." He spoke directly to people in the crowd, sharing his exasperation.

"Why kids?" he asked the crowd. "It's our future and future generation's future. Have you smelled the fish kills in the Indian River

Lagoon? Have you seen the damage from Hurricane Matthew? Those are results of climate change. Scientists say if climate change continues, sea-level rise will be even worse than it already is. Florida is at sea level. Florida will be underwater if climate change continues, then I won't have a home. And that's scary. So far, my court case has gone through two levels of court. The government and the fossil fuel industry have tried to stop my case from going to trial, but they did not succeed. So, at the end of the year, my case will be going to trial. This is a landmark case. Science is real, and climate change is real. What are you doing about it? Thank you." He flashed a big smile, his green eyes sparkling.

The crowd erupted in applause.

He'd nailed it.

Marching Ahead
April-June 2017

Julia knew that the work the 21 plaintiffs took on could be challenging and isolating. So, Our Children's Trust found opportunities to bring the youth together. At the end of April, Levi and his mom, Jayden and her mom and sister, and a bunch of the other plaintiffs traveled to Washington, D.C., to join the People's Climate March. Our Children's Trust rented a house so they could bunk together.

The plaintiffs had a busy week. Levi was invited to speak on a panel with former vice president Al Gore, who made the documentary on climate change *An Inconvenient Truth*. The panelists sat on a stage in a large hall in big black armchairs, chatting. Al Gore was on the far left, wearing a suit, and filling the chair. Levi sat next to him. In his jeans and gray T-shirt that said: I AM THE FUTURE, he looked like a little prince on an oversized throne.

The MC introduced Gore, then Levi. "We're longtime buddies," Al Gore quipped.

Levi nodded, laughed, turned to the crowd, and delivered his remarks, spot on.

The plaintiffs also met with members of Congress about the lawsuit. Isaac was surprised by how much he loved doing this. He talked with an aide to a Republican senator from a small county north of Jacksonville. The aide, who was not a climate skeptic but was skeptical of the lawsuit, asked about the remedy the plaintiffs wanted. People in his county worked in oil fields, factories, and plants. "What would their future look like?" he asked. Isaac pointed out that many skills required for coal mining or handling liquefied natural gas were also needed to build and run solar power plants or geothermal plants. Legislation could include training to transition workers from a fossil fuel energy system to a renewable energy system. "Your constituents would be making more money and the work would be cleaner," Isaac told him. Isaac could see him getting more on board with the idea.

During a quiet moment back at the house, the group did a team-building exercise, with each person sharing something good in their lives, something they were looking forward to, and an obstacle. Jayden offered that the best thing in her life was being involved in the lawsuit. Her biggest challenge: the opposition she faced in her hometown. The loss of her best friend stung. "It's very hard to, like, socialize because where I live has a bunch of oil workers," she said. "People don't want their kids talking to me or they don't want to talk to me." The others nodded. They had all faced some ugliness, even from peers.

Julia felt the difficulties the kids faced profoundly. When it was her turn to share her challenge, she took a deep breath. "[It's] what you just said, Jayden, and knowing—this is going to make me cry —the hardships you all go through."

After everyone spoke, they had a big group hug. Jayden reveled in it, laughing. "I didn't expect to fit in with the group because I've always been so different from everyone else around me," she said. "But I fit right in, like a puzzle piece."

The day of the march dawned with record heat, oddly fitting for a demonstration in support of the science of global warming. The heat did little to deter the 200,000 people gathered on the National Mall in front of the Capitol.

When it was her turn to speak to the crowd, Jayden climbed onto a huge stage with a giant sound system wearing a bright red "Defend, Resistance" bandana. "Last August, we woke up to half a foot of water streaming down our house due to climate change and the loss of the wetlands," she said. When she talked about being part of the lawsuit against the government on climate change, the crowd erupted in applause. "Thank you, Jayden!" a man in the crowd called out. Jayden smiled.

After the speeches, the crowd began the march toward the White House. Isaac and Zealand walked together, taking turns carrying a backpack and banner. An ice cream cart rolled along next to Levi. It was hot, and he was sweating buckets. He pulled his shirt over his head to get some air on his back and belly and joined in the chanting.

"Climate change is not a lie! Please don't let our planet die!"

"No more coal! No more oil! Keep your carbon in the soil!"

The chanting was so loud that Levi felt like the ground was rumbling.

He could barely breathe from the heat, his throat was raw from yelling, he was sweating, his feet hurt, and his arms were sticky from eating ice cream. "It was just so great," he said.

The march ended with the crowd surrounding the White House, chanting: "What do we want? Climate Justice! When do we want it? NOW!"

Jayden yelled her heart out with two other plaintiffs: Jaime Butler, the Navajo nation member forced from the reservation, and

Aji Piper, who was also a plaintiff suing Washington State. The three young people held before them a long white banner with a message for President Trump: "See you in court."

On May 1, 2017, the 21 got one step closer.

Judge Coffin recommended denying the government's request for interlocutory appeal, noting that appeal before a trial "would put the cart before the horse." Judge Coffin "emphatically rejected" the notion that climate change could only be addressed by Congress and the executive branch, not by the courts. Indeed, he said that the courts were the branch of government "particularly well suited for the resolution of factual and expert scientific disputes" about climate change, which was "quintessentially a subject of scientific study and methodology, not solely political debate." The government's admissions about climate change had, "if anything . . . enhanced" the kids' claims. Further, if the young people prevailed, the judge was sure the courts could offer relief that wouldn't "micromanage" federal agencies.

The trial judge, Ann Aiken, still had to approve Judge Coffin's recommendation. If she did, they would head to trial.

Then, the opposition did an about-face. On May 26, 2017, ThinkProgress led with this headline: "Fossil Fuel Groups Try to Flee Landmark Lawsuit Before It Goes to Trial." On the day fossil fuel industry representatives were supposed to give the court their position on the science of climate change and turn over the documents Julia had requested, they withdrew from the suit. "We are confident that the U.S. Department of Justice will rigorously defend its position and that the court will conclude that setting national environmental policy is the role of Congress and the president," they stated. They likely were also reluctant to reveal details about their knowledge of climate change.

The move was a relief to the youths' legal team. "We didn't want them in the case, and we thought they would fight us really hard," Julia said. "They ended up being the easy ones 'cause they walked away." Now the legal team only had to provide evidence on the climate change facts that the Obama administration had not agreed to in their briefs.

On June 8, 2017, Judge Aiken issued her ruling about the early appeal.

"Defendants' motions to certify the November 10 order and opinion for interlocutory appeal are DENIED."

"Defendants' request for a stay is DENIED . . ."

Evacuate, Evacuate!
June–September 2017

The victory was short-lived. On June 9, 2017, the Trump administration filed a rare and rarely successful motion called a petition for a writ of mandamus. The mandamus petition asks a higher court to command a lower court to do its duty. "It's actually a petition against the judge," Julia explained to the 21. "It's telling the judge that she so abused the process and so abused her discretion that her ruling needs to be immediately appealed."

The government argued that by not dismissing *Juliana*, Judge Aiken and Judge Coffin were failing in their basic responsibilities. They wanted the next level of court, the Ninth Circuit Court of Appeals, to command them to dismiss the case. In essence, the government claimed that there was a horrible emergency to stop—and that simply having a trial was that emergency. "It's hard to express how extraordinary this is," Julia said.

In July, the Ninth Circuit Court of Appeals responded by staying, or temporarily halting, the case until they figured out what to do about the government's appeal.

But climate change would not wait.

While Julia and her team worked to fight the unexpected and unusual petition, a huge storm called Irma was brewing in the Atlantic.

Levi and his family were glued to the screen, watching the devastation that Hurricane Irma wreaked on some small Caribbean islands. Wind roared, debris flew, tall trees leaned, bent, and snapped. Waves crashed and turned streets into rivers.

The hurricane barreled toward Levi's home, and he was scared. The governor of Florida ordered roughly seven million people to evacuate, including Levi's family.

Levi helped his mom tape the windows and move furniture and rugs away from windows and doors in case wind busted them open. They hauled sandbags, stacking them in low-lying areas next to the house, and even dug trenches to collect overflow from the gutters.

Then they loaded up the car. "You have to take anything you can't live without if the entire house disappeared or if the roof was ripped off and everything was ruined," Levi's mom told him.

For Levi, that meant his books.

Levi stuffed some clothes and lots of books into a bag. As he lugged the bag to the car, it felt like a ton of bricks. He also packed a box of treasures, rocks he had collected, cool feathers, other things he had found that he wanted to keep safe. But there were other things in his room that he was worried about. "What about all this stuff?" Levi asked his mom, pointing to his other books, toys, and the ribbons he had won at swim meets.

"Move what is most important to you up high," his mom said, "in case the house floods."

He shoved everything he could on top of dressers and on the high shelf above his closet. When those were full, he piled stuff on his bed. Levi was terrified. "I didn't know what would happen. I didn't know if I was going to have a home or if everything was going to be destroyed."

They drove almost 200 miles north and inland to Gainesville, to his grandma's house. The adrenaline and excitement of hustling around, preparing for the hurricane, wore off. Then came the worst part. The watching and waiting.

The family huddled around the TV as footage of waves pummeling the barrier island flashed across the screen. Storm surges rose up and flooded neighborhoods they recognized. Wind howled, roofs flew off buildings, and cars floated down rivers.

Levi clung to his mom as these horrible things happened to his town, feeling powerless to do anything. Would his house survive? Would flooding destroy all his stuff and make his house unlivable?

He watched water sweeping over Merritt Island, which was near his home. A map of the flooding filled the screen. A road just a minute walk from their house was underwater. "Oh crap," Levi's mom muttered.

Eventually, the wind and rain subsided and the storm moved on. Levi wanted to get home as fast as possible, but he also dreaded what he might find. He and his mom hoped their house was all right but couldn't tell much from news reports. "Not knowing is the worst," Levi said.

As they approached his neighborhood, Levi peered out the car window looking for signs of what their street and their home might be like. Trees were down. Signs were down. Fences, branches, and roof shingles littered the area.

They drove slowly with all the other traffic around fallen branches and trees and pieces of destroyed houses. When they finally got to their street, debris clogged storm drains and water flooded the whole area.

But their house was still standing. Screens on the windows were shredded. They could tell that water had gotten into the garage. But they couldn't tell how high it went or whether it was in the house as well.

Levi stepped out of the car into the steamy heat, struggling between rushing in and holding back. What would he find inside?

His mom opened the front door.

The living room was dark but seemed dry.

Levi flicked on the light switch. "No power," he said.

They stepped in, looking for damp areas and signs of water.

Then Levi bolted to his room. He ran around touching everything, his books, his bed.

Everything seemed okay. But he still felt shaky and anxious. It was a close call.

Irma was not the only hurricane to pummel the United States that fall. Hurricane Harvey pounded Louisiana and Texas, and Hurricane Maria devastated Puerto Rico. Scientists strongly linked this string of record-breaking storms to climate change, as warming ocean air and waters intensified the storms' wind speeds and increased rainfall.

The burden on the nation was heavy. These three disasters alone cost the United States more than $300 billion. That would have been enough to pay for four years of public college or university tuition for all 13.5 million students enrolled in the United States.

After what he experienced, Levi was impatient for the next court date. Even though his home survived the storm, several homes nearby were destroyed. He wanted nothing more than to look the judge in the eye. "They had to realize now how serious all this is," he said. "They have to do something."

Desperate to Do More
August–November 2017

Miriam, studying abroad in Sweden, was heartbroken when they heard about Levi's traumatic evacuation. Worried, scared, and angry, they remembered something that happened after one of the Eugene hearings. Miriam's mom and sister had ended up alone in an elevator with Sean Duffy. The lawyer stared down at the ground in total silence. He wouldn't meet their eyes.

Inspired by the rhythm and patterns of the birds chirping, Miriam grabbed their mandolin, plucked out a lick, and wrote "Birdsong" to Sean Duffy and the other government lawyers:

> *tell me what are you trying to do?*
> *we want a future we thought you would too*
> *tied up in this system that may be true*
> *but we all have choices, which side are you gonna choose?*
>
> *maybe it's wealth that you seek*
> *I don't understand it I'd rather be free*
> *the rivers and minnows and big noisy geese*
> *and beautiful goddamn trees, I know what I need*
>
> *where I once swam now dry cracked and broken*

trying to breathe, my lungs fill with smoke
playing to birdsong alone on the mountain
where did the wilderness go?

I used to think you were trying to kill us
now I see you just don't care if we die
we fight for a future no matter how hopeless
at least I can meet your eyes

With climate change marching on, putting them all at peril, Miriam couldn't sit still and just wait for the courts to do something.

Activists in Germany ran multiple actions a year targeting fossil fuel infrastructure called "Break Free of Fossil Fuels." Every three months or so thousands of Germans shut down coal mines in an effort they dubbed Ende Gelände, which meant "here and no further."

Julia continued to have mixed feelings about civil disobedience, which she shared with the plaintiffs. "Peaceful, nonviolent acts of civil disobedience that don't hurt anyone, even if they disrupt people's lives, play an important role in movements," she admitted. She told the plaintiffs that it was their decision whether to participate. But she asked them to take into consideration that being a plaintiff in this high-profile case was an important role in the fight for climate justice.

The weight of climate change felt heavier than the danger of arrest, and Miriam boarded a bus with some young activists from Sweden. During the twenty-four-hour ride to Germany to join an action, Miriam wondered if they would be arrested and if Julia would be mad. Mostly Miriam hoped the German protest wouldn't affect the 21's case happening so far away in another country.

With a determined group of people from several European countries, Miriam hiked into a dusty open pit coal mine. The group surrounded one of the excavators, pressed together, holding hands. With the protestors in the way, the company had to stop mining.

Police charged in, grabbing Miriam and many others. They loaded the protesters—sweaty, dusty, and jostled together—into paddy wagons, and drove away.

Here we go again, Miriam thought. How strange to be on both sides of the legal system, addressing the climate crisis as a plaintiff and a defendant. They hoped that someday their work as a plaintiff might create a legal defense for direct activists. A legal concept called the "necessity defense" holds that someone may not be liable for a crime if it was necessary to avert a greater harm. Establishing a constitutional right to a stable climate would give activists strong legal legs to stand on. "If the way you've been mining coal threatens my life, my health, my future, stopping your big coal scooper becomes a matter of survival and a matter of rights," Miriam said.

Miriam also wondered whether the direct action could be used as evidence in the case. "The threat of the climate crisis has made me put my body on the line," they said. "I've already lost jobs from having a criminal record. Did climate change make me go nuts? Then push me to break the law? Then fuck up my future? It's a really dark way of putting it, but it's possible."

The paddy wagon pulled to a stop, and the doors opened. Instead of taking the protesters to jail, the German police stopped at a distant field and let everyone out.

Soon after, Miriam attended the 2017 United Nations Climate Change Conference, or Conference of Parties (COP23) in Bonn,

Germany. Miriam was roped into a live international TV press conference with some other activists. After the scrappy and dangerous direct action at the mine, it felt odd to put on formal clothes. They walked into a room filled with big TV cameras and sat at a long table with name tags and mics at each spot. To Miriam, it felt surreal.

Every other activist on the panel pulled out a speech, but Miriam hadn't prepared anything and stumbled through their remarks. Miriam was uneasy about their role as a leader and a spokesperson. "I feel strongly that this is not about me," they said. "But someone says, 'Here's the mic and you gotta say something and we're all listening to you,' but it's a weird place to be in because you're like, 'Wait, should you be listening to me? Do I have the answers?' No, I don't. I'm really not any better than you, I'm not any more special than you are."

They felt a duty to muddle through. "Environmentalism can be perceived as something for middle-class white people to engage in if they choose, like a trivial thing not relevant to other people," they said. "But it's not trivial, especially for communities of color." Miriam's extended family, who live in India, have hosted climate refugees in their homes. People of color and LGBTQ people are often marginalized by discrimination in housing, exclusion from opportunities, and violence. Their precarious position in the world can make them more vulnerable in disasters caused by climate change. "I feel strongly as a person of color, as a queer person, as a person from a more working-class background that this is our fight and that I can put a different face on the climate movement," Miriam said. But how could they do it better?

After the press conference, indigenous activist Dallas Goldtooth, who was part of the Standing Rock/Oceti Sakowin Camp protest to the Dakota Access Pipeline, offered Miriam some tips. Break what you want to say down to three main points, Dallas said, because you can remember three main points. That way you can be ready to speak without having to read anything.

Toward the end of the conference, Miriam learned that the lawsuit was taking another step forward. In December, the Ninth Circuit Court of Appeals in San Francisco would hear oral arguments about the government's writ of mandamus. The justices already had in hand a letter from Judges Aiken and Coffin calling the issues in *Juliana* "vitally important" and declaring that they "do not believe that the government will be irreversibly damaged by proceeding to trial."

Miriam would not be able to leave school in Europe to attend the hearing but would watch, hopeful, from afar.

The Cost of Speaking Up
December 2017

Early December was a busy time for students, with end-of-the-term tests and holiday celebrations. But eighteen of the twenty-one plaintiffs planned to fly to San Francisco for the hearing.

Nathan had to choose between attending the hearing or his high school's winter dance. He was a senior and realized he had never been to a single one. Being part of this lawsuit meant missing part of what it meant to be a teenager. He lost the freedom to "be chaotic," to experiment, to make mistakes. "It's hard to do that when you are the public face for something really important," Nathan said. "There is an emotional toll to all this."

Other plaintiffs also struggled with making space for everything they wanted to do in their lives. "There are definitely times that have been overwhelming because I have sports and school and friends and family and miscellaneous things like clubs, and I have the lawsuit to think about and what I can do right now to help the lawsuit in any way I can," Sahara said. "It can be a lot."

But it would all be worth it if they could have a trial and finally tell the court and the world that enough is enough, that the time had come for the United States government to stop supporting the fossil fuel industry and start listening to science.

Observers of *Juliana* were beginning to think the trial could actually happen. A reporter for Mashable called *Juliana v. United States* "The little climate case that could," observing: "Many experts have consistently underestimated the likelihood that this suit would reach this far, considering how other judicial approaches to address climate change have failed. If the 21 young people succeed in getting a judge to order the Trump administration to alter its pro-drilling, climate-denial policies, they will have succeeded where no environmental activists or international allies have, simply by alleging a constitutional violation of their rights. While this is an unlikely outcome, it gets more and more plausible with each passing legal proceeding."

The case had also moved from the small district court in Eugene, Oregon, to a bigger stage. The Ninth Circuit, as the largest federal appeals court in the United States, covered the entire West Coast. Important groups such as the Sierra Club, the League of Women Voters, and the Union of Concerned Scientists stepped up to support *Juliana* by filing amicus briefs. Also known as "friend of the court" briefs, these documents from parties not in the lawsuit offer information or arguments that the court may want to consider before ruling. *Juliana* was now on a national—even international—stage.

The hearing would not be about the substance of the case. That was what the trial was for. This hearing was to address the government's mandamus claim that *Juliana* had no legal merit, and that Judge Aiken made an extreme mistake in ruling that the 21 could go to trial.

To prepare for the oral argument, Julia went to the website of the Ninth Circuit to watch videos of hearings held by the three judges she would face: Sidney Thomas, Marsha Berzon, and Alex

Kozinski. She observed their questioning styles, how they preferred their questions answered. She asked herself: Who is this human being who is going to hear this case? How can I deliver the ideas so that they will hear them and understand them in the best possible way?

Her read was that Judge Kozinski posed the biggest challenge. He would be highly active in the hearing, steering the arguments with probing questions. She poured over opinions he had written, especially in cases that involved young people. She took notes so that she could point to his own words. She was determined to have him really understand why the youth had a right to go to trial.

As the hearing neared, she felt ready.

Julia wanted to practice her oral arguments in a setting similar to what she might face at the courthouse. So, on the Friday before the hearing, which was scheduled for Monday, December 11, 2017, she visited her law school, U.C. Law San Francisco, for a "moot" or pretend court.

The rehearsal went well, but at 4 p.m., co-counsel Phil Gregory was scrolling through his emails and the news when his face dropped. "No," he muttered. "Not now."

"Prominent Appeals Court Judge Accused of Sexual Misconduct," read the headline of a *Washington Post* article. Phil handed Julia his phone. Six women, clerks and junior staffers, had accused Judge Alex Kozinski of inappropriate comments and contact. Julia closed her eyes and whispered, like a prayer: "Oh my gosh, oh my gosh, not right now."

What did it mean for their oral argument, which was scheduled to start in three days? Would the court cancel Judge Kozinski's hearings while they evaluated these serious allegations? If they didn't, what would the environment in the courtroom be like? Would anyone even be able to concentrate on the arguments?

The clock ticked toward 5 p.m., when the court would close for the weekend.

The legal team heard nothing. They had to assume that the oral argument would proceed as scheduled.

Julia was apprehensive all weekend. What would it be like to be a woman arguing a case before a judge accused of sexual misconduct?

Many of the young plaintiffs were awed by San Francisco, with its undulating hills, massive vistas of the bay, and grand bridges bustling with honking traffic. Approaching the courthouse through throngs of scurrying pedestrians, they knew they were no longer in the small town of Eugene.

The granite courthouse loomed over the block with imposing arched windows and intricately carved moldings. The plaintiffs hustled up the steps, straightening their clothing, taking one more sip of water or downing one more snack. Then they pushed through heavy bronze doors.

The first-floor hallway, which ran the length of the building and the length of the block, was majestic with huge marble columns leading to a high vaulted ceiling. Elaborate chandeliers sparkled above.

As the plaintiffs took it all in, their chatter subsided, their footsteps echoing on the ceramic mosaic tile floor below. Up on the third floor, they entered Courtroom One, the most elaborate room in the building. Its walls were white marble with carvings of cupids, fruits, and flowers. Sun shone through stained-glass windows. Smooth columns with intricate cornices lined the room.

The three judges, all white, sat high up on leather chairs behind a long, dark wood desk. Chief Judge Sidney Thomas, bearded, balding and wearing glasses, was in the middle. Judge Marsha Berzon, with wavy short brown hair, was to the right. Judge Alex Kozinski, who had tufts of white hair and a broad forehead, was on the left.

Now that the case was in the Ninth Circuit Court of Appeals, Deputy Assistant Attorney General Eric Grant stepped in as the government's lawyer. He was a heavy hitter who had served as a law clerk for U.S. Supreme Court Justices Warren Burger and Clarence Thomas and had argued cases in front of the Supreme Court. Built a bit like a football player, white, with a wide mouth and straight white teeth, he was a member of the Federalist Society, a group of conservatives "founded on the principles that the state exists to preserve freedom, that the separation of governmental powers is central to our Constitution, and that it is emphatically the province and duty of the judiciary to say what the law is, not what it should be."

Since the hearing was on the government's motion, Eric Grant, wearing a dark suit, stepped to the oversized wooden podium to speak first. "Echoing the Supreme Court, this Court has said that the remedy of mandamus is a drastic and extraordinary remedy reserved only for truly extraordinary cases. This is such a case," he said. "It is really extraordinary because plaintiffs seek unprecedented standing to pursue unprecedented claims in pursuit of an unprecedented remedy."

The 21 didn't entirely disagree. They lived in extraordinary times when climate change endangered their very lives. They needed an extraordinary remedy.

Eric Grant continued: "According to plaintiffs' complaint,

virtually every single inhabitant of the United States has standing to sue virtually the entire executive branch to enforce an unenumerated constitutional right to a climate system capable of sustaining human life and to enforce that right by means of a judicial order."

Judge Berzon interrupted: "Of course the usual answer to all of that is, well, then they'll lose . . . So why is this extraordinary in the sense that the ordinary processes of litigation should not be followed?"

Good question, Julia thought. Judge Berzon seemed to get how bizarre this appeal was.

Eric Grant detailed the burden of preparing witnesses for trial. Chief Judge Thomas interjected: "What you've described is what happens in courts all the time."

That's two judges who get it, Julia noted.

Judge Kozinski brought up the government's assertion that there were no legal precedents, no earlier court rulings, to support the youths' case but said, "There always has to be a first case."

Julia took a deep breath. When it was her turn, she would try to keep the judges focused on the rules. If she could convince them that it was up to Judge Aiken, the trial judge, to hear the evidence first, they had a good shot at winning this.

The government complained about the burden of discovery, how many documents they might be asked to turn over. But Judge Berzon pointed out that disputes about discovery can be resolved by the district court.

Eric Grant argued that the district court would be overstepping its bounds by holding "the trial of the century." And, he said, the law was on the government's side; they shouldn't even have to prepare for a trial.

"Well, but if we granted the motion here," Judge Berzon said, "why don't we grant it to the next person who comes in and says the same thing?"

Judge Thomas agreed. "We'd be absolutely flooded with appeals from people who think that their case should have been dismissed by the District Court."

"There is a logical boundary, Your Honor," said Eric Grant, "and those other cases do not involve, again, virtually the entire executive branch."

"Well, it may surprise you," Judge Thomas countered, "but we do get a lot of suits that are filed in this circuit and other circuits against everybody in the government, and lots of the time they're dismissed by the District Court, but sometimes they're allowed to amend, sometimes they're allowed to go forward."

Then it was Julia's turn. She approached the podium. "Your Honors, we know of no federal court ever dismissing a constitutional case on the grounds of mandamus. It would be extraordinary and unprecedented for the Court to do so here—"

Judge Kozinski interrupted her: "There's much unprecedented about this case. So, saying unprecedented is not going to help much . . . in some ways saying it's unprecedented sort of undermines your position because it may suggest we need to take unprecedented action."

Julia stiffened. She was not arguing that *Juliana* was unprecedented. She was saying that it would be unprecedented for the appeals court to jump in and stop the case before there was even a trial. All judges were supposed to follow precedent and the rules of the court.

Judge Kozinski asked several questions about a case called *Bellon,* a climate case that had been dismissed because the fossil fuel emissions in question were so low.

"I'll answer the latter part first," Julia said and launched in.

Judge Kozinski interrupted. "You're answering the second part of my question."

"I am," Julia replied.

But Judge Kozinski seemed to want her to answer the first part: How was *Juliana* different from *Bellon?*

So she did. "*Bellon* involved emissions that represented six percent of Washington state's emissions . . ." Julia began. "And here, in this case, the emissions that are at stake are the emissions that result from the national fossil fuel energy system that is—"

He interrupted. "In the entire world?"

"No, Your Honor. Just—"

But he seemed to want to get her to agree with what he said. "Right?" he demanded.

Isaac felt bad for Julia. "Judge Kozinski was just talking over her like some reality TV show courtroom," he said. "He was purposefully trying to mess up her flow."

Always careful with her words and alert, Julia became even more vigilant. She tried to explain that the court found that the emissions in *Bellon* were "scientifically indiscernible," while in *Juliana,* the U.S. emissions represented 16 to 25 percent of global emissions.

Judge Kozinski then pointed out that there has never been a case granting "the constitutional right to avoid global warming."

Isaac noticed that Judge Berzon tried to take control of the conversation, asking her own questions. If the other judges on the panel try to shut you up, it's because you are overstepping for sure, Isaac thought.

But when Julia tried to address Judge Berzon, Kozinski jumped in again: "You never answered my question . . ."

"Yes, Your Honor. Well—"

"You may not remember . . ."

"I will. And I'll—"

The plaintiffs started passing each other notes. "What the hell?" and "Why does he keep interrupting?" Kozinski was more aggressive than Julia had seen him in any of the videos she had watched. She was frustrated that he didn't let her complete a full sentence and that he didn't seem to be listening to her answers anyway.

"It got so intense," said Isaac. "Like the tension in the room was just really, really high."

Miriam, watching a video of the hearing from Sweden, also noticed the strange dynamic. "One of the judges was terrible to Julia," they said. "He interrupted her, didn't listen to her arguments, was like 'You're saying this,' and she's like 'No, I'm not saying that. I said something different.' There seemed to be something going on between this male judge and the female lawyer representing kids, belittling her, not taking her seriously."

At another point, Judge Kozinski asked Julia to cite which case demonstrates that the government has an obligation to manage federal land in a manner that controls systemic pollution. "I don't know of a case like that," he said.

"It's not a case, Your Honor," Julia offered. "It's the U.S. Constitution and the Fifth Amendment substantive due process clause."

"So, this is an interpretation of the Constitution that the District Court came up with. Right? There's no case saying there is such a right." He pointed out that in the two-hundred-plus-year history of the country, there had never been a case saying that the United States has to manage federal lands to improve environmental conditions. "Right?"

"Well, Your Honor, I'd like to point you to a dissent you wrote in *Lipscomb versus Simmons* . . ."

Judge Kozinski looked surprised. "I could have been wrong, you know. I could have been wrong."

"Well—"

"It was a dissent. I'm often wrong."

Julia pushed on. "Your Honor, what you said in that dissent was that the brunt of the State's policy [in question] falls on the children who, after all, have no say in the matter. Children are too important and far too vulnerable for us to permit the State to trifle with their lives in this fashion."

"Quote me, huh?"

Isaac was worried things would get even worse. "I was like, oh, my god, hopefully he doesn't like walk out of the room or something because he's so mad."

Julia went on to explain that the federal government's support of the fossil fuel energy system was depriving the youth of their rights to life, liberty, and property.

"No different than anyone else," Judge Kozinski said. "Whatever harm they're suffering is the same as everybody else in the country . . ."

"Actually, they are suffering different harm, and the federal defendants have admitted in various documents that children are disproportionately experiencing the impacts of climate change, and will going forward.

"In addition, Your Honor, they will live far longer than you. They will live to late in the century when the seas are projected by these federal defendants to be ten feet higher. . . . So the significance of the harm, the monumental threat that these injuries pose to these plaintiffs is very distinguishable from the rest of the country."

After more back and forth, Judge Kozinski questioned whether a district court should establish something as important as a constitutional right. "Isn't that the kind of stuff we leave to the Supreme Court to tell us?"

Julia welcomed the question. It is the district courts' role to hear and record the facts of the case that will be used to decide whether the government's actions are unconstitutional, she said. She pointed out that five district courts had developed records on the infringement of the equal protection rights of Black children before the Supreme Court's historic ruling in *Brown v. Board of Education.*

What would happen, Judge Kozinski wondered, if the district courts ruled that climate change should be handled in a certain way and the federal government had a different plan. "Can [the government] just ignore what the District Court says?"

"They can't . . ."

"The decision is made in Oregon, not in Washington, D.C."

"Your Honor, to the extent that government can't violate *Brown v. Board of Education* and have segregated schools any longer, if government acts in ways that deprives individuals of fundamental rights, then they can't do that."

The judge pressed again: If the district court says something and the government says something different, the court prevails? "That's your answer?" he asked.

"Well, Your Honor, I think it's a little bit more complex than that because, again—"

"How much more complex can it be?"

Julia pursed her lips but nodded slightly. She would not get rattled. She tried to explain, calmly and respectfully, that if a district court ruled that a right has been violated, the federal government would still have flexibility to decide *how* to address it.

"I don't know why you're running away from it because that's your position. I mean, why are you running away from it?" Judge Kozinski pressed.

"I'm not running away from it, I'm—"

"That's your answer."

She agreed. "[Government action] would be reviewed for its constitutionality."

"Because this is a constitutional right, the District Court would decide."

"That's correct."

Julia was exhausted and was well over time. Judge Thomas asked her to sum up.

"We simply ask that the Court lift the temporary stay and send [our case] back to the District Court so that these young people can go to trial and present their historical and scientific evidence and make their case."

"All rise," the courtroom deputy boomed.

Judge Berzon and Chief Judge Thomas filed out the courtroom door behind the bench. When Judge Kozinski reached the door, he turned his head, looked right at Julia and smirked.

After the hearing was over, the plaintiffs had no idea which way the ruling would go. The judges had put Julia through the wringer, but she stood strong and made compelling arguments. Was it enough to clear this big hurdle?

The stakes felt higher than ever. A reporter from the San Francisco website Resilience wrote: "If the government prevails at this point, then *Juliana v. United States* will be halted in its tracks, pending what I would call a 'Hail Mary Reprieve' by the U.S. Supreme Court (SCOTUS). If, however, District Court Judge Aiken's opinion is upheld, then it will arguably be on its way to becoming the most important environmental case of the century—perhaps of any century."

The kids didn't know how long they would have to wait for a ruling, a few weeks, a few months, a year?

Things moved quicker on the sexual harassment allegations against Judge Kozinski. Three days after the hearing, Chief Judge Thomas began a formal misconduct inquiry. The following week, Alex Kozinski announced his retirement from the bench. Julia's oral argument was the last Alex Kozinski would ever hear as a judge. Was he aware of that during the morning of unrelenting questioning? Julia wondered. Did she win his vote on the panel of three judges? Who would replace him?

U.S. Supreme Court Chief Justice John Roberts immediately ordered a broad review of how the nation's court system handles harassment, leading to sweeping changes. The women were heard and women in the future would have some protection.

Would the same ever be true for the young plaintiffs?

A Dizzying Flurry of Motions
March–July 2018

On March 7, 2018, Julia was on a video interview with Kaia Rose, director of *Climate Countdown,* describing how the youth were waiting for a decision on the mandamus petition.

"We're hopeful we'll have a decision this month," Julia said. "Fingers crossed for this week . . ."

Her cell phone rang, and her head and hand swiveled toward it. "I have to take this," she said.

"Go, that's fine," Kaia said, reaching to take a sip of her coffee. "No worries."

Julia slipped in an earbud. "So, is it the decision?" She paused, listening. "No way."

Kaia put down her coffee cup.

Julia pulled the microphone wire away from her mouth and looked up at the screen: "Kaia, we just got the decision."

Then into the phone she said: "You don't have it?" She typed quickly, bringing up the Ninth Circuit ruling on her computer. "Oh my gosh, okay, okay, ready, Phil?"

And she started to read aloud from the ruling for both her co-counsel Phil Gregory and for the journalist, emphasizing key phrases: "The panel *denied* without prejudice a petition for a writ of mandamus in which federal defendants sought an order directing the district court to dismiss a case seeking various environmental remedies." She grinned and read faster. "The panel held that mandamus relief was *inappropriate* when the district court had not issued a single discovery order, nor have the plaintiffs filed a single motion seeking to compel discovery. The panel also held that any [errors on the merits of the case] were correctable through the ordinary course of litigation." She wiggled happily and finished: "For these reasons, we declined to exercise our discretion to grant mandamus relief at this stage of litigation."

Julia put a hand to her heart. "Oh my god, finally!"

Later that day, Bloomberg News ran the headline: "Teenagers Defeat Trump's Move to Kill Climate Change Lawsuit." The ruling of the three-judge panel of the Ninth Circuit—with Judge Michelle T. Friedland filling Alex Kozinski's position—was unanimous. The government must demonstrate "some burden . . . other than the mere cost and delay that are the regrettable, yet normal, features of our imperfect legal system," the opinion said, and their concerns are "better addressed through the ordinary course of litigation."

In other words, the government should stand aside and let *Juliana* go to trial.

The 21 were excited and relieved. A little over a month later, Judge Thomas Coffin set a date for the trial, October 29, 2018, to be held in Judge Aiken's Eugene, Oregon, court. The trial would be a "bench" trial, rather than involving a jury, with Judge Aiken presiding. To accommodate all the testimony, he tentatively scheduled about fifty trial days. The kids were overjoyed to finally have a chance to testify.

"It was going to be insane, like the only thing Judge Aiken was going to do for three months was show up from nine to five every day to hold this trial," said Nathan, who planned to take time off of college in Minnesota to be there.

But the government was far from done with its motions and appeals.

In May, the government filed a motion for a protective order, asking the district court to deny requests Julia and her team had made in this discovery phase. They also filed a motion to stay (or stop) all further discovery while the court considered other motions. Judge Coffin denied both motions.

In June, the government asked Judge Ann Aiken to review Judge Coffin's rulings on the motion for a protective order and the motion to stay discovery. Judge Aiken denied both motions.

Isaac was exasperated. "The tactic was delay, delay, delay," he said.

But the Trump administration was just warming up. Michael Gerrard, the director of the Sabin Center for Climate Change Law at Columbia University, observed that the Trump administration "pulled out all the stops, legally, in trying to prevent the trial."

In July, the government went to the Ninth Circuit Court of Appeals again with a second writ of mandamus request. The Ninth Circuit denied it.

Behind the scenes, Julia and her legal team considered asking the court to sanction the government. In the law, defendants have many motions at their disposal, and they can keep filing them, even filing the same ones. But at some point, filing the same motions after they've already been decided, sometimes more than once, becomes harassment, an abuse of the process, and sanctionable. "It's a hard call to know when to decide to ask the court for sanction," Julia said. She was wary of taking that step.

Also in July, Judge Aiken held oral arguments on the government's motion for judgment on the pleadings and a motion for summary judgment. In essence, the government wanted Judge Aiken to rule in their favor based on the paperwork filed, without a trial, without taking any evidence, and without even hearing from the 21 directly. Julia and her team continued to prepare for trial while waiting to hear how Judge Aiken would rule.

The kids had whiplash just trying to follow it all. "This was just one gigantic blur of meaningless hurdles," said Nathan. "I can pretty much summarize it as the government put up every hurdle known to man, and we jumped each one, so let's get to trial already."

But first they had to jump the biggest hurdle they had ever faced: The United States Supreme Court.

Lead plaintiff Kelsey Cascadia Rose Juliana (above)

Left: Julia Olson, lead attorney in Juliana v. United States *and executive director of Our Children's Trust, leaves the courtroom after a hearing.*

Levi Draheim (top) was just seven years old when he joined the case. Jayden Foytlin (bottom left) and her family in Rayne, Louisiana, suffered from a catastrophic flood during the case. Plaintiff Xiuhtezcatl Martinez (bottom right) spreads his message about climate change and racial justice through rap and hip-hop music.

Top: Miriam Oommen
Middle: Sahara Valentine
and Nathan Baring
Bottom: Siblings Miko and
Isaac Vergun

Left: U.S. Department of Justice attorney Sean Duffy leaves the Wayne Morse Courthouse in Eugene, Oregon, with another USDOJ attorney.

Above: All 21 youth plaintiffs stand outside the courthouse in 2016. From left to right, top row: Nic Venner, Journey Zephier, Jaime Butler, Vic Barrett, Nathan Baring, Jacob Lebel, Alex Loznak, Aji Piper, Xiuhtezcatl Martinez, Kelsey Juliana, Miriam Oommen, Sophie Kivlehan, Tia Hatton. Bottom row: Jayden Foytlin, Levi Draheim, Avery McRae, Hazel van Ummersen, Sahara Valentine, Isaac Vergun, Zealand Bell, Miko Vergun.

Right: U.S. District Court Judge Ann Aiken outside the courthouse.

Top: Co-counsel Julia Olson and Phil Gregory confer in court.

Bottom, left to right:
Sahara, Levi, Isaac, Nathan, Miriam, Miko, Nic, and Alex in court.

Top: NASA scientist James Hansen fist-bumps plaintiff Alex Loznak in court. Hazel sits between them.

Bottom: Avery leans on Kelsey in court.

Photo by Robin Loznak / Courtesy of Our Children's Trust

Photo by Robin Loznak / Courtesy of Our Children's Trust

Top: *Kelsey Juliana speaks at a press conference on the steps of the U.S. Supreme Court in Washington, D.C. Plaintiffs stand to the left; members of Congress on the right.*

Bottom: *Youth climate activists Greta Thunberg and Jamie Margolin sit at the plaintiffs' feet during the press conference.*

Top: Levi yells a chant during the climate march.

Bottom: Journey, Aji, and Jayden hold a banner.

Top: *Isaac Vergun greets supporters in San Francisco for oral arguments before the Ninth Circuit Court of Appeals.*

Bottom: *Sahara, Avery, and Hazel hold a banner while Jacob, Isaac, Zealand, Tia, and Vic stand behind.*

Above: The 21 outside the James R. Browning U.S. Court of Appeals building.

Right: Judge Alex Kozinski was accused of sexual misconduct the week before the hearing and retired after it.

Top right: The U.S. government petitioned the U.S. Supreme Court to try to stop the case. Justice Anthony Kennedy (top left) denied the first petition before retiring. He was replaced by Justice Brett Kavanaugh.

Bottom and facing page above: Just before trial, Chief Justice John Roberts temporarily stayed the case. While the young plaintiffs awaited a ruling, their October 29, 2018 trial date was vacated. They gathered for a mournful rally outside the courthouse on the missed trial date.

Bottom: The U.S. Supreme Court ruled in the youth's favor just days later.

Top: Julia Olson presents oral arguments before a panel of three judges (bottom) of the Ninth Circuit Court of Appeals: Judges Andrew Hurwitz, Mary Murguia, and Josephine Staton. Two of the three judges ruled to dismiss the case. Judge Staton wrote a scathing dissent. The youth have filed an amended complaint, and the case is ongoing.

Photo by Robin Loznak / Courtesy of Our Children's Trust

Photo by Robin Loznak / Courtesy of Our Children's Trust

The rally with supporters in downtown Portland after the hearing was an emotional time for the young plaintiffs and their lawyers. Journey, Miriam, and Kelsey greet supporters (above). Sahara, Kelsey, Zealand, and Julia on stage (bottom).

Top: *As the youth plaintiffs continue to fight for their constitutional right to a stable climate, they are growing into adults. This photo was taken in Eugene, Oregon, in 2016.*

Bottom: *This photo was shot in New York City in 2019.*

The Highest Court in the Land
July 2018

On July 17, 2018, as Julia was about to set off on a backpacking adventure in California's Ansel Adams Wilderness with her family, the Trump administration submitted a 111-page motion for an emergency stay of discovery and trial with the U.S. Supreme Court, the highest court in the United States. Each of the nine Supreme Court justices oversee one or more of the thirteen district courts. Associate Justice Anthony Kennedy oversaw the Ninth Circuit and requested the plaintiffs' response immediately. "When the Supreme Court tells you you have to do something, you do it," Julia said.

She started drafting the brief right away, then handed it over to Phil and Andrea for their comments while she and her family drove to California. Once there, they checked into a hotel with Wi-Fi and Julia worked nonstop on the brief for the next twenty-four hours.

The 21's legal team was worried. A decision to petition the Supreme Court is made at the highest level of the Department of Justice, by a lawyer appointed by the president called the Solicitor General. The Solicitor General argues so frequently before the nine Supreme Court justices that some people call them the tenth justice. "If the Solicitor General speaking for the government asks for something, it automatically comes with great credibility, weight, and power," Julia said. "They already have a sort of foot in the door with the Supreme Court."

Julia's brief had to be powerfully persuasive. There's an old adage that a good lawyer understands the law, but a great lawyer understands the judge. A bit of a Supreme Court geek, Julia had gotten familiar with the personalities and styles of argument of individual justices by listening to oral arguments on oyez.com, a public website with all of the Supreme Court's audio since 1955. Knowing Justice Kennedy would be the first to consider the brief, she directed some key arguments to him.

For instance, Justice Kennedy wrote the opinion in a case called *Obergefell v. Hodges,* which ordered all states to recognize and license same-sex marriages. The U.S. Constitution doesn't mention marriage as a fundamental right, yet the Supreme Court opinion did. Julia and her team suggested that the Supreme Court view the right to a stable climate in the same way. In fact, she quoted the ruling in her brief saying: "Judge Aiken recognized that [the right to a stable climate], if supported by evidence at later stages of litigation, would be, like the right in *Obergefell,* a right 'underlying and supporting other liberties' and 'quite literally the foundation of society, without which there would be neither civilization nor progress.'"

Worn out from working around the clock, Julia submitted the brief by the 9 a.m. deadline and updated the young plaintiffs. She explained that their case had landed in what was being called the "shadow docket." In the shadow docket, the Supreme Court issues orders not handled in the usual fashion. Normally, if the Supreme Court agrees to hear a case, both sides provide briefs and opposing lawyers give oral arguments before the nine justices. The justices confer and issue a written decision. In the shadow docket, some-one avoids the normal process by filing a motion for an emergency order, which can be decided with or without briefing, oral argu-ments, or even a majority of justices.

In this case, Justice Kennedy would only be reading the briefs and not taking oral arguments. He could rule on his own or get the other justices to weigh in.

The 21 knew their case could end right there, and they would never get to testify at trial. Or the most important court in the land, the Supreme Court, could rule in their favor. They had waited before, but not like this. This waiting felt weightier, more import-ant, and more stressful.

Sahara never imagined being in this situation. "Everyone has heard of the Supreme Court, it's talked about a lot and is where big cases, and big issues, and big decisions happen," they said. "I knew it was a big deal and I was like, 'Am I really a part of this?'"

Even hard-to-impress Miriam was excited and tense. "The Supreme Court accepts only a tiny number of cases, so that's a big deal," they said. "But it definitely makes you nervous because what if they throw our case out?"

That was a very real possibility. Back in 2016, when the kids overcame their first motion to dismiss, law professor James May of Widener University told the *Washington Post* that because of its pioneering legal theory and the conservative leanings of the court, if *Juliana* ever made its way to the Supreme Court, it would be "dead on arrival."

Julia knew that they were up against a lot. But Justice Kennedy, a swing voter on the Court who was retiring, could have a big impact on the case. All the youth and their legal team could do was wait and see what he would say and hope that justice would prevail.

Isaac, now 16, tried to keep himself busy, focusing on Plan B in case they lost. He threw himself into climate activism, mentoring other youth, and overseeing the planting of trees with the kid-run Plant-for-the-Planet. "With a high probability that the case would get thrown out, I had to cover all the bases I could, so I could keep working for change even if we got shut out of court," he said.

But the 21 all hoped, beyond hope, that that wouldn't happen.

The Arc Is Long
July 30, 2018

Julia backpacked into the wilderness with her family knowing that the Supreme Court might rule on the government's petition while she was out of range of cell service. "I have to let go," she thought. "It's going to be what it's going to be."

Heaving the heavy pack on her back and hoofing up the mountain trails with her family to Iceberg Lake, Julia felt the weight of her body moving across the earth. Passing lush green meadows, the family pointed out yellow, red, and purple wildflowers to each other. They gazed at jagged granite peaks called the Minarets and dove into the chilly water of crystal-blue alpine lakes, screaming and laughing. They hoped that the wildfires burning in the distance would not force them to hike out early. Julia thought about how all-consuming this legal battle was and how challenging it was to juggle the *Juliana* case while also preserving precious time with her children and sharing with them such beautiful natural places that were increasingly threatened by drought and fire. While the trip felt grounding, it also reminded her how high the stakes really were.

On July 30, 2018, after hiking out of the wilderness, the family piled in the car to head to Mono Lake. Besides being a gorgeous lake with intricate rock and mineral formations, Mono Lake was also a significant exemplar of public trust litigation. In the 1980s, Los Angeles' demand for water was draining the lake and harming wildlife. The California Supreme Court ruled that the lake had to be protected under the public trust doctrine, and the water levels stabilized.

While on the road, the car passed through an area with spotty cell service. Julia's phone rang. The call was from Washington, D.C., and she recognized the number as the Supreme Court's.

Julia was driving, so she answered on speaker.

It was the Supreme Court clerk handling the emergency stay petition. "Julia, we have a decision," she said.

Julia felt like her heart stopped. Everyone in the car got quiet.

"It will be coming out shortly, but I wanted to give you a heads-up."

Julia tried to concentrate on the road. "Okay, I'm ready."

"I'm going to read it to you. It's a short opinion."

Julia was aware of her kids in the car, listening intently.

"The application for stay presented to Justice Kennedy and referred by him to the Court is denied . . ."

"Thank you," Julia tried to say.

But the call dropped.

"Whoo-hooo!" the kids yelled. Julia was laughing and crying, and everyone was yelling and cheering as they pulled into the Mono Lake area.

As soon as she could, Julia got word to the 21 plaintiffs and her team: They had won at the Supreme Court and the trial date of October 29, 2018, still stood.

Sahara was thrilled: "Relieved, happy, excited, and super pumped up!" They joyfully shared the good news with family and friends and got a slice of raspberry chocolate cake to celebrate.

"I was like 'Thank you, thank you, thank you,'" Levi said. "It was the best feeling ever, like on your birthday, when you got the present that you most wanted, times by two million then times that by two million again."

The win meant the world to Isaac. "It boosted my faith in the justice system, showed me that justice could prevail in the end," he said. "Here we had a case where the administration was working against us, the Justice Department was working against us and being uncompromising, and we had a conservative-leaning Supreme Court, but they ruled in our favor."

For the first time in a long time, what Dr. Martin Luther King Jr. said decades ago rang true to Isaac: "The arc of the moral universe is long, but it bends toward justice."

"I was like, okay, we're back on track. Let's get this ball rolling."

For Julia and her team, that meant picking apart the Supreme Court's ruling, which was just two paragraphs long.

The application for stay presented to Justice Kennedy and referred by him to the Court is denied. That meant that though the government submitted the request to Justice Kennedy, he consulted with his colleagues. The full Court appeared to support the decision. That was a good sign.

The Government's request for relief is premature and is denied without prejudice. That meant the Justice Department shouldn't appeal to the Supreme Court when problems can be resolved in the district court. "Without prejudice" indicated that the government could petition the Supreme Court again later in the process. Given what had happened so far, they likely would.

The breadth of the respondents' claims is striking, however, and the justiciability of those claims presents substantial grounds for difference of opinion. Julia couldn't deny that the kids' claims were striking but the inclusion of the phrase "substantial grounds for difference of opinion" could signal trouble. Suggesting that there was a lot of room for a difference of opinion on whether the case should even be in the courts could prompt Judge Ann Aiken to allow review of her rulings. Judge Aiken had denied the government's early request to appeal to the Ninth Circuit (interlocutory appeal). Was the Supreme Court suggesting that she should grant it?

The District Court should take these concerns into account in assessing the burdens of discovery and trial, as well as the desirability of a prompt ruling on the Government's pending dispositive motions. The highest court in the land was directing the trial court to rule quickly on the government's requests to eliminate (or dispose of) some or all of the claims. Was that a subtle scolding or pressure directed at Judges Aiken and Coffin?

"The Supreme Court has shown a willingness here to reach down to the district court level and shake a finger at them," said Georgetown law professor Lisa Heinzerling. "That was not a good sign."

The ruling was Justice Kennedy's last order as a Supreme Court justice. He retired just days later. That meant that if additional appeals went to the Supreme Court again, they would be handled by a different justice. Julia and her team wondered who, and how that might affect their chances.

But they didn't have time for playing guessing games. With the stay lifted, they had to get ready for a trial that would commence in just three months.

Preparing for Trial
August–September 2018

Many trial scenes in movies play out like this: A lawyer calls a surprise witness to the stand. Everyone gasps. The opposing lawyer leaps to her feet. Objection! Prosecution by ambush! We had no time to prepare for this witness!

Though TV shows, movies, and books often depict surprise witnesses and last-minute evidence, these tactics are actually rare. Before a trial, lawyers on both sides of a case exchange information about the witnesses and evidence that they will present. This sharing of information, called discovery, gives both sides a chance to get familiar with the evidence so they can figure out how to address it and make their best case.

Perhaps because the government was so committed to stopping *Juliana,* they had avoided requesting discovery from the plaintiffs and their experts. Then, at the last minute, the government demanded to interview all the youth plaintiffs. As a result, both sides had to fit seven months of preparation into three. "It was crunch time. We had to do fifty depositions in sixty days," said Julia. "They [had to] depose our plaintiffs, all our experts, and we had to depose theirs."

The legal team had profoundly serious conversations with all 21 youth plaintiffs about whether they wanted to be deposed and take the stand at trial. The testimony the young people would share would have to include delicate information about their physical health, their mental health, their safety, and their security. "Once you decide you're going to share your story of how you are being harmed under oath, whatever you talk about, the government can ask follow-up questions in cross-examination," Julia explained. She wanted them to know they had complete control over this deeply personal choice. "We will have enough plaintiffs who want to testify so you don't have to testify," she told them.

Every single one said they wanted to take the stand. All 21 wanted to tell their story in court.

When some of the plaintiffs were gathered in Oregon, co-counsel Phil Gregory showed them what to expect in their deposition. They met in Our Children's Trust's conference room with its long wooden table and office chairs. He sat in the middle of the long side of the table. "You'll sit here."

He moved to a seat on the same side of the table. "And your lawyer will be here."

He switched to the other side of the table to show where the government's lawyers would be when asking questions. And he showed them where the video camera would be set up to film them.

The kids would not have to be experts on climate change or the government actions. They just needed to share their stories. "The most important rule about the deposition is to tell the truth," he said. "Each of you is a remarkable individual, and each of you has a genuine story to tell."

He also warned them that they wouldn't have control over when and if they would get to tell their story in the deposition because the government lawyers would be asking the questions. "Look," he said, "if you get a chance to tell your story, tell it. But if they don't ask you the right questions, you don't have to add anything. Just answer their questions." He assured them that if—when—they went to trial, their lawyers would give the plaintiffs a platform to be heard. And the whole world would listen.

Sahara, just 13, dreaded the deposition. "I've always been super-duper scared of public speaking, and it's been really hard being a plaintiff in a case that is getting so much attention," they said.

That summer, Sahara backpacked the Opal Creek Wilderness with some other kids. Opal Creek is a pristine Oregon forest, with white, splashing waterfalls tumbling into emerald pools. Deep green moss covers round granite rocks. Douglas fir and Pacific yew trees that have lived many hundreds of years tower like columns in a cathedral.

One morning, shortly after waking up, Sahara hiked off on their own to the peak of a nearby mountain. It was cool, the air was fresh, the views both spectacular and soothing.

Sahara thought about how they wanted to protect all natural places they loved. Their family spent long days on the Mohawk River swimming, floating downstream on inner tubes, and searching for yellow, red, and orange agates. But every spring, there was more flooding stripping the banks. And every summer, the water level dropped lower and lower. Warming waters and algae blooms were suffocating fish. Sahara was scared thinking about how the river would continue to degrade.

They also worried about the small town of Yachats on the Oregon coast where their grandparents had a place a few blocks back from the beach. On maps showing sea-level rise, it was easy to see that the house was not far back enough to survive. "It's just super sad," Sahara said.

Up on the mountain peak, Sahara started to talk to their future self, about the deposition and about testifying at trial. "Sahara," they said. "You can totally do this. You've been through some hard and stressful times before, and this is going to be another one, but you will get through it." They sent love to their future self. "You can do this," they whispered.

That August, another teenager across the globe ventured out of her comfort zone in response to the climate crisis. The Swedish 15-year-old named Greta Thunberg told her parents she wanted to skip school to protest climate change. She couldn't convince her parents, her sister, her friends, or any classmates to join her. So, she hand-painted a wooden sign—School Strike for Climate—rode her bike to the Swedish Parliament and sat on the cobblestone steps in the cold all alone.

After a few hours, some journalists snapped her picture and then left.

When the sun set, Greta packed up and biked home.

The next day, she climbed on her bike again. She settled on the Parliament steps again. Alone.

Then, someone sat down beside her.

As people began to rally around Greta and her Fridays for Future strikes, on a different continent seven lawyers from Our Children's Trust began flying all over the country to meet government lawyers to take testimony from the young plaintiffs and from experts on both sides.

A typical week of fourteen- to fifteen-hour days went something like this:

Sunday: Fly into Denver to prepare plaintiff Nic Venner for deposition. That meant role-playing and reminding Nic to think before speaking, tell the truth, and only answer the question.

Monday: Prepare an expert for deposition, drive to Boulder and prepare another expert, then prepare plaintiff Xiuhtezcatl for deposition.

Tuesday: Defend the expert's deposition and Xiuhtezcatl's deposition in Boulder. That meant keeping him comfortable during hours of intense questioning, listening closely, and objecting to any improper questions.

Wednesday: Defend the expert's deposition and Nic's deposition back in Denver.

Thursday: Fly to Kalamazoo, Michigan, to prepare another expert for deposition.

Friday: Defend expert's deposition then fly to Madison, Wisconsin, where plaintiff Vic Barrett was in college.

Saturday: Prepare Vic for deposition in the morning. Defend his deposition in the afternoon. Fly to New York to prepare another expert for deposition. And so on.

One of the particularly damning expert witnesses was Gus Speth, formerly the chair of President Jimmy Carter's Council on Environmental Quality. In that role, he personally educated the president on climate change in the late 1970s and early 1980s. Gus Speth planned to testify that there was "a tremendous amount of knowledge available at that time," and that "neglect of the issue over these past four decades is the greatest dereliction of civic responsibility in the history of the Republic."

At one point, Julia was bouncing from California back to Eugene to repack and then off to New York to prepare Gus Speth and Nobel Laureate economist Joseph Stiglitz for deposition. Stiglitz was prepared to testify that: "The fact that the U.S. national energy system is so predominately fossil-fuel based is not an inevitable consequence of history. The current level of dependence of our national energy system on fossil fuels is a result of intentional actions taken by Defendants over many years. These actions, cumulatively, promote the use of fossil fuels, contribute to dangerous levels of CO_2 emissions, and are causing climate change. The economic impacts of these actions are deleterious to Youth Plaintiffs and the Nation as a whole."

When Julia arrived in New York, she realized that she had her suit jacket and dress shoes but had forgotten her suit pants. "Wow," she realized, "I'm fried. Completely maxed. I can't even get my clothes straight."

In between flying, driving, preparing witnesses, taking depositions, and defending depositions, the kids' lawyers wrote court documents, commented on each other's drafts of court documents, or responded to documents the federal government submitted to the court. While the federal government had said they would submit around seventy documents for evidence, they ended up submitting about 1,600 documents numbering 80,000 pages. The team had to become familiar with every detail in the material. They got very little sleep.

Julia, Phil, and the rest of the team were perplexed when they deposed the government's expert witnesses. They expected testimony on climate change and its effects on wildfire smoke and asthma. Instead, government witnesses knew little about climate change and planned to testify that no one could say that the wildfire smoke exacerbated Isaac's asthma or Sahara's asthma or Alex's asthma because no one examined the kids while the wildfire smoke and asthma was occurring.

Government lawyers also tried to keep the kids' expert

witnesses—such as NASA's climate expert James Hansen—from testifying. According to Phil, an exchange at a pretrial meeting went something like this:

Government: We aren't contesting the science, so you don't need scientific experts.

Our Children's Trust: So, let's take James Hansen as an example. He has something like fifty points in his report. Will you admit to all fifty points and allow all fifty points into evidence?

Government: Well, no. We don't agree to that.

Our Children's Trust: Then we need to put Hansen on the stand.

Government: You don't because we agree with the science.

Our Children's Trust: But you don't agree with all fifty points. And on and on.

It's possible that the government had difficulty finding credible witnesses willing to testify, according to a Bloomberg article. Two government attorneys approached Ken Caldeira, an atmospheric scientist at the Carnegie Institution for Science. Ken was wary about testifying on the government's behalf. "I had a good impression of the lawyers; they said their goal was to provide the best available scientific evidence," he said. "But my name being associated may give credibility to their case, and with this administration, there's a concern about being edited and taken out of context."

Julia, Phil, and the others on the team also got a glimpse of how the opposing lawyers would handle the accusation that the government knew about the dangers of climate change and continued supporting fossil fuels anyway. "We couldn't get the government to admit that *what was in the government reports* was known by the government," Phil said.

Government lawyers even contested official reports, such as

the National Climate Assessment, assembled by multiple federal agencies as evidence that the government knew about the effects of climate change. "We wanted the government to admit that, okay, you knew the various things in this climate assessment report as of the date the report was published," Phil explained. "And they would be like, no, the only thing we'll admit is, those things were in a report that was published. But we're not going to admit that the government knew that."

So, Phil and Julia realized that they would have to find witnesses in the government who would say, "I read the report and knew the findings of the report or I read a draft of the report or I helped write the report," Phil said.

"It's a very common strategy for defense lawyers to object to everything, to deny the obvious, and to make you prove it at trial," said Phil. The strategy tends to work on juries. Not so much on judges. "I'm going to use the Latin term," he joked. "It ticks off judges."

But there was something more disturbing about this process. Though the court had sealed the young plaintiffs' depositions to protect private information, Phil attended many of them, and he was shocked by the government's behavior. "For some reason, they started asking highly technical, scientific questions," he said. Perhaps they were trying to rattle the youth. Or get the kids to say something on record that could undermine their credibility in court.

When Tia Hatton said that she and her Nordic ski team had trouble finding places to train because the snow had not been as deep where she lives in Bend, Oregon, the government asked: How many snow measurements have you taken in Bend?

They asked Miko the mathematical likelihood that the Marshall Islands would go underwater.

They asked Nic what scientific research they had done on greenhouse gases contributing to climate change.

They asked Jacob whether he had measured what the climate was like at different times in the course of human civilization.

"Objection!" the kids' lawyers exclaimed. "Vague, ambiguous, nonsensical."

Jacob covered his mouth with his hand and laughed. "No, I have not gone back and measured," he said.

Over and over, the youth's lawyers objected that questions were repetitive, redundant, time-wasting, and bordered on harassment of the witnesses.

It was brutal on the young people. The government lawyers prodded Jayden with all kinds of questions about the flood and made her relive the experience. "The nature of the questioning was almost like, 'Did this really happen to you?'" Phil said. "Like they were questioning her story."

But the government's tactics backfired. The young plaintiffs got prepared and got fired up. "Over the course of the depositions, their ability to handle the questioning improved so much that by the end they were spitting fire," Phil said. "They wanted more questions. They couldn't wait to get on the witness stand to tell the judge their story."

Mary Wood, the University of Oregon law professor, was eager for the showdown, too. "It would be hard to imagine a more consequential trial, because the fossil fuel policies of the entire United States of America are going to confront the climate science put forth by the world's best scientists," she told the *Washington Post*. "And never before has that happened."

But the Trump administration had more tricks up its sleeve.

The Home Front
October 2018

On October 5, 2018, the government filed another motion in the district court for an order to stay discovery and the trial. "This redundant motion by the Department of Justice, with no new grounds for stopping the trial, is nothing more than a show of fear," Julia told the media. "Plaintiffs will be ready to give their opening statement on the first day of trial on October 29. Our experts have booked tickets and are ready to testify."

The 21 found each new motion more annoying than the last. "At this point, it's just harassment," Kelsey said.

Jayden thought the government was panicking now that the trial was just around the corner. "The fact that they're going to such great lengths to avoid this trial shows how important it is," she said. "It shows that they know what they're doing is wrong."

While Julia and her team battled the government over whether or not there would be a trial, Levi faced a new battle of his own. On October 6, another huge hurricane stirred up by warming ocean waters began barreling toward his vulnerable home. The East Coast of the United States had not taken a direct hit from a Category 5 hurricane in about thirty years, but Hurricane Michael was growing in strength. Florida was the bullseye, with landfall expected October 10.

Levi felt like he and his neighborhood had barely recovered from Hurricane Irma, and now they faced another menace. It didn't help that he had been through this before. If anything, he was more scared. He and his mother prepped the house and did all they could to help neighbors, the elderly, and their church get ready.

Julia felt helpless, with a pit in her stomach, worrying about Levi and his family and hoping they would be okay.

Levi's family planned to shelter closer by at his other grandparents' house in Satellite Beach. Expecting heavy rains and storm surges there, Levi and his mom did everything they could to shore up the house, securing the shutters and duct-taping the edges of all the doors to keep water from seeping in.

While the family prepared, the United Nations released an Intergovernmental Panel on Climate Change report, which confirmed that the world had already warmed 1 degree Celsius since pre-industrial time, triggering more severe storms and heavier rainfall. If current fossil fuel consumption continued, the globe would warm another half a degree and reach dangerous tipping points in just a few decades.

At his grandparent's house, it felt like the tipping point had already been reached. As skies darkened and rain began to fall, Levi and his mom hustled out to get sandbags, pulling in behind a long line of cars. When they neared the front, a Boy Scout handed them a handful of bags and waved them toward huge sandpiles. As the rain got heavier, Levi and his mom took turns shoveling sand into six bags, then went through the line again for six more for a neighbor.

Soaking wet and sandy, they peered through the car windows as gusts buffeted the car. With the wind whistling around them, they lugged the sandbags into place along the edge of the garage door and other doors. Rain fell in driving sheets, and water began pooling near the house and in the yard.

"Levi," his stepdad called, "I need your help over here."

They grabbed a shovel and began digging trenches around the house. Wind pushed at them as they took turns lifting shovelfuls of wet, heavy dirt. The roar of the storm made it impossible to talk. Trees whipped back and forth. *Crack!* A large branch crashed to the ground.

Levi was terrified. His mom pointed at the trenches they had dug. Little rivers from the drain spouts now directed water away from the house. His mom and stepdad grabbed Levi and hustled toward the last unlatched door. They scrambled inside and locked the door tight behind them.

Drenched with rain and sweat, muddy and sandy, they caught their breath. The wind roared. Rain pounded.

His mom nodded soberly at Levi's grandma and glanced at the TV. "There's a tornado warning," she said.

Levi listened. He had heard that tornadoes sound like a train screaming by. He sat tense, listening for the roar through the wind and straining trees and flying debris. Flash-flood warnings and more tornado warnings ran in red banners across the bottom of the TV screen.

Then the power went out. The water and the gas shut off. Levi wanted to run and scream but he was stuck inside, wondering and worrying and wishing it would stop.

Isaac and the other kids fretted while the hurricane pounded Levi's home. "Climate change was feeling way more real," said Isaac. "Levi already lived through one horrible hurricane and now he was facing another one. Jayden has faced multiple floods. Wildfires that happened once in a while started happening all the time. I was worried about everyone, and my climate anxiety just ramped up."

The next day, at Levi's grandparents' house, the world seemed eerily still. Levi discovered a giant oak tree in one of his best friend's yards laying on its side, roots to the sky. He loved that tree, and his heart broke a little.

Wandering through the hurricane's aftermath, he noticed shingles and tree branches scattered everywhere. Neighbors struggled to tack tarps over damaged roofs, windows, and walls.

Levi lost his school. Though homeschooled, Levi attended classes at IfSpace, where his mom also worked. The high winds and rain damaged the roof, and water had poured in, triggering mold. The school was shut down permanently.

Levi tried to see a silver lining to all this loss. "It was more evidence for us to win. Come on, like, you can't deny this now. How could we not win?"

That same October, 17-year-old Miko, Isaac's adopted sister, visited her birthland for the first time. The Marshall Islands, with a combined land mass the size of Washington, D.C., are scattered over an area twice the size of California, Oregon, and Washington State combined. Flying over the Pacific, halfway between Australia and Hawaii, Miko squinted to make out the slender, arched ribbons of gold and green that floated in the ocean of blue.

A thin strip of land sprang out of nowhere, and the plane touched down on a narrow runway with beach on both sides. Miko stepped off the plane into hot, humid, salty air. Palm trees rustled and snapped in the breeze. She soon noticed how close the water was to the land, almost level with it. The nation had no mountains, no higher ground, nowhere to escape if there was a flood or a hurricane, like the one pummeling Levi.

Areas of the island just four or five houses wide showed troubling signs of erosion. Sea walls crumbled into piles of concrete blocks and metal, and abandoned shacks slumped into the waves. Sea water flooded yards and fields. Muddy salt water coated main roads. Even cemeteries had begun washing away. Seeing all the destruction saddened and scared Miko.

She met family members and many kids her age. She was heartbroken to hear about the fear they all carried. But she also noticed how differently people there talked about climate change. Addressing it was not optional, the way it seemed to be in the United States. Instead, people said: "What can we do to reduce our wasteful ways of living?"

She also listened to how passionately people advocated for removal of nuclear waste dumped on their lands and for climate justice. "The Marshallese are not helpless," she realized. "[They] are fighters."

Sorrowful that she lived so far away from this amazing place where she had such a strong connection, Miko felt even more fervent about speaking up for herself and her people. "It's important for me to be a part of this lawsuit so that I can represent the Marshall Islands, too," she said. "This isn't my only hope of getting justice for my people, but it's a start. We could do so much if we got the United States government to take responsibility for its contributions to climate change. When I see government officials make decisions that impact my people, that's what really gets me hyped up—hyped up to stand up and go testify and use my voice. I fight to make sure that the actions of the country that I live in don't negatively affect other places, like the place I was born."

On the trip, she also visited schools, talking with students about climate change and the lawsuit. In one class, inspired by students, she told them: "I'm going to wear the Marshallese flag to court." Everyone burst out in applause.

In another class, the teacher wanted to share with Miko all the students had learned about climate change. They talked about the rising seas.

"What happens when the water comes up?" the teacher asked.

"We will go underwater," a student replied.

"And what happens if we go underwater?"

"We die," someone replied.

Miko closed her eyes and took a deep breath.

"We're going to trial on October 29," she told them. "Save the date."

Countdown to Trial
October 2018

October is deep into fall term for most high schools and colleges. The plaintiffs began carving out time for the trial.

Isaac told his high school teachers he would be gone to Eugene for four to six weeks. "They were pretty supportive," he says. Nathan made plans with his college professors to make up the work he would miss when he traveled to testify. Aji, from Seattle, had considered getting a job that fall, but he wanted to attend the whole trial, so gave up on that idea.

Levi often juggled his homeschooling around the lawsuit, but the trial would mean a bigger sacrifice. As a strong swimmer on his club team, he had been competing in the USA circuit and had a dream of making it to the Junior Olympics.

That fall, he qualified for the next step, the Area 6 meet. He was thrilled to have a chance to test his speed at this level, especially in his best race, the 50-yard backstroke. But the meet was scheduled for a few days after Halloween when he needed to be in Eugene for the trial. Levi gave up his spot at the meet. "This really sucks," he said. "But it's like a small sacrifice for the greater good, right?"

Despite the sacrifices the 21 had to make, as the trial date neared, the excitement was palpable. "It felt like we were going somewhere," said Miriam. "It felt like we were taking the next step deeper into this."

Media interest in the suit skyrocketed. A *New York Times* reporter rented an apartment in Eugene to be there to cover the trial. "Everything was just getting bigger and bigger," said Sahara. "We were getting closer and closer."

"It felt very powerful and symbolic to be going to trial," Isaac said. "Not only did we jump through all the hurdles that the Justice Department threw at us, but we overcame all the delays and other excuses. It meant that the courts were finally ready to accept and hear what we had to say. And the truth is that the government would be put on trial. They were going to have to defend their actions for the past fifty-plus years and admit that they were exacerbating climate change. It was the moment that every single environmentalist all around the world had been awaiting for so long."

"There's a fierce urgency now to work through a climate recovery plan," Montana activist Jeff Smith told NBC. "This trial has the potential to break through the logjam."

People compared the case to *Brown v. Board of Education* and told Kelsey Juliana that as the lead plaintiff in the case, her name was going to go down in history books. "I can't comprehend that," Kelsey said.

But the road to trial was still bumpy. On October 12, the government filed a third writ of mandamus with the Ninth Circuit, hoping to stop the trial. "The most powerful government in the world sure is scared of a group of young people armed with the truth," New York plaintiff Vic Barrett told the press.

On October 15, District Judge Ann Aiken ruled in the kids' favor on the motion for judgment on the pleadings and for summary judgment. In other words, she refused to rule before trial. As long as the Ninth Circuit Court of Appeals didn't stop it, the trial could proceed.

Julia, Phil, and Andrea and their team continued prepping their forty-plus witnesses and scheduling them to travel to Oregon from all over the world. Julia wrote, rewrote, and practiced her opening statement, which she would give on the first day of the trial. Phil drafted questions to examine the first witness, and co-counsel Andrea Rodgers prepped to examine the second. They prepared charts and PowerPoint presentations to help make their case. Flights and hotels were booked. Excitement among the plaintiffs grew to a fever pitch.

Then, on Friday October 19, ten days before trial, Phil was on the tarmac at Dulles Airport after having finished some depositions and just before flying out to do more. His cell phone rang. It was Julia. The day before, before even hearing from the appeals court decision on mandamus, the government asked the U.S. Supreme Court for another emergency order to stay the trial. The case was back in the shadow docket. The Supreme Court clerk had called Julia. Chief Justice John Roberts had granted an administrative stay, temporarily, to consider the government's arguments.

Phil could hardly believe it. They were so close. "We are right on the verge of opening statements with the judge banging her gavel and turning the courtroom over to the attorneys to present arguments and evidence," he said.

The move was, to put it mildly, unusual according to observers. "They're going to trial and the Supreme Court reaches way, way down into the lower court and says, 'Not so fast,'" Georgetown's Lisa Heinzerling said.

Phil, Julia, and Andrea were outraged that they hadn't even been given a chance to respond. "The government leapfrogged the Ninth Circuit Court of Appeals in asking for a stay and Chief Justice John Roberts granted it without even the courtesy of asking for our position," Phil said. "The rug was pulled out from us without Justice Roberts even hearing from the youth plaintiffs."

The team didn't have time to dwell on the feelings of injustice. "We have no control of what the government does," Phil said. "We can scream and yell and say, 'Look at how they are abusing the system!' but at the end of the day we have to prepare our reply."

Julia immediately notified the young plaintiffs. The order was an administrative stay, what Julia called "a light pause," while the Supreme Court decided whether to put a longer stay in place. "There's no way the Supreme Court is going to stop our trial ten days out," she told them. "The Supreme Court is going to look at it, they are going to see that this is crazy, they're going to deny the stay, and we're going to have our trial."

Their reply brief was due the next week. Phil and Julia and the team didn't want the stay to last that long. So, they worked all weekend, all day and all night Saturday and Sunday, forgoing sleep, fueled by chocolate and kombucha, and submitted their reply brief early, on Monday.

The Justice Department was usually silent on ongoing cases, but Acting Assistant Attorney General Jeffrey H. Wood commented on *Juliana* during a speech. "Beyond the legal defects, the fallacies of the plaintiffs' policy approaches are significant," he said. "They are ignoring the clear fact that the United States is the global leader in environmental protection. Indeed, the United States leads the world in greenhouse gas reductions, and the United States is the global leader in the development of new energy technologies that are helping to reduce emissions."

The youth wondered how anyone could call the United States "the global leader in environmental protection" when it had historically contributed more to global warming than any other nation and continued to be the world's second-biggest emitter of carbon.

The legal team crossed their fingers that the Supreme Court would move quickly, remove the stay, and let the trial move ahead. After all, in the three years since they filed *Juliana,* the kids had overcome three motions to dismiss the case in the district court, two in the Ninth Circuit, and one in the Supreme Court. They needed just one more victory to go to trial.

Garrett Epps, who teaches constitutional law at the University of Baltimore, said the youth should have their day in court. "Our world is burning in front of our eyes, and what *Juliana* tells us is that our children know it," he said. "The government fears these 21 children; it asks the Supreme Court to tell them they do not even deserve a chance to fail."

While everyone waited to see what would happen, the plaintiffs began arriving in Eugene. The kids, teens, and young adults were happy to see one another, and their lawyers still thought prospects for a favorable decision were good, so energy was high. Everyone had the sense that, "We were finally going to get to do this!"

Out-of-towners stayed in a big house with lots of bedrooms, porches, and burritos. Our Children's Trust stocked the fridge with, Levi said, "Like two hundred burritos."

The atmosphere in the house was exuberant. Levi and Xiuhtezcatl covered the carpeted stairs with big pillows upholstered in slippery material. Then Levi tucked himself into a laundry basket and careened down the stairs, hollering happily.

Levi's mom kept holding up plates and foil rappers, yelling: "Whose burrito is this?"

"One of the most important things I've learned from this lawsuit is what happens to a burrito when someone sits on it," Levi said, cracking up.

Levi also explored what he called "the finer points" of being a little brother to the older plaintiffs. "You mess with their stuff and annoy them as much as you can," he said. "But not too much." He and Isaac played the punching game. "We just lay back and randomly punch each other."

Isaac found the most joy in these in-between moments with his co-plaintiffs, when he could just connect with the other kids, chill, relax, hang out, and talk about music or sports, school, movies, and other normal stuff.

Kelsey, now 22, lived just down the road from the plaintiff house and headed over each morning to help with breakfast, and hang out. She was there the morning Levi ran down the hall waving cash and yelling, "I got money! I got money!" It was the tooth fairy.

The next morning, he found more money under his pillow and Kelsey admitted she put it there.

"Aw, thanks, Kels," Levi said, and gave her a hug.

Levi considered the other plaintiffs to be his siblings. "I've spent so much time with them, I know so much about them," he said. "They are always looking out for me, and they are always there when I need them."

The 21 would soon need one another more than ever.

35

VACATED

October 2018

Mid-afternoon on Wednesday, October 24, 2018, just five days before trial, Julia asked the chaperones to call the kids together in the plaintiff house.

"Everybody, gather up," Levi's mom Leigh-Ann yelled. "We have an important announcement." Isaac and Zealand were blasting some music for Hazel and Miko. Leigh-Ann popped her head around the door. "Can you turn it down? We're rounding everyone up to talk."

The kids tumbled into the big living room, plunked on the couches and sprawled on the floor, lounging on the pillows and leaning on one another. Someone poured chips and popcorn into bowls around the room.

Levi was scampering from kid to kid and bowl to bowl when Julia walked in. He stopped in his tracks. "She had this look on her face. We knew something was up," he said.

Levi worried that the restaurant where they were getting dinner had canceled. "That was the worst thing I could think of."

But it was much worse than that. Just moments before, at 3:18 p.m., Julia and her team got an email notice from the district court. As she read it, her heart plummeted. Everything felt dark as if a heavy steel door had slammed in their faces just as they were about to cross the threshold.

Julia spoke carefully. It's not over, she said, but they have paused our case. She struggled to hold back tears. It was an indefinite pause.

Everyone erupted with questions:

"What do you mean?"

"But the trial is on Monday!"

"Are they even allowed to do that?"

Julia tried to explain that because the Supreme Court had not yet lifted the stay on the case, District Court Judge Ann Aiken had to cancel the trial date.

"What did she say?" someone asked. "Read what she said."

"'Scheduling Order by Judge Ann L. Aiken. Pursuant to the United States Supreme Court's Order staying this case, all trial dates and associated deadlines are hereby VACATED. This Court will schedule a status and scheduling conference when the stay is lifted. Ordered by Judge Ann. L. Aiken.' That's it."

"What the heck?" Levi exclaimed. "What's the reason? This doesn't sound right to me."

Isaac just sat there "completely decimated." This trial is never going to happen, he thought. *Juliana* will just disappear like every other environmental lawsuit in the United States. Ordinarily quite talkative, he didn't say a word. Strangely, he felt guilty. "I felt like we let so many people down, which was weird because it wasn't necessarily my fault or anything," he said. "But I felt accountable and like maybe somehow I could have done more."

Levi completely lost his appetite. "It's like you got the birthday present you always wanted, like a really cool dirt bike that's electric. Times that by two million. And then it gets taken away. That's what it feels like."

Our Children's Trust put out a press release immediately and their phones just lit up. Everyone was talking at once, answering reporters' questions, conferring on next steps.

"The Trump administration for well over a year now has been trying every tool to try to stop this case from going forward," Julia told the press.

Phil riffled through some court documents and jumped in. "During a recent eight-year period, the Supreme Court received more than nineteen hundred applications similar to what the federal government filed here, and they granted none of them," he said. He also blasted the government for filing motions in all three levels of court at the same time: the district court, the appeals court and the Supreme Court. "Legal scholars will tell you that rarely, rarely happens. And it's happened to us twice this year."

"The Trump administration is scared to put the climate science on trial, and also they are worried as to the type of order Judge Aiken will issue, which will require them to address the catastrophic problems these young plaintiffs and the children of America face due to the national fossil fuel energy system," he added.

In some ways, things were easier for the lawyers, distracted by the work they had to do preparing their next legal move.

While the lawyers were swept up into a blur of activity, the kids hugged one another and cried. And wondered:

"What are we going to do?"

"Are we going home?"

Julia didn't have many answers. "We'll still go down to the courthouse, we'll do a press conference and rally—just not the trial, not yet."

Sahara wasn't at the plaintiff house, so they learned by email. They barraged their parents with questions, most of which the adults couldn't answer. "How could this be in our grasp and then taken away?"

Avery was in her bedroom when she heard. "They have delayed trial," her dad said. For the next few days, Avery hardly functioned. She felt "clumsy, fumbly, and huffy"—so full of anger that she could do no more than eat and sleep.

Later, all the kids gathered at the plaintiff house, and Julia asked them to write down what they were feeling. Maybe some would share their thoughts at the rally. Isaac wrote and wrote. "But I did not want to tell anyone. I did not want to speak," he said. "We had such high hopes and then literally in one minute all those just went down the drain."

The next day, the young people got together privately to talk about what had happened. They shared their feelings of being crushed and hugely disappointed. They cried and hugged some more. "We're all so emotionally and mentally interconnected," said Nathan. "We needed that time together to have that privacy, to grieve."

But they also knew that they were the public face of the case. They would have to cope with the media and the world while they grieved. In the end, they decided that they would all attend the event commemorating the lost trial date, a kind of memorial service. They would do their best to handle this difficult moment together.

Rather Be in Court
Missed Trial Date: October 29, 2018

On October 29, everyone glumly dressed in the clothes they had picked out to wear for the opening day of the trial. Even Levi had trouble eating breakfast.

The weather was miserable, drizzling and cold and overcast. They drove solemnly to the courthouse, like a funeral procession. Our Children's Trust had been expecting thousands of people from Oregon and beyond to rally there on the first day of trial. Even with the trial date canceled, a large crowd had gathered, bigger than the crowds at the early hearings in Eugene. Supporters held tall banners that declared: "Fierce Urgency of NOW!" and "Give Science Its Day in Court!" and "Let the Youth Be Heard!"

As the plaintiffs stepped out of the cars, everything felt off. Where climate rallies were usually full of cheering and lively chatter, this group of people bundled in ponchos and huddling under umbrellas was eerily quiet, mournful. The kids trudged up the steps, aware of how the courthouse doors had been closed to them. They turned to the crowd, which broke out in applause. Instead of making the kids feel better, it made them feel embarrassed. What are they even clapping about? Nathan thought. It's not like we've accomplished anything.

Aji opened with a mournful song while the plaintiffs stood close together and despondent with the courthouse looming dark and gray behind them.

Phil Gregory approached the podium and bellowed: "These young plaintiffs have raised their voices! Let the experts testify! Let the courthouse doors be open! This is not just the trial of the century. This is the trial for the *future* of this century. This. Is. No. Ordinary. Lawsuit!"

Julia's words for the crowd were quieter but just as passionate: "In our brief filed with the Supreme Court one week ago, we quoted Chief Justice John Roberts, who recently emphasized the critical importance of our independent judiciary: 'Without independence, there is no *Brown v. Board of Education*. Without independence, there is no *West Virginia v. Barnette,* where the Court held that the government could not compel schoolchildren to salute the flag.' And those words give me hope and faith today that the court will do the right thing."

Most of the kids wore dark, somber colors. But Miko had wrapped herself in the royal blue Marshallese flag and had a traditional crown of flowers on her head. Levi, still just 11 years old, wore a bright blue sports coat. He stepped forward. Dwarfed by the podium, he spoke emphatically. "I am a kid, so I'm very impatient," he said. "And I'm impatient for a very good reason . . . I have *personally* had to evacuate *my home* because of hurricanes. I have seen fish kills on *my beach.*"

Twenty-one-year-old plaintiff Jacob Lebel told the crowd: "The wildfires around my farm in Oregon keep getting worse. The winters keep getting warmer, the salmon keep dying, the seas keep rising, and our politicians keep lying."

Nathan looked tall and grown-up in a navy suit, light-blue shirt, and dark-blue tie. He was an awkward 15-year-old when *Juliana* was filed—now he was 18 and in college and felt more strongly about the lawsuit than ever.

"I still believe our justice system will prevail," he told the crowd, his voice emotional, yet strong and proud. "I still believe we have the capacity for change even when the future looks bleak. I still believe in the power of youth voices and the power of youth activism."

As he spoke, he heard some chanting off in the distance, so he paused.

Voices echoed a few blocks away.

"Whose streets?"

"Our streets!"

They got closer and slightly louder.

"We are the future!"

"We are the future!"

Then, the chanting stopped. A massive group of students, more than a thousand, from South Eugene High School and the University of Oregon, emerged into view moving silently toward the courthouse.

Everyone at the rally watched as the solemn group approached. Nathan—the whole crowd—felt their presence.

Suddenly the sun broke through the clouds.

The rally burst into applause.

"We. Are. The. Future!" The students chanted, their voices reverberating off the sleek courthouse.

"We. Are. The. Future!"

Nathan, the other plaintiffs, and many supporters began crying.

"It was magical and mythical and really, really, really emotional," said Nathan. "The young people came and breathed life and hope into the rally."

For ninety more minutes, undeterred by intermittent rain, students took the stage and shared spoken-word poetry and music. They gave speeches filled with fire.

"The power of the people is more powerful than the people in power!" Xiuhtezcatl rapped in a stirring speech.

"We rally for our right as American citizens to a fair trial," Miriam said. "No matter how much the federal government might try to deny us that right, we WILL have our day in court."

This wasn't over yet.

After the rally, the out-of-town kids began packing up. Levi and his mom had to fly home to Florida on Halloween, so he donned his homemade Captain Climate costume and hoped to get back in time to do some trick-or-treating.

Their flight was supposed to get in at 4 p.m. but was delayed. They didn't stumble into the house until two in the morning. Levi missed the trial and he missed trick-or-treating.

"We're just kids," Levi said. "We're not adults. But we have to do this because so many things are wrong in this world because of adults. We have to take action to be able to even have a future. But this is not a kid's job. It should not be a kid's job. I'm doing it because I absolutely have to."

"It was a tough time," said Isaac. "The loss of momentum, the emotional toll. I put a lot of my time and my effort into the lawsuit. That setback took me down a couple notches."

It was hard for Sahara to handle, too. "I had all my other life still going on. I still had school and family and friends," they said. "Everything else was going on as if nothing had happened, you know?"

Everyone wondered, what would happen with the lawsuit now?

Too Little, Too Late
November 2018

On Friday, November 2, 2018, just four days after the trial was supposed to commence, the Supreme Court issued a three-page order, denying the government's request for a stay. The youth had prevailed again.

But they'd lost the October 29 trial date.

"I'm not gonna lie," said Levi. "I was pretty confused. First, we have a trial date, then we don't have a trial date, then the Supreme Court rules in our favor, but what does that even really mean? What is going on here?"

This time, instead of being impressed and excited, Miriam was annoyed. "The case was just bouncing around the courts, like ping-pong," they said.

Other plaintiffs had the same reaction. "I didn't see it as something great," said Nathan. "It was more like, yeah, the government's motions are obviously junk and have nothing to do with the law and everything to do with delaying because Trump is trying to get as many fossil fuel projects through as he can. So yeah, it was like, thank you, I'm glad the Supreme Court ruled that this was BS. Now back to business."

Isaac felt like they were endlessly treading water. "What's the point in the Supreme Court saying that we can proceed if we have nothing to proceed to?"

"I want to trust that we are truly on track for trial without having further delays," Kelsey told NPR. "But these defendants are treating this case, our democracy, and the security of mine and future generations like it's a game. I'm tired of playing this game."

The Justice Department, uncharacteristically, issued a statement. "The Supreme Court order is without prejudice and recognizes ongoing appellate proceedings in the lower courts," it said. "We are pleased that it sets a path for the Justice Department to continue efforts toward dismissal of this improper case." The legal term "without prejudice" indicated that the Supreme Court's decision was neither final nor permanent. The defendants could file more motions to try to stop the case. In other words, the 21 could expect more of the same.

Morale hit an all-time low. Even the most hopeful of the plaintiffs felt more pessimistic about the lawsuit. Many checked out, missing calls with Julia and the team and the other plaintiffs.

Though Julia was not their parent, she felt very protective of them, and worried about their mental health, especially when instead of working to fix climate change, their government was increasingly making their world ever more dangerous.

That fall, the Trump administration opened the Arctic to offshore oil and gas drilling. It lifted restrictions on drilling across millions of acres of protected sage grouse habitat in eleven states. And it eased restrictions on greenhouse gas emissions from coal in hopes of spurring construction of new coal plants.

Kassie Siegel, the director of the Climate Law Institute, commented: "We're all in a bus speeding toward a [climate crisis] cliff, and the administration is driving," she said. "And the Trump administration is flooring it."

Things went from bad to worse. On November 21, the day before Thanksgiving, under pressure from the higher courts, Judge Ann Aiken reversed herself, allowing the Ninth Circuit to review her previous rulings. "Bullied into submission," is how Georgetown Law's Lisa Heinzerling characterized it. Journalist Lee van der Voo called Judge Aiken's move "a dare." The district judge seemed to be saying to the circuit court: "You want the case? Take it."

The young people and their legal team were crushed. "Losing the trial date was such a blow," said Phil. "And this was a tougher blow. We had had so much momentum and now it was just gone."

Julia searched for a way forward. "There are always letdowns and hardships and losses and times when things don't go the way you thought they should," Julia said. "And you have to take that and learn what there is to learn from it and go at it again or pivot and go in a different direction." But what direction should they take?

Days later, the federal government quietly released a report that made the 21's case for them. The Fourth National Climate Assessment stated that climate change "presents growing challenges to human health and quality of life, the economy, and the natural systems that support us." Intensifying impacts—heat waves, heavy precipitation, flooding, ocean acidification and warming, forest fires, and ever-dwindling sea ice, snowpack and soil moisture— threaten "Americans' physical, social, and economic well-being."

The next day, the federal government released another report that pointed a finger of blame squarely at themselves. The U.S.

Geological Survey found that over the last decade, 40 percent of coal production, 26 percent of oil production, and 23 percent of natural gas production came from federal public lands and waters. In fact, roughly a quarter of U.S. carbon dioxide emissions were from drilling and mining the federal government permitted on public lands. The U.S. government was clearly a part of the climate change problem.

Then the youth got wind of something that really boiled their blood. On November 28, former President Obama spoke at a fundraiser for Rice University's Baker Institute in Houston, Texas. Dressed in a tux and smiling broadly, the former president expressed his pride at the United States joining the Paris Agreement. But he seemed even more proud of his record on supporting the fossil fuel industry.

It was all caught on YouTube.

"I know we're in oil country and we need American energy," he said. The crowd cheered.

"You wouldn't always know it, but it went up every year I was president," he said. "That whole—suddenly America's like the biggest oil producer and the biggest gas producer—that was me, people."

He was right. Oil production grew by almost 90 percent while he was in office.

Julia wished more Americans were aware of things like this. "Part of what's been going on for fifty years is this really tight network of money and people in positions of power, in government and in the fossil fuel industry, all working toward the same goal, which is keeping fossil fuel interests alive," she said.

To the youth, it was just so painfully obvious that climate

change was so much less of a political issue than people realized. Democrats and Republicans both had close ties to the fossil fuel industry. No matter what they said in public, both parties supported this ongoing, deadly fossil fuel system.

Action outside the political system was the only way to stop the madness.

This Has to STOP
November 2018-March 2019

On the day after Christmas, the Ninth Circuit agreed to review the case.

"This was really, really saddening to us," Phil shared. "We all have a sense of urgency on addressing climate change. All this delay while the courts make up their minds about whether or not we can go to trial is not helping anybody."

In fact, Phil was really worried about Julia. He'd seen her get beaten down by blow after blow. First the tragedy of losing the trial date. Then on the eve of Thanksgiving, Judge Aiken's reversing herself and asking the Ninth Circuit to review that case. And now the Ninth Circuit agreeing to review it. She seemed exhausted. "Julia tries to look for the reasoning, the rationale, behind what is going on," he said, "and those decisions didn't make sense in terms of how the law is supposed to work."

The youth were struggling, too. Julia checked in with them. "Just wondering how you're feeling with everything that has happened with the case," she asked. "I know that it has been a totally rough, emotional time for me, going through all this and getting so close to trial and the setbacks."

"A reoccurring feeling is hopelessness," said Sahara.

"I feel wiped . . . ," Aji shared, "across the board just feeling like we're running against the clock, and we don't actually know how much time we have left."

The team had to find a way to re-energize. Phil knew Julia was at her best when she was taking action. And she and the 21 young people were keenly aware of the urgency of the climate crisis. They needed to find a way to speed things up.

In February, the team unveiled a new approach. It's been said that the best defense is a great offense. That strategy—filing motion after motion after motion—seemed to be working well for the government. The legal team would take a page from the government's playbook. Instead of just reacting to the government's motions, they would file a motion of their own in the Ninth Circuit Court of Appeals: An Urgent Motion for Preliminary Injunction.

Sahara loved how the legal team always had something up their sleeves. "No matter what obstruction the government throws at us, they find a way forward," they said. But Sahara wasn't clear about what an injunction was, so they asked Avery's dad. He explained that as the plaintiffs were waiting to see if they would get their day in court, the government was free to lease more public lands for fossil fuel extraction, approve more pipelines, and support the burning of fossil fuels. As long as the government delayed the trial, they could continue making climate change worse.

The kids' lawyers would argue that this was not fair. An injunction would stop the government from taking new steps to support fossil fuels until the courts decided the case. The injunction could also act as an incentive for the government to speed things up rather than throwing obstacles and delays at the case. That totally made sense, Sahara thought.

For Nathan it was nerve-wracking. "I was definitely uneasy

about the idea of like, potentially, grinding Alaska's economy to a halt." But he felt they had no choice. While in college in Minnesota, Nathan was tracking two horrifying phenomena becoming more commonplace back home in Alaska. Thawing permafrost left melted water under the surface. When it froze in the winter, the ground bulged upward. Summer thawing caused the hillocks to collapse, forming boggy lakes. These pimples and pockmarks called "thermokarsts" were spreading. Permafrost thawing on slopes were also causing mushy landslides, stripping mountains bare. Climate change was scarring one of the most beautiful places on earth, and Nathan knew the government was free to make everything worse.

"One of the best ways to get a hearing, one of the best ways to get the government to stop putting up every hoop known to man would be to make them have some skin in the game. And they had absolutely none, up until now," Nathan said. "They could just keep doing what they wanted, as long as they could delay us." Plus, he figured: "In some situations, the law is only as powerful as your money to keep it going. So, if the government has endless money to throw at delay, then they really have no incentive to come to the table. So, okay, well, this is what is necessary to put people's feet to the fire. Let's at least halt the bleeding."

On February 7, 2019, Julia and her team filed the motion. Citing the federal government's own recent and damning reports, it asked the Ninth Circuit Court of Appeals to bar the U.S. government from allowing any new leases, permits, or approvals of any fossil fuel projects until *Juliana* was decided. No new mining of coal on federal lands. No new offshore oil or gas exploration or drilling. No new building of fossil fuel infrastructure such as laying new pipelines or building new plants or export facilities. The injunction would halt roughly one hundred new fossil fuel projects, including sixty pipelines, thirty-two natural gas and coal terminals, and one oil export facility. It was a temporary, but important, attempt to protect the status quo.

If the motion were granted, it would halt, for instance, a scheduled sale of new oil and gas drilling leases in almost eighty million acres in the Gulf of Mexico. Those were the very waters that endangered Jayden and her family.

The government questioned why the plaintiffs waited three years to ask for an "urgent" injunction. But Julia addressed this in her brief: "Plaintiffs made every effort to avoid seeking preliminary relief by moving the case swiftly to trial; Defendants made every effort to prevent Plaintiffs' case from being decided, all the while accelerating fossil fuel development and increasing [greenhouse gas] emissions . . ."

Filing for an injunction demonstrated grit, according to observers. "I think the aggressiveness of the *Juliana* plaintiffs as a strategic matter is a good thing," commentator Joel Stronberg wrote. "Whether it makes any difference in the outcome of the case is another matter."

The Department of Justice called the move a stunt. "Plaintiffs' request for an emergency injunction reinforces the view of many that this lawsuit is more about attracting attention to an issue than about actually obtaining judicial relief," said Jeffrey Wood, who had worked at the Justice Department's environmental division.

But to the youth, it was far from a stunt. They were desperate to slow climate change. To them, letting the government take actions that would make things worse was not an option.

Julia had to dramatize this for the judges. The brief pointed out government plans to approve new offshore oil and gas drilling in 98 percent of coastal waters by 2024. It quoted one expert who would testify that "the United States is expanding oil and gas extraction on a scale at least four times faster and greater than any other nation and is currently on track to account for 60% of global growth in oil and gas production." Burning of these fossil fuels could release as much carbon as a thousand coal-fired plants.

The plaintiffs' brief also dramatized how urgent the crisis really was, how loudly the climate change clock was ticking. "What we do *today* will influence the stability of ice sheets for the next 30–40 years with enormous consequences for the nation's shorelines and marine resources," Eric Rignot, the nation's leading expert on ice sheets wrote in supporting documents. "We are running out of time."

A biologist and climate expert noted that: "Continuing U.S. emissions at the present level for even two years will make it progressively more difficult to stabilize the climate system this century in order to preserve the critical components for human life on this planet."

The young people wanted their voices heard in this effort, too. Some plaintiffs submitted declarations—impassioned pleas—in support of the injunction.

"I am so frustrated that we haven't had our trial yet," Levi wrote. "I don't think it's fair that we have to wait so long when every year the climate change impacts I am experiencing are getting worse."

He described the hurricanes, losing his school, and wading through eighteen inches of water in his front yard. "This was a very hard experience for me," he wrote. "I can't believe I had to evacuate from my home two years in a row, and I am scared this is going to happen even more because of how climate change makes hurricanes stronger and more frequent."

Plaintiff Aji Piper's declaration brimmed with anger and sadness. "If we had started the trial on October 29, the trial would be done by now. Instead, our case is in limbo," he wrote. "The feeling I have inside of me is a horrible feeling . . . I would describe it as the lead-up to complete despair."

Aji shared how he had suffered through two summers where climate change–induced wildfires shrouded his home in Seattle in smoke. Stuck inside, he was terrified that this would be the new normal.

"Sometimes every hour of every day feels like there is more pressure building. I have been waiting for over three years to get the climate science evidence and our stories into court, to have our case heard, and to start the process of healing our climate. All the while the clock has been ticking, and the pressure has been building."

"And it is not as if we are standing still," Aji wrote. "We're not." Every day the U.S. government was taking steps that would worsen the climate crisis.

To rally even more support for the case, the team started a campaign called #JoinJuliana, asking other youth affected by climate change to sign on to a "friend of the court" brief called an amicus brief. Social media postings with this invitation "just blew up," according to Nathan. Signatures from young people all across the country piled up hour by hour, going viral and reaching into the thousands.

In just eleven days, 24,137 young people under the age of twenty-five representing all U.S. states, the District of Columbia, and several territories signed on to the brief. More than 8,000 kids from 140 countries also signed the brief, which said:

"Children are people and citizens. The Constitution protects the fundamental rights of children as fully as it does the rights of adults. The Constitution states clearly it intends to 'secure the Blessings of Liberty to ourselves and our Posterity.' We *are* the Posterity the Constitution protects . . . The government's fossil fuel policies and actions threaten to push our climate system over tipping points into catastrophe."

Many of the young people who signed on to the brief included comments describing how climate change had hurt them and why they support the lawsuit.

"Due to climate change, I am growing up in a world where I don't know if I have a secure future on this planet, and where I don't know if the ecosystems and life on this planet will be able to survive. The homes, health, happiness, and culture of many people are being destroyed. Animals are going extinct. The weather is unpredictable and damaging. The plaintiffs in *Juliana v. U.S.* are boldly working to end these issues in a powerful and effective way, and I wholly support them. The futures of all organisms on Earth are on the line."
—E. W., 13, North Carolina

"I want to be able to live my life without fearing about whether or not the world I know today will exist in 20 years. I am tired of being scared of the future that I should be excited for. I want to travel, I want to find love, I want to have kids, but will that ever happen because of climate change?"
—G. J., 14, New Jersey

"As the ones who will have to bear the load of climate change later on, our voices deserve to be heard by the government. We deserve the right to a future, one that won't be shortened because of how we have hurt our planet. The government has the power to reduce emissions and help our planet. We have the right to be heard, and they must listen to us."

—S. H., 21, Tennessee

39
Backlash
Spring 2019

On June 4, 2019, a three-judge panel of the Ninth Circuit Court of Appeals would convene in Portland, Oregon, for a hearing on the government's interlocutory appeal and the youth's motion for preliminary injunction. Once Julia learned that three new judges would hear the oral arguments, she started doing research on them, watching videos of them in action questioning lawyers in other cases. From reading Judge Andrew Hurwitz's opinions and watching other cases, Julia thought she had a shot at convincing him.

She also greatly admired Judge Mary Murguia, a pathbreaker for Latina women on the court. But she had one worry. Judge Murguia was next in line to be Chief Judge of the Ninth Circuit. "Sometimes, when someone is a pioneer and seeking to move their way up and feeling the weight of that position, it can make them risk averse," Julia said. Judge Murguia might be sympathetic to the plight of the young plaintiffs but also not want her ruling overturned by the Supreme Court. She might seek some way out.

The third judge, Josephine Staton, was a district court judge sitting on the appeals panel as a visiting judge. That meant there were no appeals court oral arguments including her that Julia could review. But some of her rulings in the district court showed that she was an excellent writer and did not shy away from making hard decisions with political implications.

Julia's overall assessment of the hearing: They had a good shot with this panel, but she would have her work cut out for her.

In the meantime, media attention for the case picked up. National outlets covered *Juliana*, including *People, Teen Vogue, O Magazine* and *National Geographic.* "A lot of people will tell us that 'no matter what happens, you've already won because you're winning in the court of public opinion, and you've elevated the voice of youth, and you're bringing so much more attention to the climate movement,'" said Julia. "I completely disagree with that. I think that those successes represent incredible and valuable progress, but we haven't won until governments around the world are no longer allowing our world to be powered by fossil fuels, and until we've stopped the ice sheets from melting."

The CBS program *60 Minutes* aired a segment about the case, calling it "interesting" and potentially "life-changing." The host fired off some hard-hitting questions at Julia: "You're talking about a case that could change the economics in this country—"

Julia interrupted: ". . . for the better."

"But other people would say it would cause huge disruption."

"If we don't address climate change in this country, economists across the board say that we are in for economic crises that we have never seen before."

The host probed about why the government didn't want to go to trial. "They will lose on the evidence," Julia said. "They know that once you enter that courtroom and your witnesses take the oath to tell the truth and nothing but the truth, the facts are facts and alternative facts are perjury."

To comment on the significance of the case, CBS brought in

Ann Carlson, professor of environmental law at UCLA. "If the plaintiffs won, it'd be massive," she said, "particularly if they won what they're asking for, which is: Get the federal government out of the business of in any way subsidizing fossil fuels and get them into the business of dramatically curtailing greenhouse gases . . . That would be enormous."

And why, the host asked, had this case gotten so far?

"The lawyers have crafted the case in a way that is very compelling," she said. "You have a number of kids who are very compelling plaintiffs who are experiencing the harms of climate change now and will experience the harms of climate change much more dramatically as they get older. I think the hard question here is the law."

Shortly after the *60 Minutes* segment aired, the *Washington Times* ran a story with the headline "Youth Climate Strike Sparks Debate on the Use of Students as Props." It quoted James Taylor, senior fellow for environment and climate policy at the conservative Heartland Institute: "They're putting the emotional and mental health of young people at risk so they can use them as pawns for their own political agendas," he said. "[They] should be allowed to be children, should be allowed to enjoy life. And certainly it's good that they're aware of scientific and political issues, but to use them in a manner that has them fearing they're not going to have an inhabitable world is borderline abusive."

The young people were outraged. "They're not listening to us," Xiuhtezcatl said on a national public affairs television show. "We have personal investment in this. We have stories of how we've already been affected. We have burning passion within us. It doesn't take a degree or any amount of years on earth to know what is right and what is wrong."

His message to adults: "Either get on our side or get out of the way."

The *Wall Street Journal* ran an opinion piece with the harsh title: "On Climate, the Kids Are All Wrong; and a band of ignorant brats shall lead them." In it, an investment manager wrote: "Letting children lead the way on climate change would be a recipe for disaster . . . From following the Pied Piper into a medieval forest to sailing off with Pinocchio to Pleasure Island to shoplifting candy from Willy Wonka's chocolate factory, children tend to make bad choices, which is why we don't let them run things . . . ," he wrote.

With the higher profile came greater criticism on social media, too. On Facebook, a photo of Isaac, Miko, and some others enjoying a takeout meal got comments like: "What kind of activist are you if you use plastic?" People also criticized the young people for the carbon emissions of the planes they flew on to get to their hearings. "We try our best to try to eliminate fossil fuel emissions, but the problem is really the system that gives us no choice!" said Isaac. The comments were upsetting, but he tried to let them roll off. "I don't respond 'cuz that's just going to escalate and distract from what really matters—which is getting the government out of the business of supporting fossil fuels."

The hecklers' logic pissed Miriam off. "I'm not causing climate change because I drive a truck or use disposable plastic," they said. "I do my best to limit carbon as much as I can but it's not my fault, it's the systems that are in place."

The criticism, the endless waiting, the ever-worsening climate crisis weighed heavily on Miriam. Their music shifted from folk punk to hard-core punk. Faster, louder, and angrier. No catchy mandolin licks, just pounding drums, guitar, and bass with ragged distortion. No singing. "I just scream," they said.

Levi's mom told him not to read the online comments. "The people who bother to comment are either great supporters or very harsh critics," she said. But she monitored them with dismay. "People have been very mean, very rude, and have even made nasty comments about the kids' physical appearance," she said. She and other parents noticed that trolls directed their most hateful comments to the Indigenous youth and the youth of color.

The parents took direct heat, too. "Oh, why can't you just let them be kids?" people asked.

"But nobody's forced any of these kids into this," Levi's mom said. "They are super passionate about the environment, and they know a ton about it, way more than I do."

The young people hated how these comments patronized and infantilized them. But they tried to ignore them. Seeing other plaintiffs stand up strong, time after time, no matter what, inspired Isaac to care less about what people thought of him. "When Kelsey or Aji got an unwelcoming crowd or some rude people, they just let it go right out of their heads," he said. "They know that the majority of people care and support them, so they don't give the haters any validation. You just do the job that needs to be done."

And now the job at hand was preparing for the upcoming hearing.

Bigger Than Ever
June 2019

In June 2019, the young plaintiffs began packing to travel to Portland. They were excited to see one another after nine months, relieved the injunction would be taken seriously, and worried that the Ninth Circuit would stop the case.

A Bloomberg Law article laid out the stakes: "A trio of federal appellate court judges could breathe new life into the case or kill it altogether."

Observers were eager to see what would happen. David Uhlmann, who heads the environmental law program at the University of Michigan, told the *New York Times:* "In my heart, I love this lawsuit. Everything that's compelling about this lawsuit from the beginning is even more compelling today."

UCLA environmental professor Ann Carlson, who had been skeptical of *Juliana* at the beginning, was now rooting for the kids. "If the Constitution doesn't protect your right to live in an environment that will protect your life, then what does it protect?" she told the *Los Angeles Times.*

The plaintiffs checked in to their hotel in downtown Portland. Late-spring sun shone down on the buildings and bustling sidewalks, light-rail trains and streetcars dinging bells as they passed. Rooms high in the hotel had peekaboo views of the pointy summit of Mount Hood. Usually coated white with snow, the volcano was strangely brown due to severely low snowpack.

The young people hadn't seen one another for a while, and it was awkward at first. Isaac launched into a conversation about some recent music by Khalid. One by one he pulled kids in, until they were standing together relaxed, talking, and laughing.

Sahara's arm was in a sling, and everyone asked about it. Sahara rowed for their high school's crew team and during a recent work-out, they biked up a mountain with members of the boys' crew team. "I toasted a bunch of them," they said. Flying down the mountain, at a hairpin turn, a truck with a trailer blocked their path. Sahara swerved off the road to avoid it, crashed into a ditch full of poison oak, and broke their collarbone.

"Ouch!" the others exclaimed.

Levi was in heaven because there was a boba tea place across the street. The owners were supporters of the case, so they gave the kids metal straws and said they could come over for free refills anytime. Levi gulped down "boba tea by the bucket!"

The plaintiffs were happy to see Julia, too. She had miles of paperwork, legal arguments to polish and practice, but she hung out as much as she could, eating and joking around with them. "She's just one of the kindest, sweetest people I know," said Levi. "Always willing to talk or go get something to eat, always willing to deal with our shenanigans."

Behind the scenes, Julia was steeling herself for another tough court battle. She believed very strongly in the law, arguments, facts, and evidence and just the whole theory behind the case. She believed immensely in the 21 young people. "The last piece is believing in myself and my ability to carry all this forward," she said, "and to communicate it effectively in oral argument and to make the judges understand."

The evening before the hearing, everyone met for pizza and to make signs for the rally after. Someone called Julia up front. They blasted her favorite song "I Will Wait," by Mumford & Sons. She started dancing and her husband joined her and soon everyone was dancing. "In the moment, everybody was like, 'Oh my gosh, we're gonna do this thing,'" said Levi's mom.

The hearing was at 2:00 p.m. the next day, so the plaintiffs had a few hours in the morning to hang out. As they were scarfing down some breakfast and ironing their clothes, someone yelled: "Hey! Look what Leonardo DiCaprio tweeted!" The kids huddled around a cell phone and read what the actor had written: "#AllEyesOnJuliana today as the 21 young people who filed the *Juliana v. U.S.* lawsuit present their argument to the Court of Appeals in Portland, Oregon, about why this case should continue to trial. Watch the livestream," with a link. The 21 were psyched.

The youth had a bunch of other big hitters supporting them. The American Academy of Pediatrics, more than a dozen other medical organizations, and more than seventy doctors and scientists, including former U.S. Surgeons General, had filed briefs with the court on behalf of the 21. And just days before the hearing, top public health experts published a letter in the prestigious *New England Journal of Medicine* stating: "As the *Juliana* plaintiffs argue—and we agree—climate change is the greatest public health emergency of our time and is particularly harmful to fetuses, infants, children, and adolescents."

After lunch, everyone donned their court-wear. Levi dressed in "the coolest tuxedo ever," light gray with a bright pink shirt. Isaac wore a hip black button-down and gray suit jacket. The rest put on their coats and ties, dresses, skirts, and flowy pants.

When the young plaintiffs stepped out of the hotel to walk to the courthouse, hundreds of kids from city and suburban middle and high schools around Portland greeted them. Isaac was surprised and delighted to see so many students from his high school: "Kids who seemed more focused on other interests, staying in their lane of sports or academics or whatnot were taking their first climate action."

Crowds also began gathering in nearby Director Park, an open-air city block park set among a Nordstrom, a movie theater, and some other tall buildings. Expecting overflow, the court allowed projection of the hearing onto a big screen there, among the bubbling fountain, oversized chess boards, and metal patio tables. Across the country, watch parties like this one drew crowds of supporters.

To Isaac, it felt like a turning point. "It just seemed to be an exponential increase in youth awareness and youth turnout," he said.

As the young people and their lawyers walked through the city streets to the courthouse, other youth lined the route, cheering and giving high fives. The plaintiffs were pumped. "All these young people made it so much more meaningful," Nathan said.

Nearing the entrance to the sixteen-story Hatfield Courthouse, the group passed through a line of modern limestone columns. When they opened the door, the tone shifted completely. "You go from a big crowd of cheering people and then you enter the courthouse and in a split second it's quiet," said Nathan. "You're in this expansive, echoing hallway and no one is there with you. It's just us and Julia, in our suits, and you feel kind of alone."

"Do We Get to Act?"
June 4, 2019

Courtroom etiquette had become second nature to the plaintiffs. They filed into the wooden benches and rose when the three judges entered. Clothed in their black robes, Mary Murguia, Andrew Hurwitz, and Josephine Staton sat together at the high bench with dark wood paneling all around them.

The government's lawyer, Jeffrey Clark, approached the podium first. He was white with arched eyebrows, a receding hairline, and a wide forehead. Gripping the sides of the podium, he began. "We believe [this suit] is a direct attack on the separation of powers . . ." he said, referring to the three branches of the federal government, each with their separate roles. The government was arguing as it had all along that the courts can't remedy climate change because it would interfere with the work of the legislative and executive branches.

To explore the nuance of the separation of powers, Judge Hurwitz posed a hypothetical, speaking slowly, almost musing. "Assume we have rogue raiders coming across the Canadian border into the Northwest and they're kidnapping children of a certain age and murdering them and the White House refuses to do anything and Congress doesn't act. Can those people go to court to compel action? Your answer, I take it, has to be no, doesn't it?"

The youth listened carefully because the scenario captured painfully how the government was leaving them to suffer and no one seemed willing to do anything about it.

"My answer is no, because that's not the [role] of the judicial branch, Your Honor," the government lawyer said. "So the remedy, however painful it might be . . . is the political remedy of removing them from office."

The judge leaned in a bit: "Even if [they] will suffer all the damage before that can occur?"

"Yes, Your Honor."

Ouch, the young plaintiffs thought. Julia also worried about this line of questioning. She needed Judge Hurwitz on their side, and he seemed to think their case was about government inaction.

Judge Murguia turned the discussion to legal standing and the three criteria the youth had to meet to have the right to a trial: injury, evidence that government caused the injury, and redressability, whether courts could do anything to fix it.

Legal terms like "standing" and "redressability" no longer confused or intimidated Sahara, Isaac, Levi, and the other kids. They could tell the difference between a stronger argument and a weaker argument. Miriam, previously bored to sleep, now found the hearings fascinating.

The government lawyer, Jeffrey Clark, said: "Sure. So, we think that all three elements are flunked."

"Flunked" is not a legal term and Judge Murguia grinned. "You used the term 'flunked.'" she said.

"I'm sorry?"

"You used the term 'flunked," she repeated and gestured to the young plaintiffs. "I think there's a lot of students in the courtroom that might be sensitive to that particular term."

A few spectators chuckled quietly, but the attempt at humor rubbed some of the young plaintiffs the wrong way. How could she compare flunking a test with losing this case—and their security and their future?

Judge Hurwitz summarized where he thought the case stood in terms of standing: "These plaintiffs claim injury in fact. They claim causation from the lack of action on climate change."

Miriam couldn't believe it. Julia and the team had been arguing for *years* about the concrete *actions* the government took to support fossil fuels. And still, this judge thought the case was only about the government not doing enough to stop climate change. That's what frustrated Miriam about the court system. "There is so much energy, so much momentum, so many good ideas, and so many good conversations that happen outside the court," they said, "then we get into the courtroom, and we have judges that don't understand the basic premise of our argument!"

It was a red flag for Julia, too. It sounded like Judge Hurwitz had adopted the government's lens on *Juliana,* echoing the false descriptions from the government briefs. She had to get him to see this differently.

Judge Hurwitz rubbed his chin. He was inclined to acknowledge that the young plaintiffs had been injured. But he wondered what the courts could do about it without interfering with the executive and legislative branches. If the courts couldn't issue a remedy, the kids had no standing to sue. The judges would have to dismiss *Juliana.* It alarmed Julia to sense Judge Hurwitz easing into this position.

Jeffrey Clark nodded, agreed, and said it was "radical" for "one district court judge" to "impose a plan on basically the entire executive branch of the country."

Judge Hurwitz leaned back. "Your argument isn't about one district judge." He spread his arms wide. "Your argument is about the judiciary writ large, is it not?

"You're quarreling whether any judge sitting anywhere, any number—the three of us, nine on the Supreme Court, or one on the district court—can deal with this issue. Correct?"

"We are certainly arguing that . . . ," the government lawyer said.

Judge Josephine Staton, who had been quiet so far, stepped in. The courts did not have to be able to completely fix the problem, she said. "Lessening the harm would be sufficient."

Jeffrey Clark pointed out that the young plaintiffs wanted the courts to require the federal government to create a comprehensive plan to address the climate crisis. He called it an "incredibly substantive, structural injunction."

"But courts have issued structural injunctions in the past," Judge Staton said, nodding. "Correct?" And instead of waiting for his answer, she cited a case where the court ordered a detailed, complex remedy. This made Julia think that Judge Staton could imagine the court being involved in a solution here.

The vibe of this hearing reminded Isaac of the first hearing. As the government lawyer and judges parried, Isaac swung back and forth between being hopeful and worried. He had no idea which way this ruling would go.

When it was Julia's turn to present, Judge Hurwitz asked her to explain why the kids had a Fifth Amendment right to a safe environment. In other words, how was the climate linked to the rights of life, liberty, and property found in the constitution? Julia began by citing Judge Ann Aiken's recognition of a right to a climate system that sustains human life.

Judge Hurwitz shot Julia a skeptical look. Clearly the lower court's ruling was not enough. Julia had to convince this panel here, now. "What cases can you give me that suggest that *inaction* by the federal government deprives somebody of a substantive constitutional right?" the judge asked.

Julia, noting with dismay that governments' misrepresentation of her argument had just been stated by the judge, brought up the concept of state-created danger. The Supreme Court has ruled that when the government creates a danger, it is liable for injury to life, liberty, and property.

Judge Hurwitz became suddenly animated. "But can a state create a danger by failure to act? That's what I'm asking. I understand when the state goes out and puts a cone on the highway, and you run into it, they're responsible for it because they've created the danger. But your argument here is that the danger is created by the *inaction* of the federal government in these areas."

Julia leaned in. "No, Your Honor. That's not—"

"Well, let me finish. Let me finish. To the extent you are arguing that, I think you may be arguing it and you may think you're not. Can you cite me any case that says that the *inaction* by government creates a danger?"

Miriam found the line of questioning ridiculous. It's like he hasn't been listening at all! they thought. Miriam knew that people were supposed to respect judges but found it hard to respect someone who didn't seem to have carefully read the briefs and couldn't follow what Julia was saying. Honestly, they thought, how did you get to be a judge if you can't listen to a basic concept?

But Julia continued, answering his questions calmly. "No. I don't think the Fifth Amendment provides plaintiffs with a claim for pure inaction. But it does provide them a claim when the government has *affirmatively acted* to promote a fossil fuel energy system and to allow federal public lands to be extracted—and almost 25 percent of U.S. emissions come from federal public lands. And when the federal government controls the system, facilitates it, subsidizes it, promotes it, as it does, that creates a claim for a substantive due process violation." Watching Judge Hurwitz's face, Julia thought he was persuaded.

The judge changed direction with a question related to what remedy courts could offer in this situation. He raised both hands in front of him. "Let's assume you win. We get to the end of the case—I always like to ask people this—and you're writing the judgment, what does the judgment say?"

Julia nodded. "The judgment says that these defendants . . . have violated these plaintiffs' Fifth Amendment rights to life, personal security—"

"And must therefore . . . do what? You're not asking for damages, so tell me what the relief is."

"So, the decree, the injunctive decree, that plaintiffs seek is for the defendants to use their existing authority and the planning mechanisms that are already in place to prepare a national energy plan that transitions the nation away from fossil fuels."

Judge: "And who judges the adequacy or inadequacy of that plan?"

Julia: "So . . ."

Judge: "Judge Aiken?"

Julia: "Yes. Judge Aiken."

She elaborated with examples from other cases where judges oversaw court-ordered plans.

Judge Hurwitz squinted slightly. "Could the plan that you foresee be undertaken without any congressional action?"

Julia nodded. "Yes, Your Honor. In fact, we have expert evidence in the record as to the feasibility of the remedy, the economic viability of a remedy in this case, and there's abundant statutory authority that the executive branch already uses to manage the national energy system . . ." In other words, the federal government can move the country to clean energy using the tools it already has. No new laws would be needed.

As Levi sat and listened to Julia, he found it "really, really compelling." He hardly squirmed at all.

But Julia feared she had not convinced Judge Hurwitz.

Judge Murguia wondered aloud if the courts had done anything like this, on this scale, before. Julia was glad to have this question. "So the defendants, they would be ordered to do this much like in *Brown versus Board of Education*, [where] school districts and states were ordered to desegregate entire school systems, or in *Hills versus Gautreaux*, [where a federal agency] was directed by the Court, along with state and local agencies, to desegregate public housing." She gesticulated with her hands, punctuating her points. "So, whenever there's a government system that is causing such catastrophic infringement to fundamental rights, it is actually the duty of the court, starting with the district court, to issue a decree that can redress that constitutional violation."

As Isaac watched the questioning closely, he felt hope creep in. "I was like, oh, they are in our favor," he said. "They're asking the right questions and they're not trying to stop us." But he knew that could change any minute.

"You present compelling evidence that we have a real problem," Judge Hurwitz said, laying both hands on the desk. "You present compelling evidence that we have inaction by the other two branches of government."

Ugh, there was that word "inaction" again, Miriam noticed.

"It may even rise to the level of criminal neglect," the judge added.

Okay, that's promising, the kids thought.

Judge Hurwitz clasped his hands and looked at the other judges on the panel. "The tough question for me, and I suspect for my colleagues, is: Do we get to act because of that?"

Julia's deepest frustration is when she can't make someone understand her argument, when she can't seem to land it in a way that convinces them. She pointed out once again that this was not a "failure to act" case.

Judge Hurwitz rubbed his chin. "So it's not the government's *inaction* here that you attack. It's the government's *action*."

"That's correct."

What a test of Julia's character, Miriam thought. She's keeping her cool and making her arguments and defending our position.

Julia and the judges batted some other legal ideas around, concepts that she had covered in other hearings and other briefs. When it was time to close, Julia took a deep breath and said, "If we look back on the twentieth century, we can see that race and sex discrimination were the constitutional questions of that era. And when our great-grandchildren look back on the twenty-first century, they will see that government-sanctioned climate destruction was the constitutional issue of this century."

The judges listened carefully, their expressions serious as Julia continued. "We must be a nation that applies the rule of law to harmful government conduct that threatens the lives of our children so that they can grow up safe and free and pursue their happiness and that is what the founders intended.

"So, we respectfully request that the Court lift the stay and remand for trial."

Julia couldn't shake a deep sense of foreboding. She thought Judge Staton was with her but worried about Judges Hurwitz and Murguia. She tried to shake it off, hoping that when the judges reviewed all the briefs and conferred that they would see what needed to be done.

Jeffrey Clark closed, repeating arguments the government had made before. Then the hearing was over. Everyone stood as the judges left the courtroom.

Julia and her two co-counsels Phil and Andrea slipped into a room down the hall to debrief alone. The lawyers were upset, worried about how the ruling was likely to go. After they vented, they joined the youth in the hallway.

Together they stepped outside.

Let the Youth Be Heard!
June 4, 2019

Filing out the courthouse doors, the 21 and their lawyers met a crowd of young supporters cheering wildly. Seeing all the young faces showing so much passion hit Miriam in the heart. "We came out of the courtroom after having the experience of that judge not getting what we've been explaining for years and then stepping out in front of thousands of people who DO get it, who are pushing society in the direction it needs to go." Emotions swelled and Miriam's eyes welled up.

Julia hugged the kids and looped arms with Hazel and Levi. Together, with the warm spring sun shining, they headed to Director Park with throngs of young supporters surrounding them clapping and cheering.

The young plaintiffs and their parents were in awe of their lawyer. "Julia just kicked ass in the court room," said Levi's mom Leigh-Ann, "then she just walked arm in arm through Portland, just marching with them."

Director Park, where a giant screen had shown the hearing, was packed with people with huge bright blue and white banners declaring "Let the Youth Be Heard!" and "Give Science Its Day in Court!" and "Gov Knew!"

A marimba band, friends of Sahara, scooted into place on the big stage and started playing. People swayed and danced and cheered. "Let the Youth Be Heard! Let the Youth Be Heard!"

Miriam thought the rally was "nuts." Their parents, siblings, and friends were all there along with several thousand other people.

"What an incredible, lighthearted, happy scene," said Nathan.

Sahara smiled broadly, arm in a sling. *This just feels right,* Sahara thought. *We're going to win; it's the right thing, and it's going to happen.*

Plaintiff Vic Barrett, 16 when the lawsuit started and 20 now, wore a smart dark suit, white sneakers, and round sunglasses. His face shone in the sun as he stepped forward, grabbed the mic, and spoke to the crowd:

"What's happened here today, and what's been happening with youth climate movements around the world, is part of a larger narrative . . . What it is to be young is being redefined every day. It's always been a time of change and growth and discovery. And now it's all about that and more. It's about laying down the groundwork to ensure a healthy world . . .

"We spent another day in court facing our government, the apparent strongest government in the world, showing fear of young people and showing fear of facts. We're learning every day that we're the ones who must secure our future. We must do the work. We must take to the streets. Being young is being an activist today and cheering each other on.

"So, I want my two cents today to be dedicated to the youth who showed up, not just to the youth who are up here. Thank you for the sacrifices I know you're making every single day when you wake up. For the school days missed. For the moments on the bus where all of a sudden, you're like, 'Damn, climate change is a terrible issue.' I just want to tell you: Keep going even when it seems like you can't, when everything is telling you to stop. Because we have *all* the power. We have *all* the tools. And we have *all* the stake in this issue."

The youth left the stage feeling buoyed, but they felt older, too. Nathan told *CBS* in an interview that the case had gone on so long that they had to change their social media hashtag #KidsvsGov to #YouthvsGov. "I think eventually it's just going to have to be #AdultsvsGov," he said.

The plaintiffs gathered back at the hotel, happy to simply be together again. "We were all pretty hopeful," said Sahara. "We thought our prospects were good."

But were they?

Shaun Goho, of Harvard Law School, shared the kids' optimism, telling Bloomberg Law that "the only way they lose is if the court basically concludes that no one ever has standing to bring cases about climate change."

But EPA administrator Andrew Wheeler said in a speech: "I don't think it's going to go much further." And Jeffrey Wood, formerly of the Justice Department, said: "The panel—though concerned with global climate change—seemed to have real heartburn over plaintiffs' claim that the entirety of U.S. energy policy is unconstitutional to the extent it allows or promotes the use of fossil fuel energy.

"It's hard to imagine any court accepting that argument."

If the court did, it would be huge. "If they rule in favor of the plaintiffs," a reporter for *Vice* wrote, "it will set in motion a chain of historic legal events that could ultimately force a climate-denying president to adopt an aggressive plan for limiting greenhouse gases."

Experts like Michael Gerrard, of Columbia University, could not predict which way the ruling would go. "There's no real telling and there's no deadline," he told the *Los Angeles Times*.

This uncertainty was tough on the plaintiffs. "It's been a huge emotional roller coaster," said Sahara. "With lots of ups and downs, definitely some really big downs." But there was another part of the whole quest that was really challenging, they said, something less obvious. "There are a lot of points in this case where we just have to wait. We just have to sit on our hands really waiting for someone else to decide what will happen to our lives."

Demanding Action
August-September 2019

Young activists all around the world were becoming less willing to wait for adults to do something about the climate crisis. Across the globe, young people demanded action, making themselves heard in bigger ways than ever before. That September, Swedish teen Greta Thunberg, the youth groups Zero Hour and Earth Guardians, and others planned a massive mobilization effort called Global Week for Future. As part of the effort, activists including some of the *Juliana* plaintiffs gathered in Washington, D.C, to testify to Congress and to lobby for climate action.

At a hearing of the U.S. House of Representatives Climate Crisis Committee, members of Congress sat in two rows of seats arched across a wide room. Youth witnesses faced them, poised to testify at long wooden tables with name cards and slim black microphones. When Greta Thunberg hustled in with her signature braid over one shoulder, wearing a pink tee and light plaid shirt, photographers followed her like paparazzi, shoving their cameras close to her face. She slid in place before her mic in the row of testi-fiers including plaintiff Vic Barrett. Jacob, Xiuhtezcatl, and Kelsey sat behind them watching and listening.

Greta's opening statement was characteristically short and biting. "I don't want you to listen to me," she said. "I want you to listen to the scientists." She slid a copy of the United Nation's "Global warming of 1.5°C" report across the table toward the representatives. The report stated that allowing the Earth to heat by 1.5 degrees Celsius is "not considered safe," something the plaintiffs had known for a long time. Even the 1 degree C the Earth had already warmed was harming health, flooding homes, and burning communities. Allowing 50 percent more warming "poses significant risks to natural and human systems," the report stated.

"I want you to unite behind the science," she finished sternly, "and then I want you to take real action."

Plaintiff Vic Barrett, a first-generation American living in New York, testified about what he and his family stood to lose because of climate change. "If we keep going on with business as usual, both Honduras and New York, the places where my family and I are from, will forever be lost to the sea," he said.

Two other youth climate activists shared the fear and despair that their generation lives with every day, the glaring need for immediate action. One said: "The fact that you are staring at a panel of young people testifying before you today, pleading for a livable Earth should not fill you with pride. It should fill you with shame. Youth climate activism should not have to exist. We are exhausted because we have tried everything."

Later, *Juliana* plaintiffs and some supporters from Congress held a press conference on the steps of the U.S. Supreme Court. The sky glowed bright blue behind the majestic white marble courthouse with its eight rows of long columns. Seven of the young plaintiffs stood tall beside an equal number of members of Congress. Greta Thunberg sat on the steps, legs crossed.

Cameras clicked as Kelsey approached the podium, which had

a "Let the Youth Be Heard" banner below it. She gazed at the crowd before her and took a deep breath. "I find myself this week and today in a state of mourning," she said. "I feel extremely let down by history, by the decisions of our elders past. I feel old. I'm twenty-three years old, I've been doing this for more than half my lifetime." As the oldest plaintiff in the lawsuit, she felt responsible for the younger kids. "We are asking those individuals who seem to be putting guns to the foreheads of all youth to not only not pull the trigger but remove your weapon."

She shared what it's like to be in this fight saying, we are "asked to make great sacrifices . . . to put ourselves into these huge places of responsibility and burden." She wanted the audience and the members of Congress to appreciate the "sacrifices on our emotional states." Young people have had to "show up time and time again, begging for our dignity, begging . . . not only to survive, but to thrive," she said.

As Nathan listened, he felt a pit in his stomach. Over time he had come to realize the struggle behind Kelsey's happy face, how hard it was for her, for all of them, to keep up the energy. On this trip, he and Kelsey had had deep conversations about how tired they were of being told that they were "a beacon of hope" by adults. He gazed at Greta sitting at their feet and remembered something she often said: I don't want your hope, I want you to feel the fear and to DO something.

Kelsey did see one cause for celebration: all the young activists. She smiled at the young people by her side and sitting in front of her. "When I started out, there was no one. It was me banging down the halls of my school. And now we are a collective banging down the halls of Congress and the streets all around the world."

Vic Barrett was up next. He, too, seemed somber. "I'm young. I'm trans. I'm Black. I'm Indigenous. I am Latino," he said as clouds, both white and gray, drifted by. "Every aspect of my identity puts me at increased risk from the impacts of climate change. My ancestral home is threatened by climate change and will be underwater in my lifetime if nothing changes. I was born into a world in which my future and my past are uncertain, born into a world where my inheritance is slipping into the sea, where people, my people are going extinct." A light breeze fluttered the paper where he had written his speech. "That is why I'm here today. To fight for my community and all those impacted by the injustice of climate change, a crisis they did nothing to create. Like Greta so bluntly put it, our house is on fire. And we need all hands on deck to put it out. We need people in the halls of Congress, in the courts and in the streets."

The next day, young people took to the streets in a protest the likes of which had never before been seen on this planet.

44
STRIKE!
September 20, 2019

On what should have been a typical Friday, students in every class of Sahara's school put down their pencils and books, got up and walked out. Sahara hustled out to the front of the building quickly to help organize. As a member of South Eugene High School's Earth Guardian 350 environmental group, Sahara had led protests like this before—but this reached a different level. "More and more and more kids just poured out the door," they said. Sahara spotted many friends and acquaintances who hadn't attended environmental events before. Sahara waved to them all and thanked them for joining the climate strike.

Hordes of students marched through town calling out:

"There's no planet B! There's no planet B!"

and

"What do we want?"

"Climate Justice!"

"When do we want it?"

"NOW!"

Students marching from South Eugene High School merged with groups from other area high schools, swelling the crowd. "We might be rivals in football or basketball or whatever, but none of that mattered as the yelling and chanting got louder and louder," Sahara said. "It was super powerful."

That day, inspired in part by Greta Thunberg's Fridays for Future and organized primarily by youth, young people, rich and poor, of every color and faith, on every continent, walked out of school and into the streets, united in a global cry demanding that adults in charge stop ransoming their future. They drew handmade signs and held massive banners. They yelled through bullhorns and chanted in unison. For hours, sweaty, tightly packed, and enraged, they filled block after block in thousands of cities and towns in all fifty U.S. states and more than 150 other countries.

"You had a future, and so should we!" yelled young people in New York City.

"Our streets flood, so we flood our streets!" screamed students in Texas, recently swamped by Tropical Storm Imelda.

Young voices across the globe cried out for change—and fast.

"Adults are like, 'Respect your elders,'" 13-year-old Jemima Grimmer of Sydney, Australia, told the *New York Times.* "And we're like 'Respect our futures!'"

On the steps of Pennsylvania's state capitol, a student begged the crowd: "Act as if your survival is at stake because it is! Act as if your future is at stake because it is! Act as if your kid's life is at stake because it is! Act as if your health is at stake because it is!"

Four million people raised their voices, making this the largest environmental demonstration in the history of the world.

Still, it made no discernible difference. Fossil fuel projects continued to move steadily ahead, paving the way for more and more carbon dioxide to be pumped into the atmosphere, smothering the planet.

No Other Choice
November 2019

Once more, the interminable impasse moved Miriam to put their body on the line. In the predawn hours of November 4, 2019, Miriam and five other activists struggled into tight white-and-red dry suits and donned bright red caps. Through the dark and thick fog, they trudged toward several inflatable motorboats waiting in the Columbia River near the Port of Vancouver, Washington. Hauling dry bags, helmets, headlamps, hammocks, climbing ropes and chains, they crossed the parking lot toward the boats, gravel crunching underfoot and the chains clanking.

Miriam and their fellow activists were trying to stop the expansion of the Trans Mountain Pipeline, which carried dirty crude oil from Alberta in the interior of Canada to British Columbia for export to the U.S. and Asia. Steel pipes for the 700-mile expansion would be shipped along the Columbia River on the bulk carrier, the *Patagonia*. If protesters from the direct-action group Portland Rising Tide and kayakers in the Mosquito Fleet could stop shipment of the pipes, maybe they could stop the expansion.

Before boarding a small motorboat, Miriam talked to a reporter covering the direct action. "Part of why I'm here is to just give them a little reminder that they can play with us in the system, but we don't have to stay in the system to have our voices heard."

The possibility of arrest loomed over Miriam, and they knew a second offense on the record could screw up their future. Recently three job applications had been denied because of the railroad action arrest. Miriam also knew that stopping a huge ship from docking was potentially dangerous. Would the pilot see the protesters soon enough to avoid crushing them into the dock? And of course, there was the worry about how an arrest could affect *Juliana v. United States.*

Miriam and the other five protesters lowered their gear and themselves into small boats, which motored into the darkness. The boats skimmed over the black water to the four-story-high pier where the *Patagonia* would dock. They maneuvered to a piling that had a long metal ladder leading from the water to the top. Two activists hopped off and headed up the ladder. At the next piling, heavy gear strapped to their back, Miriam reached for a rung and swung themselves up. They slowly climbed the ladder, clipping in from rung to rung and pausing to catch their breath and calm their galloping heart. About ten feet below a large cleat where the massive ship would tie up, Miriam secured a hammock chair to the ladder, shimmied into place and waited, breathing heavily. A young woman hauled herself up and locked in below them. The *Patagonia* could not dock without crushing them.

The woman below yelled up to chat, but Miriam felt too freaked out. "I might actually just need to sit here in quiet for a minute," they said.

The sun rose, and so did the breeze blowing across the frigid water. Activists in kayaks paddled into place between the three pilings where Miriam and the others dangled overhead.

The *Patagonia* was due shortly, and workers in hard hats began to arrive on the dock. Leaning over the edge to eye the protesters, they grumbled about the disruption to their work and joked about peeing off the dock onto the protesters' helmeted heads.

Miriam, from a blue-collar background themselves, thought about the impact this direct action had on the dockworkers and deckhands. They thought about how direct action pushes everyone out of their comfort zones. Everything Miriam did, the direct action, the marches, the lawsuit, was meant to shake things up so people would notice that the world was not right, that we needed to do something to fix it, and soon.

Someone above yelled: "Trump! Four more years!"

Miriam and the others stayed quiet, letting their bodies speak for themselves.

Someone radioed for the police and Coast Guard. A patrol boat motored over.

Off in the distance, a ship blasted its foghorn. The *Patagonia* emerged from the fog, a massive 600-foot long blue-and-red hull, being pushed toward the dock by a tugboat. It blasted its horn again and again, as if the sound could move the protesters out of the way. The kayaks below looked tiny, and the six activists chained to the pier smaller still. The horn, even louder now, blasted again. Miriam winced and covered their ears.

More Coast Guard, firefighters, and police arrived by boat and neared the dock.

We'll be arrested for sure, Miriam thought.

"Come down!" an officer yelled through a bullhorn. "Clear the pier!"

Miriam and the others watched the massive ship filled with pipes looming over a growing group of smaller government vessels.

Eyeing the kayaking protesters and the other activists hanging like tear-drop-shaped cocoons from the long pilings, Miriam waited, shivering in the cold.

Eventually, without notice, the *Patagonia* changed course and began to move quietly down river. Flanked by a procession of official boats, like floating bodyguards, it headed for an alternate pier.

Miriam sighed. With the ship and police officers gone, there was nothing left for the protesters to do there. Kayakers paddled off. Miriam and the others disassembled their hammocks and climbed down to the waiting boats.

The resistance slowed but did not stop the pipeline expansion. Frustrated that even putting their bodies on the line seemed to have little impact, Miriam wondered if anything young people did would make a difference. Miriam and the other plaintiffs held out hope that the Ninth Circuit Court would come through for them. But they had been burned before.

The Ninth Circuit Rules
January 2020

On January 17, 2020, Nathan got a notification on his phone with news about the lawsuit. Headlines blazed across his screen:

"Court Quashes Youth Climate Change Case Against Government," screamed the *New York Times* headline.

"Court Tosses Landmark Climate Change Case Brought on Behalf of Youth," *Rolling Stone* reported.

"Appeals Court Kills 'Climate Kids' Lawsuit," according to Legal Reader.

"Headlines just pounded in," Nathan says. "Climate kids get SQUASHED, DESTROYED, WRECKED. It was like a bomb went off—BOOM!"

Though it was a frigid outside, Nathan stumbled out to his backyard for air. He sat on the porch steps and his head fell into his hands. Then he recorded a message to his friends on his phone: "Hey, everyone. So, I just woke up this morning to the news that we had the case dismissed, at least at face value. That's what all the major headlines are saying."

Kelsey, who was in her car when she heard, burst out crying: "I don't understand the full implications of this, but it feels like, like a death. It feels very scary."

The Ninth Circuit court judges had voted two to one to dismiss

Juliana. "Reluctantly, we conclude that [the requested] relief is beyond our constitutional power. Rather, the plaintiffs' impressive case for redress must be presented to the political branches of government," Judge Hurwitz wrote for the majority. The kids' motion for an injunction to halt any new fossil fuel projects was denied, too.

The panel unanimously acknowledged the reality of climate change. "The record leaves little basis for denying that climate change is occurring at an increasingly rapid pace," the opinion said. "Copious expert evidence establishes that this unprecedented rise stems from fossil fuel combustion and will wreak havoc on the Earth's climate if unchecked."

Indeed, the judges admitted that "the problem is approaching 'the point of no return.' Absent some action, the destabilizing climate will bury cities, spawn life-threatening natural disasters, and jeopardize critical food and water supplies." The record also established that the federal government knew about climate change and that their contribution "is not simply a result of inaction."

In other words, the kids were right—about everything their lawsuit contended. The panel even acknowledged that "in some circumstances, courts may order broad injunctive relief while leaving the 'details of implementation' to the government's discretion." This has happened in past cases and can continue to happen in future cases.

But the two judges in the majority, Hurwitz and Murguia, worried that action by the court would jeopardize the separation of powers. The judiciary would have to "pass judgment" on a government plan that involved both the executive and legislative branches, and "the court would be required to supervise the government's compliance with any suggested plan for many decades."

Judge Hurwitz dismissed the case "reluctantly," and even closed by saying that he hoped that the lawsuit spurred Congress and the executive branch to action. "The plaintiffs have made a compelling case that action is needed; it will be increasingly difficult in light of that record for the political branches to deny that climate change is occurring, that the government has had a role in causing it, and that our elected officials have a moral responsibility to seek solutions," the opinion stated. "The plaintiffs' case must be made to the political branches or to the electorate at large, the latter of which can change the composition of the political branches through the ballot box."

Tell that to Levi, Sahara, Avery, Hazel, Zealand, Isaac, and Jayden, and all the other kids still too young to vote, Nathan and Kelsey thought. Tell that to kids not yet even born, who would inherit a burning planet.

Julia shared the plaintiffs' outrage and their exhaustion. At times like this, she wished she could stay in bed or crawl into a tent in the mountains to escape from everything. But she couldn't and she wouldn't. Instead, she hustled to counter the narrative that was spreading through the media about the ruling.

"This is far from over," Julia told the *Washington Post*. "That the judiciary cannot act as a check on two branches that are causing an existential threat to the lives of these young plaintiffs, to America's children, and to the future of our nation is an idea that would make our founders roll over in their graves."

"The idea that [youth plaintiffs'] only recourse is to go to the very branches of government that are violating their rights when half of them can't even vote is a preposterous notion," she told the

New York Times. Julia knew it would be an uphill battle to explain to reporters and the public that the Ninth Circuit wouldn't have the last word on this and that there were still many plays left in the case.

Still, news of the dismissal quickly circulated everywhere. Levi's mom had friends all around the world, and people from England, Hong Kong, and other places sent her texts and emails about the case being done, being over.

She tried to explain that only one aspect of the case was over, that the courts wouldn't force a plan to address climate change. "If you look at the history of the case, there were lots of moments where the same kind of thing happened, where the judges were like 'Nope not going through,' or 'Failed this time,'" she told them. "That has happened multiple times."

"But for whatever reason," she said, "this particular time, maybe the wording of the headline from a big media outlet and the speed in which it spread, everybody just said, 'Oh, it's totally over now.'"

Miriam's parents also read some headlines. "Oh, no," they texted. "What happened? What now?" Miriam's cell phone lit up with friends texting: "How do you feel?" "Are you okay?"

Miriam didn't understand everyone's reaction. The case was endlessly bouncing around in the courts so how big a loss could this be? Then they started reading the media coverage.

"This is a very serious blow to the case, perhaps a fatal blow," Jennifer Rushlow, an associate dean for environmental programs at Vermont Law School, told Yahoo! News.

Michael Gerrard of Columbia University put it this way: "For now, all three branches of the federal government are sitting on their hands as the planet burns."

A lawyer with an energy lobbying firm told the *Washington Post:* "I know that climate activists are disappointed, but the result is not a surprise to any lawyer in the country. No U.S. court has ever even come close to ordering the kind of relief that the activists were seeking in this case."

"With today's decision, the question of how to deal with climate change is now squarely before Congress. Under our system of government, that's where it belongs."

The press quoted Jeffrey Clark, the lawyer who argued the case for the defendants, saying the government was "pleased with the outcome."

Julia set up a video call to discuss the ruling but in the meantime, the plaintiffs texted and emailed one another articles.

Sahara was really upset and frustrated and felt powerless. They worried about the impact this coverage could have on all their supporters, all the people counting on them. "I didn't want readers all over thinking it was over because there were still other avenues we could take, weren't there?"

On the video call, emotions ran high. The youth asked questions and some shed tears of frustration. The lawyers emphasized what they had said in the email: This does NOT mean the case is over. Even though the media are saying the case is finished, we are your lawyers. We are telling you that the dismissal does not mean that the case is completely over.

"I don't really think in terms of failure," Julia said. "I think in terms of partial wins and partial successful steps forward. Everything we are doing is about moving the law forward."

The legal team encouraged the youth to read the powerful dissent written by Judge Josephine Staton. This opposing opinion offered a searing critique of the majority's reluctance to address the constitutional question at hand. "In these proceedings, the government accepts as fact that the United States has reached a tipping point crying out for a concerted response—yet presses ahead toward calamity. It is as if an asteroid were barreling toward Earth and the government decided to shut down our only defenses. Seeking to quash this suit, the government bluntly insists that it has the absolute and unreviewable power to destroy the Nation," she wrote.

"My colleagues throw up their hands, concluding that this case presents nothing fit for the Judiciary," she continued. But the courts, she said, have not only the right to intervene—they have the responsibility to intervene when presented with an infraction to fundamental rights that is so momentous. "The injuries experienced by plaintiffs are the first small wave in an oncoming tsunami—now visible on the horizon of the not-so-distant future—that will destroy the United States as we currently know it," she wrote.

And "unlike the majority, I believe the government has more than just a nebulous 'moral responsibility' to preserve the Nation." She added: "When fundamental rights are at stake, individuals 'need not await legislative action,'" and "courts serve as the ultimate backstop."

She pulled no punches. "The majority laments that it cannot step into the shoes of the political branches, but appears ready to yield even if those branches walk the Nation over a cliff.

"Where is the hope in today's decision? Plaintiffs' claims are based on science, specifically, an impending point of no return. If plaintiffs' fears, backed by the government's *own studies*, prove true, history will not judge us kindly. When the seas envelop our coastal cities, fires and droughts haunt our interiors, and storms ravage everything between, those remaining will ask: Why did so many do so little?"

Kelsey read the last paragraph of the ruling through her tears: "I would hold that plaintiffs have standing to challenge the government's conduct, have articulated claims under the Constitution, and have presented sufficient evidence to press those claims at trial. I would therefore affirm the district court. With respect, I dissent."

The kids and their parents didn't know what to think of the dissent. "It was very frustrating because we were so close and yet so far," said Levi's mom. "One judge was on our side. What would it have taken to convince one more judge and switch the decision in a completely different direction?"

Paul Sabin of Yale thought the dissent could have an impact in the long run: "If the situation worsens, as is likely, the courts may grow more receptive to these claims. It was a 2-1 decision, and one already can imagine a different scenario in which a different set of judges might have reached a different result," he told *Time*. "The courts are still coming around to the necessary role that they may have to play. A dismissal now does not mean a dismissal forever."

But the dissent did not change the ruling. For now, the court was telling Judge Aiken to dismiss the case.

Levi was devastated. "How can they not see that all the facts are there?" Levi wondered. "How can they just dismiss us like this?"

The case was dismissed without prejudice, which meant that the youth could try again. And the youth could also appeal. Julia acknowledged their grief about this setback and also told them to stay strong, to not give up, that they were going to keep going, keep pressing, keep doing everything they possibly could. Every dissent, and every ruling in fact, gave the lawyers information that helped them further develop the case, she told them.

She reminded them that they had actually won every legal argument the government threw at them, except one. The three judges rejected almost all of Jeffrey Clark's arguments. Julia had even convinced Judge Hurwitz that it was not a case about "inaction."

The legal team insisted they would immediately explore what arguments, evidence, or angle they could use to overcome the judges' objection. Was there a way to reframe things to keep the case alive?

Still, Levi was despondent. His mom tried to comfort him. "Your lawyers are going to keep pushing this and pushing this as far as they can possibly go until every avenue has been exhausted," she told him.

"How will it move forward?" he asked. "And when?"

"Sometimes decisions like this take a very, very, very long time," she told him. That was really hard for an 11-year-old to hear, especially one who had been trying to halt climate change for nearly half of his life.

Levi and the other plaintiffs mourned and wondered: What could their lawyers do—what *would* they do—to bring the lawsuit back to life?

PART III
Can the Youth Resurrect Their Case— and Save the Planet?

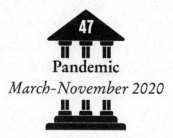

47

Pandemic

March–November 2020

A few days before the ruling, China reported that a man had died from a strange pneumonia-like virus that had infected dozens of people in Wuhan. Just after the ruling, a 30-year-old man returning to Washington State from Wuhan checked into a hospital with similar symptoms. It was the first confirmed U.S. case of COVID-19, a highly contagious, deadly virus that quickly shackled the country and the world.

By the end of March, more than a thousand people in the United States had died of the coronavirus. Cities and states across the country went into lockdown—including the courts. The Oregon federal courts canceled in-person hearings and transitioned to telephone and video. They focused mostly on "essential" criminal cases. No matter what Julia's next step would be, the courts would likely not move quickly on the youth climate lawsuit.

"Our case was already taking so long," Sahara said. "There were so many things slowing it down and now this!" They were frustrated. "I could actually use a stronger word than frustrated."

Nathan felt like he had no emotional juice left. "We were all kind of wallowing in this feeling of impending doom where nothing was happening," he said.

Meanwhile, the virus upended the youths' lives. Their middle schools, high schools, and colleges closed, sports and theater and other activities were canceled. They faced stay-at-home orders and couldn't see friends or even some family members.

The 21 were trying to figure out how to continue with their lives but realized pretty quickly that everything had changed. Even video meetings about the case petered out. "I felt pretty shut off," Sahara said. "It was really hard not seeing the plaintiffs. I really missed, like, all of them."

The pandemic pushed Miriam to reflect on what was most important in life. After graduating from college, Miriam was a musician and environmental activist living in Seattle. But they felt less connected to nature than they did as a kid. With the pandemic spotlighting how fragile life could be, Miriam wondered: What's it all for? Wanting to deepen their connection to nature, Miriam moved to an off-the-grid camp near the Oregon coast, where they could trade labor for housing. But to check in on the case, they figured out where to park to get Wi-Fi.

Being in limbo took its toll on Isaac. Over the course of the case, he felt like he spent surprisingly little time in the courtroom or getting rulings or doing other related work. The rest of the time was waiting. In those five years, he graduated high school and was trying to juggle transitioning to adulthood with keeping engaged in the case. It wasn't easy.

In the fall, Isaac attempted remote classes at Howard University, in Washington, D.C., from his family's home in Beaverton, Oregon. He had picked where to go to college with the lawsuit in mind. "In D.C., I would be perfectly located for anything Julia needed done," he said. "I would be right there! I wanted to speak on behalf of Julia and the plaintiffs in Congress or with representatives to be an instrument to nudge elected officials to support our lawsuit." But that couldn't happen with the world in the tight grip of the pandemic.

Levi became a big brother during the pandemic. He adored his new baby sister Juniper Rue, holding her on his lap during video interviews and talking about how we *had* to address the climate crisis to keep her healthy and safe.

The 21 and their legal team were painfully aware that one thing would not wait for the pandemic to end—climate change. The world continued to warm with devastating consequences. Seas had already risen up to seven inches and were predicted to rise up to three feet. Megadroughts threatened water and food supplies. Ninety-nine percent of the world's coral reef could be destroyed, and one third of the Earth's plants and animals could go extinct. "I worry perpetually about the clock ticking," Julia said.

That fall, Oregon burst into flame. Extreme drought and high winds whipped up multiple infernos that spread rapidly through forests and obliterated small towns. "It was apocalyptic," said Sahara. "Dystopian." White cinders floated down from the sky like snow. The ash coated everything. The home state of many plaintiffs in the case had the worst air quality in the world.

Because of their asthma, Sahara retreated to their bedroom, which had an air filter. Day after day, Sahara woke up to more of the same. Suffocating gray sky, ash-filled air, another day grounded. Their crew team workouts, even indoor ones, were canceled. "First the case stalling, then COVID, then this. It was like a triple whammy, almost too much to bear," they said.

Sahara felt called to do more to inspire people to take climate change seriously. They took a step they thought they'd never take.

"If there are requests for interviews or speaking opportunities," Sahara told Our Children's Trust, "please send them my way."

Julia watched closely as evacuation orders from the wildfires approached Eugene. She ordered air purifiers, taped all their windows and doors, and ordered an over-the-head respirator for trips to the grocery store.

As the wildfires spread, forests on each side of the camp where Miriam lived burst into flames, enveloping the area in dense smoke. "This shit is REAL," they said. So real that they had to pack up everything they would need in an evacuation. Storing the bags in the truck, ready to go, didn't ease Miriam's anxiety. They hardly slept, hearing crackling in the dark, convinced their house was going to burn down. "It was terrifying," they said. "If our forest burns, our home burns."

In the previous four years, fewer than one hundred homes were lost to wildfires in Oregon. That fall, fire destroyed more than 4,000 houses. That's at least 4,000 families who lost everything, who became homeless in what seemed like a blink of an eye.

Miriam struggled with exhaustion but couldn't call it burnout. "Burnout suggests that there is something else I can be doing. But I can't just go to a regular job, save up money, buy a house, and start a family," they said. "That's just not in my future because I can't trust that the climate system will be stable enough for that to happen."

The youth and their lawyers also nervously awaited the 2020 election. Would Trump, the climate-denier-in-chief, stay in office? If so, they could expect the administration to continue blocking their attempts to secure their rights to life, liberty, and property.

But if a climate-friendly candidate won, someone serious about ending the climate crisis, that could change everything. Maybe the new president would stop the procedural maneuvering that was keeping them from going to trial. Or maybe he or she would settle out of court with real commitments to ending the climate crisis.

At the beginning, the Democratic field was wide open, including Washington Governor Jay Inslee, who was running with climate change as his top priority, and Senator Bernie Sanders, who publicly supported *Juliana* and embraced a Green New Deal, which would tackle economic inequities and climate change together.

But the youth and their lawyers knew not to get their hopes up. "It's not hard for Democratic presidential contenders to go after Trump's record on climate," said a reporter at the *New Republic*. "Anyone vying for the party's nomination, though, will have to confront Democrats' own legacy of looking out for the fossil fuel industry." In fact, youth represented by Our Children's Trust were suing Governor Inslee over climate change. And at a time when the U.S. government spent $20 billion subsidizing fossils fuels, the Democratic National Committee deleted from its party platform a pledge to end tax breaks and subsidies to the fossil fuel industries.

Maybe, no matter what happened with the election, it would be business as usual. Maybe their only hope would still be the courts.

Only time would tell.

A New Administration
November 2020–February 2021

Joe Biden, a moderate who had served as Vice President under Barack Obama, won the Democratic nomination.

On the campaign trail, Biden frequently referred to the climate "crisis," and promised "no more drilling on federal public lands, period. Period, period, period." He bragged about being "one of the first guys to introduce a climate change bill, way, way back in '87," when he called climate change "an existential threat." But no true legislative action tackling climate change followed.

And he was part of the Obama administration which oversaw the expansion of fossil fuel production in the United States. So, the 21 couldn't really be sure of Biden's stance on climate—or on their case.

In the contentious presidential election, Biden prevailed.

Trump falsely claimed repeatedly that the election was stolen. Department of Justice attorney Jeffrey Clark, who argued for the government in *Juliana* before the Ninth Circuit Court of Appeals, met with the defeated president to find ways to keep Congress from certifying the election.

And in terms of climate change, things got worse. Before leaving office, the Trump administration offered seventy-nine million acres in the Gulf of Mexico for drilling and rushed to auction drilling rights in the Arctic National Wildlife Refuge.

The attempt to overthrow the election failed, and on January 20, 2021, Biden was sworn in. On his first day as president, he rescinded the permit for the Keystone XL pipeline. Within two weeks of taking office, Biden recommitted the United States to the Paris Agreement on climate change, halted new permits for oil and gas production on federal land and waters, and promised to address climate change in every department under his control.

Many people assumed that with a Democrat in office, they didn't have to worry about climate change anymore. "What's frustrating about getting a more liberal president in office is that it'll make people think that everything is fine," said Miriam. But it was far from fine.

The year 2020 tied with 2016 as the hottest year on record. Even with President Biden's actions, the United States was nowhere near cutting greenhouse gases enough to stabilize the climate.

It still seemed like the lawsuit was the best chance for making real and lasting progress. "Change through the courts is just so important," Isaac said. "Even though it can take a long time, it can work. And we really need that."

What *Could* the Court Do?
February–March 2021

Meanwhile, the young people's legal team had tried asking the entire Ninth Circuit Court, with its dozens of judges, to review the 2-1 dismissal by the three-judge panel. In February 2021, the court declined. With the panel's ruling to dismiss *Juliana* still standing, the team had three options: let the case die, send the case to the U.S. Supreme Court for the third time, or try something new.

A reporter at Bloomberg Law asked Julia if she would appeal to the Supreme Court. "If I told my clients, 'Look, people think we should cut our losses and accept this loss because it's not too bad,' my clients would reject that advice," she said. "And rightly so."

But observers worried that a third review by the U.S. Supreme Court would be reckless, especially since liberal Justice Ruth Bader Ginsberg was replaced by Trump appointee Amy Coney Barrett. "The general rule, of course, is you don't want an adverse Supreme Court decision, and it's as simple as that," said Seth Jaffe, an attorney who tracks environmental lawsuits.

"This is the most conservative Supreme Court we've seen in the modern age of environmental law," Vermont Law School professor Pat Parenteau observed. "There is no chance of a favorable decision from this court."

But Julia didn't represent environmental law professors, or

the legal community, or even environmentalists generally. She represented 21 young people who had been injured by their government's contributions to climate change and whose injuries were only going to get worse. "I have an ethical obligation to my young clients," she said. "I do not see any benefit to them in not pursuing the appellate channels we have to at the end of the day deliver justice to them."

Nathan and some of the other plaintiffs were torn about appealing to the Supreme Court. Maybe they could prevail. And even if the justices ruled against the youth, at least it would be on the record. Any dissenting opinion could be a basis for change down the road. But their lawyers had always told them that if the Supreme Court ever heard the case, they should hear it after trial when all the facts had come out in the light of day. And Nathan worried about the possibility that a harsh final judgment from the highest court could be "used as a hammer to destroy every other environmental lawsuit." It seemed prudent to pursue other options first.

So, Julia unveiled a new tactic to the plaintiffs: amending the original complaint.

"It's really, really normal when you're a lawyer, that if a court kicks you out on something, for plaintiffs to seek amendment of their complaint to try to fix the error identified by the court. It happens all the time," Julia said on a video call. In other words, it's like saying, Judge, we don't agree with what the Ninth Circuit Court did, but we'd like to adjust our complaint a little bit to meet the concerns of the Ninth Circuit so we can still go to trial.

Julia and her team had already won everything they needed to proceed to trial except for one thing. The courts ruled that the young people had been injured and that the government was at least partially responsible. They only lost on the issue of whether the courts could redress, or make right, the injury.

The Ninth Circuit had ruled that courts could not require and oversee a huge climate recovery plan. But maybe, Julia explained, the courts would be willing to offer more limited relief that was squarely in their wheelhouse—simply declaring that the young people had a constitutional right to a stable climate. Courts offer "declaratory relief" all the time, she said. Many of the most important Supreme Court decisions of constitutional law have been declaratory judgments, including *Brown v. Board of Education*, which declared "separate but equal" to be unconstitutional. Other actions by the three branches of government may follow but "the first step and the most important step is the declaratory judgment," she said.

If they took this approach, *Juliana* would not solve everything at once, which they had hoped it would, but open the door to progress. That's because declaring rights would set important limits on government policy. "It tells the political branches that you have to operate within this particular constraint, so that you are in compliance with the Constitution, which is the most significant law of the land," Julia said.

The plaintiffs agreed it was a good idea. The lawyers would remove the request for the court to oversee a climate recovery plan and just ask for declaratory relief. By satisfying the three prongs of standing—the youth were injured, the government contributed to that injury, and the court could offer relief in the form of a declaration of plaintiffs' rights and government wrongs—*Juliana* could proceed to trial.

The lawyers filed the motion to amend the complaint on

March 9, 2021. The new approach infused the legal team and the 21 with energy and excitement.

Nathan was so psyched that he penned an op-ed that ran in the *Register-Guard*. He wrote: "As the Constitution directs and as the scientific gravity commands, it is past time we had our day in court. We hope to see everyone in Eugene soon, for trial."

To Isaac, this changed everything. It felt like forward momentum after being stuck for so long.

Some observers were surprised and pleased. This case is "never say die," Vermont Law School professor Pat Parenteau told *NPR*.

But for this strategy to work, Judge Ann Aiken would have to allow them to amend their complaint. She scheduled a hearing for June 25, 2021.

The young people crossed their fingers, but they couldn't help but worry, too. So much was riding on this hearing. "Pretty much every single time we have a hearing it's a pretty stressful two hours," said Isaac. "The stakes are so high, and the pressure is so high and there is no room for error. Anything Julia said, if it's just slightly wrong, that could be the end of everything."

Settlement?
May 2021

In another twist, on May 13, 2021, the 21 got a second option. Judge Ann Aiken ordered the young plaintiffs and the U.S. government into settlement discussions. With *Juliana* still alive, both parties had incentive to try to find common ground to resolve the dispute.

Miriam had mixed feelings about settlement discussions. On the one hand, settlement could get them out of legal limbo and finish the case with some concrete action. "But my concern is that we'll end up with a nice agreement where nobody really does anything," they said.

Nathan was more optimistic. "It's an incredible opportunity," he said.

The youth all agreed that they wanted a seat at the settlement table, to present their views, and to see what the government was willing to offer up. Julia and Phil assured them that they didn't have to agree to anything they didn't want. So, the youth and lawyers started working up their initial offer, outlining terms they would and would not accept.

Because of pandemic restrictions, the talks would happen by phone and videoconference. To facilitate the discussions, Judge Aiken asked Judge Coffin, the first magistrate judge who heard *Juliana*, to come out of retirement to act as the intermediary.

The 21 were excited to have Judge Coffin because he was so familiar with the case.

Under court rules, the whole thing had to be hush, hush. When
the media asked, the young plaintiffs offered: "No comment." The
kids who were now adults couldn't even talk to their families about
the discussions. They couldn't share any possible settlement terms
with anyone until the judge wrote them into a court order. They
couldn't even talk about who was taking part in the negotiations.
Nathan likened it to the part in the musical *Hamilton,* when only
a few people making important decisions on the founding of the
United States were "in the room where it happened."

The legal team would not put all their eggs in one basket. After
all, the government had fought this case tooth and nail. Dan Farber,
a University of California Berkeley School of Law professor, told
Reuters that the government would not agree to a deal that recognized new rights for fear of future lawsuits.

And the young people might not accept anything less.

"What's it to you?"
June 2021

As the date for the hearing on the motion to amend the complaint neared, Phil obsessively checked the U.S. Supreme Court's website for new rulings. It was the end of the court's term, and Justices were releasing opinions daily. Something in one of their newest rulings could help—or hurt—their case. He wanted to be prepared.

A few days before the hearing, they found something. A case called *Mahanoy Area School District v. B. L.*, dealt with the free speech rights of a 14-year-old cheerleader. Since the ruling protected a fundamental right—free speech—Phil and Julia wondered if the court's opinion could help their case. The night before the hearing, Phil and Julia read the case together, deciding whether to bring it up with the judge. Julia stayed up late figuring out how to incorporate the ruling into her oral argument.

June twenty-fifth dawned scorching hot in Oregon, where Judge Ann Aiken would preside over the hearing. The U.S. National Weather Service issued an excessive heat warning. "Dangerous temperatures of 98 to 103 likely, with temperatures locally 104 to 110." Such heat was unheard of in Oregon—and seemed even more bizarre in June. With projected temperatures 15 to 30 degrees higher than normal, weather forecasters all across the Pacific Northwest called the situation "unprecedented."

Indeed, much of the west was in the grip of a powerful and long-lasting climate-change-triggered heat wave endangering forty million people. Phoenix hit 117 degrees, breaking the previous record by three degrees. Death Valley, California, reached a dangerous 128 degrees. The region was so hot that walking barefoot gave people third-degree burns, and asphalt roads melted and buckled. In Nevada, the National Weather Service tweeted the warning: "Long duration heat waves are DEADLY." That's because extreme heat overwhelms the body's ability to maintain a steady temperature. As core body temperature rises, cells break down and organs fail. Children are most vulnerable to heat because they spend more time outside being active and can't regulate bodily temperature as easily as adults can.

If the world continued consuming fossils fuels at the current rate, things would just get worse. Scientists projected that average summer temperatures in the west could climb *6 degrees* by 2050. The number of days of extreme heat in the United States could triple.

How appallingly fitting, the plaintiffs thought, that their hearing on whether they had the right to fight their government's contributions to climate change would happen on a day of record-breaking heat.

The morning of the hearing, Julia and Phil met in the conference room at Our Children's Trust, where binders of evidence and legal documents lined the walls. Julia reviewed her arguments, especially the new material on the cheerleader's case she had added the night before.

Phil clicked over to the U.S. Supreme Court website and noticed that just that morning, the Court had issued a new ruling on a case called *TransUnion LLC v. Ramirez*.

Could this ruling help or hurt their case? Scrolling through the pages, Phil saw that the case was about thousands of people who brought a class-action lawsuit against a credit-reporting company that incorrectly identified them as potential drug traffickers or terrorists. The court had ruled on which people really had standing to sue.

Juliana could only move forward if the amended complaint gave the 21 standing to sue. So, standing would be a central issue in today's hearing.

Huh, let me print this, Phil thought. After grabbing the pages from the printer, he sat down at the conference table where Julia was reading her notes.

The clock ticked toward 10 a.m. as Julia rehearsed and Phil studied the opinion.

Suddenly, he started hitting Julia on the arm. "Oh my god," he said. "You got to, you've GOT to hear this!"

And he read: "Plaintiff must have a 'personal stake' in the case—in other words, standing. To demonstrate their personal stake, plaintiffs must be able to sufficiently answer the question: 'What's it to you?'"

She looked up from her papers. "You're kidding."

"It's right here," he said, stabbing at the printout. "What's it to you?"

She peered over his shoulder at the printout. "What's it to you?" she said, a grin spreading across her face. "Oh my god, What's it to you?! Thank you, Justice Kavanaugh!"

With just minutes left before the hearing, Julia and Phil

highlighted parts of the new opinion for Julia to refer to and jotted out some notes to reframe her oral argument. Energized and convinced they were on the right track, they dialed in.

Because of the pandemic, the hearing took place by telephone. The young plaintiffs phoned in to a call-in line, from their bedrooms, dining rooms, and dorm rooms. At 10 a.m. the phone line erupted with people calling in from all over the country: Beep, beep, beep, beepbeepbeepbeeep.

Once the beeping settled down, Judge Aiken opened the hearing. It was the plaintiff's motion, so Julia began. "Your Honor, how our nation's children and adults speak, move, love, vote, worship, assemble, learn, and behave in our world is a function of the rights we hold and those we are denied. For our rights to endure in the face of government policy threats, they need to be declared."

It was an eloquent start. Some of the plaintiffs got goosebumps.

She jumped right in by describing the two-day-old ruling from the U.S. Supreme Court on *Mahanoy Area School District v. B. L.* The case was brought by a 14-year-old cheerleader who dropped the F-bomb in a Snapchat post she made off-campus. "F*** school f*** softball f*** cheer f*** everything," she wrote. The school cut her from the junior varsity squad and suspended her for the vulgar language. Defending her constitutional right to freedom of speech, she sued. While the courts have allowed schools to limit speech that disrupts the school environment or that invades the rights of others, the cheerleader's lawyers argued that these exceptions should not apply to speech made outside of school.

The school reversed its policy on suspension for the off-campus speech, and the young woman graduated. But to the young woman, the case was not resolved. She wanted the court to tell schools that they could not interfere with students' freedom of speech when they were not even on campus.

The Supreme Court awarded the girl $1 in nominal damages. The one dollar indicated that she was right, that the school had interfered with her right to freedom of speech. And the ruling was a powerful declaration of constitutional law.

The climate kids' motion was similar, Julia argued. They were now asking the court "whether they too have constitutionally protected rights that have been invaded by their government," she said.

She explained her thinking: If the court ultimately "declares the nation's energy system policies and practices unconstitutional, the Government will change those policies and practices to stop the constitutional violation." That, she argued, was a powerful remedy.

Judge Aiken seemed impressed: "That intervening Supreme Court case changes somewhat the complexion of everything."

Julia and the young people were encouraged.

Julia knew that the government would argue that Judge Aiken should dismiss *Juliana* because the Ninth Circuit had already dismissed it. So, Julia addressed that. "We don't need to argue whether the Ninth Circuit got it right or got it wrong," she explained. "We need to look at what they didn't consider and did not rule on." Since the 2-1 ruling didn't address the 21's newly amended complaint and its specific requests for declaratory judgment, the court could look at the remedy issue anew, in light of new Supreme Court opinions.

Judge Aiken asked a question about another recent case. Julia answered it and then dropped the bombshell. "Just today, Your Honor, another decision came down . . ."

She described what Justice Kavanaugh wrote in the ruling about who gets standing in a lawsuit: "Plaintiffs must have a personal stake in the case and, to demonstrate their personal stake, Plaintiffs must be able to sufficiently answer the question, 'What's it to you?'"

The phone line crackled with static, but Julia pushed on. "And that question—'What's it to you?'—is very, very clear here."

The young people were amazed at how Julia was able to take a ruling just handed down that morning and turn it into a strong argument for their case.

Judge Aiken seemed surprised and impressed. "I try very hard the mornings of expected opinions to be attuned to them coming down, and I was getting ready for this case and had an earlier hearing and did not know that case came down," she admitted. She appreciated Julia's "eloquent summary of the argument and the essence of the case: 'What's it to you?'"

The young people listening in felt a tug of hope. What did the case mean to them? Everything.

Then, the government had the floor.

Sean Duffy, the government lawyer who had handled *Juliana v. United States* earlier, came out swinging. "I'm going to go straight to the bottom-line issue before the Court today. The Ninth Circuit has decided this case and ordered that it be dismissed," he said. "There is nothing left for this Court to do but to dismiss the case."

There was nothing really different in this amended complaint, he continued. Originally, the plaintiffs had asked the courts to declare a constitutional right to a stable climate (declaratory relief) and for the courts to oversee a climate relief plan (injunctive relief). And they lost. Now the plaintiffs were just asking for the same thing again. Plus, he added, "Plaintiffs' injuries will not be redressed merely if the Court declares government action to be unconstitutional."

The 21 completely disagreed with him. Ruling that the government's actions were unconstitutional would be a huge relief to the youth—and would give them hope.

Judge Aiken seemed more interested in the "What's it to you?" idea. "I guess I'm thinking a little bit out loud," she said. "The new case today—'What's it to you?'—these young people have certainly thrown down that question."

Sean Duffy admitted that he hadn't read the new Supreme Court decision.

"It's clear to me that . . . these cases from the Supreme Court changed the complexion of the case in significant ways," Judge Aiken added.

Sean Duffy tried to convince the judge that the Ninth Circuit's order to dismiss *Juliana* applied to the amended complaint, because they both "have the Court essentially commandeer the energy policy of the United States."

"I would disagree with that," Judge Aiken said. She was fully engaged now. "I don't think [declaratory relief] directs anything. What it does is it gives guidance to the federal government about, again, stepping up and protecting the constitutional rights that have been discussed."

She continued. "So what is interesting in this case is—and what I think many people have not understood—is a district court is a place where the facts are developed and the facts are laid out," she said. "If the facts and the trial on those facts were out there, I strongly suspect . . . that before the Court could even act there may be both executive and legislative action that begins to redress and address the damage done to the rights that have been expressed by the 21 young people . . ."

She continued directing her remarks to Sean Duffy. "I'm also trying to get you to focus on how this case, moving forward with an amendment—given what the Supreme Court has said in the two most recent cases and the way this case is postured . . . is, frankly, not such a, shall we say, a controversial request on the part of the plaintiffs."

The government lawyer disagreed, arguing vigorously that if the Ninth Circuit wanted to allow the plaintiffs to amend their complaint, "there would have been some language in that opinion to that effect."

Julia was tired of Sean Duffy's same refrain and misrepresentation of legal procedure. The government continued making the same arguments they'd been making for six years from the Obama administration through the Trump administration and now to the Biden administration. They just continued to say these young people don't have a right to be in court instead of grappling with the fact that for hundreds of years the U.S. Supreme Court has been declaring constitutional rights and wrongs. And amending a complaint is as common as brushing your teeth.

Julia wished Sean Duffy would be more honest and delve deeper. Rather than just carrying out the old Department of Justice command to challenge standing, she wished he would ask himself: What is right here? What is justice? What does it really mean to represent the people of the United States?

Judge Aiken lost her patience with the government's lawyer, too. "Well, we're going to agree to disagree on that point, because, let me tell you, having been on the bench a long time, when they want to dismiss with prejudice [which allows for no amended complaints], they do that," she said. "When they don't, they leave it open. And this was left open."

Sean Duffy continued to argue for dismissal, wrapping up with: "We do not disrespect youth and the important cause that they take up, but the place to take up that cause is not the courtroom but instead with their elected representative." The young people on the phone line wanted to scream. Levi can't vote. Neither can Avery or Hazel or Sahara or Zealand. Neither could the kids of the future.

Julia rebutted him. "Mr. Duffy says that the energy system is up to the political branches and that these young people need to go convince their elected officials or they need to go to the polls and vote to change that system," she said. "There's no other instance where a constitutional right, a fundamental right, is being violated that plaintiffs are told to go to the polls!

"Every decision the Government has made about the energy system today and for the past fifty years has been, to this point, solely up to the political will of the majority," she continued. "And those policies and practices, which Defendants admit are endangering these plaintiffs, have never been evaluated for their constitutionality . . .

"We do not ask the Court to commandeer the nation's energy system. We want the Court here to do its job—to hear the evidence on both sides, find the facts, declare the rights, and, if Your Honor finds violations of those rights, to also declare them. And what the Plaintiffs truly want is for the political branches of government to stop infringing their rights and to make policy decisions that are protective of them."

She brought her argument home, to Oregon, where the judge, like everyone else in the Pacific Northwest, faced a week of unbearable heat. "As we head into over 110-degree temperatures this early summer weekend in Eugene, Oregon, and a summer again ravaged by drought, with looming threats of another vicious wildfire season, there's a new draft report by the United Nations that just came out, and it said, quote, 'The worst is yet to come affecting our children's and our grandchildren's lives much more than our own.'

"Six years into this case these plaintiffs are still being individually harmed by their government's policies and practices, and only a declaration by this Court of their constitutional rights and the Government's violation thereof, after all of the facts are laid bare, will truly begin to protect their rights and redress their ongoing injuries."

And she rested her case.

Judge Aiken gave the government the last word. Sean Duffy seemed irritated. "It's not Mr. Duffy who said that the energy system is up to the political branches," he said. "It's the Ninth Circuit who said that definitively in its opinion."

Judge Aiken listened carefully and directed her final comment to him: "I was hopeful that your argument might have been different today. But I'm prepared to go forward and make my decision on this case."

Georgetown Law professor Lisa Heinzerling, who had been following the case, found Julia's arguments "persuasive."

"It seems like Julia Olson did everything she could have done," she said.

The 21 were awed, as usual, by how eloquently Julia spoke for them. And they were stunned by how open the judge seemed to the amendment. Did they dare hope that their case would be resurrected?

Things Heat Up
July–November 2021

As the young people and their lawyers waited for Judge Aiken's ruling, climate change continued to ravage the planet.

July broke the world record for the hottest month on Earth. The heat wave packed emergency rooms across the Pacific Northwest with people dizzy and drenched with sweat, stumbling in or wheeled in on stretchers. Doctors struggled to stop patients' muscles from breaking down and their livers and kidneys from failing. As many as 800 people across the region died from the heat.

A public health official in Seattle was blunt. "Climate change is a health emergency," he said. "And reducing greenhouse gas emissions is literally a matter of life and death."

In August, while the 21 waited, a monster storm brewed in the Gulf of Mexico. With water temperatures in the gulf three to five degrees Fahrenheit higher than the average, Hurricane Ida picked up power and moisture. Meteorologists forecast as much as twenty inches of rain for areas in Ida's path.

The Category 4 hurricane hit Louisiana with whipping winds and huge storm surges. It wrought destruction across Alabama, Florida, Georgia, Mississippi, and Texas. Families lost power and access to clean water. Conditions were dire. "The schools are not open. The businesses are not open. The hospitals are slammed.

There's no water and there's not going to be electricity," Louisiana governor John Bel Edwards told people. "If you have already evacuated, do not return here."

The storm blazed up the eastern seaboard, dumping huge quantities of rain and triggering massive floods. Some areas got as much as four inches of rain in one hour.

In New York City, the scene was apocalyptic. Water gushed down subway stairs, as if they were waterfalls. Stations filled up with foaming, murky water. Major avenues resembled filthy rivers with cars, taxis, and buses sticking partway above the flood waters. People waded thigh deep in water as dead rats and garbage floated by.

"It was terrible," Yvette Baker, 34, told reporters from Bloomberg. "The water was so high. They had one rowboat trying to save all these people. People were screaming for help."

Power outages hobbled New York, New Jersey, Pennsylvania, and Connecticut. Forty-seven people died. "The storm and its death toll served as grim reminders that weather once considered freakish is striking with regularity, threatening the viability of all coastal economic centers," the Bloomberg reporter wrote.

New York Governor Kathy Hochul tweeted: "Climate change is happening right now. It is not a future threat. It is a current threat."

While the East Coast was waterlogged from extreme rainfall, the vast majority of the West suffered from extreme drought. Parched forests erupted in fire, long before peak wildfire season. Some wildfires were so large they created their own weather systems, stirring up windstorms with speeds exceeding eighty miles per hour, tornadoes, and dry lightning thunderstorms.

In mid-August, the Dixie Fire and the Caldor Fire ripped through the towns of Greenville and Grizzly Flats outside Sacramento, California. Leaping, scorching flames blackened homes and cars. Metal road signs curled in the heat. Thousands evacuated as the fires raged, exploding in size and power in just days. Aggressive winds fanned roaring flames, and the Caldor Fire tore toward South Lake Tahoe, forcing more evacuations.

"It's important for [everyone] to understand the severity of how our climate-driven conditions are altering the environment and are making these fires move faster and making them more complex and, ultimately, more dangerous than anything we've faced in the past," said Mark Ghilarducci, director of California's emergency services.

Thick smoke across the region drove kids indoors. Summer camps, sports, and family trips were canceled. Family members with respiratory problems feared for their lives.

For the first time ever, a water shortage was declared on the Colorado River, an essential supply to forty million people in seven states. This, too, was the result of climate change. The snowpack that fed the river had dwindled. Rainfall had dropped. Dry soil soaked up any rain before it could replenish waterways. Extreme heat evaporated water all around.

"Climate change has loaded the weather dice against us," Katharine Hayhoe, a climate scientist at Texas Tech University, told the *Washington Post*. "These extremes are something we knew were coming. The suffering that is here and now is because we have not heeded the warnings."

The dangerous impacts of climate change were reaching nearly everyone: "Nearly 1 in 3 Americans live in a county hit by a weather disaster in the past three months," the *Washington Post* reported.

"On top of that, 64 percent live in places that experienced a multi-day heat wave."

Without drastic and immediate change, things would get worse according to a report released by the United Nations in September.

And who would be hurt the most by this pile-up of climate disasters? Young people, according to a generational study of climate change published in *Science* that same month. A child born in 2021 would suffer an average of *five* times as many climate disasters in their lifetimes as their grandparents, including twice as many wildfires, 1.7 times as many tropical cyclones, 3.4 times more river floods, 2.5 times more crop failures, and 2.3 times as many droughts. Today's kids could expect to face twenty-one to thirty-nine deadly heat waves. The grim reality young people faced was even worse, the authors said, considering sea-level rise and coastal flooding would also be more frequent and more severe.

And there was little relief in sight.

Internationally, nations who signed on to the Paris Agreement gathered in Glasgow, Scotland, from October 31 to November 12, 2021, to get countries to do more to stop global warming.

As the nations negotiated, climate chaos struck all over the planet. The worst dust storm in history whipped through Uzbekistan. Temperatures soared to 111.6 degrees Fahrenheit (44.2 degrees Celsius) in Mozambique. Record snow fell in China and record rain fell in Australia and Japan.

Still the international negotiators backed away from phasing out coal power and only agreed to reduce the powerful greenhouse gas methane by 30 percent by 2030.

"Try harder," Mia Mottley, the prime minister of the island nation Barbados, begged members of the summit. "Try harder."

The final Glasgow Climate Pact didn't even meet the original Paris Agreement target of limiting warming to 1.5 degrees Celsius (2.7 degrees F), which climate scientists said was not safe anyway. "Our experts say island nations will disappear at 1.5 C," Julia said. "Greenland ice sheets will not survive long term at 1.5. These temperature increases, 50 percent hotter than today and growing, are not protective of human rights or our planet." In fact, pledges put the world on track to warm 2.5 degrees C (4.4 degrees F), which would unleash far more severe climate change effects on people, wildlife, and ecosystems.

Meanwhile, the 21's legal team was getting nowhere in settlement discussions with the Biden administration. "After the first thing they pitched, I was like, yeah, no, nothing's gonna happen," Nathan said.

Sahara felt the same way. "It was very obvious that they weren't going to budge at all, they were just trying to completely shut us down," they said. "It was pretty frustrating because it could have been a way forward, but the doorway seemed closed."

On November 1, 2021, Our Children's Trust announced they were walking away from settlement discussions. "While I am unable to share specifics from these confidential talks, I can say, without reservation, that we came to the table in good faith and sought to participate in a productive discussion on behalf of our young clients," Julia said. "However, it takes the participation of both sides of the table to have meaningful communication and seek solutions. When and if the Biden administration wants to talk to the youth about their case, they will be ready. Right now, our goal is to get to trial as fast as possible. This is an emergency. A crisis. And yet these words still fall short in describing the climate situation and its devastating impact on these young Americans. We eagerly await a ruling from Judge Aiken on our amended complaint, which, if favorable, will put us back on track to trial."

The 21 truly had all their eggs in one basket. They were counting on Judge Ann Aiken to rule in their favor on the motion to amend the original complaint. It was now the only path forward.

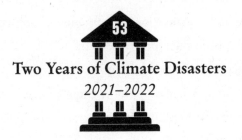

Two Years of Climate Disasters
2021–2022

On November 18, 2021, nearly fifty members of Congress sent a letter to the president asking his administration to stop opposing the *Juliana* youth. "I urge President Biden to stand in solidarity with these young people and end the efforts of his administration to impede their path," said New York Representative Mondaire Jones. "It's time our federal government finally aligns its actions on climate change with its rhetoric and takes the bold action necessary to avert climate catastrophe." More than 165 organizations advocating for public health, children, and the environment sent a similar letter.

There was no response from the Biden administration and no word from Judge Aiken on the motion to amend.

In December, climate change triggered three peculiar weather disasters. Towns from Pennsylvania to Texas set record-high winter temperatures, with many 20 to 30 degrees warmer than normal. This warmer weather drummed up rare thunderstorms, which triggered a rash of freakishly large and long-lasting tornadoes. The twisters tore a 250-mile path from Arkansas to Kentucky, yanking up trees, roofs, and walls, hurling debris five miles in the air, and killing at least eighty-eight people. "It looked like a bomb dropped on our town," said one survivor. Hitting well outside peak tornado season, it was the deadliest tornado event in December in U.S. history.

In drought-plagued Colorado, record-breaking warmth set the stage for a bizarre winter wildfire. An unusually strong windstorm whipped the flames into a fury. The blaze roared through suburban Boulder, torching more than a thousand homes, making it the most destructive fire in the state's history.

December also brought "icemageddon" to Alaska. Officials coined the term when the state experienced record-breaking high winter temperatures—as high as 66.9 F (19.4 C)—followed by the heaviest rainfall in decades. The deluge froze and more snow dumped on top. "I have never seen anything like it," said Nathan, who was home for winter break from college. Fairbanks in the winter was usually very cold and very dry. But during this break, he shoveled every day, sometimes twice a day. Roofs collapsed all around town. Moose that couldn't walk in the thick snow and ice congregated near roads. Alaska Fish and Game predicted that most of the moose calves born that year would perish.

It was a terrifying end to a terrible climate year. National media characterized the deluge of weather disasters as "unprecedented," "extraordinary," and "unsettling." And they pointed to one clear cause: The last seven years on Earth were the hottest in recorded history.

Climate change, a *Washington Post* analysis found, was reaching nearly everyone, everywhere. In 2021, more than 90 percent of the U.S. west of the Rockies suffered drought. Roughly 80 percent of Americans sweated through a heat wave, more than 40 percent lived in places slammed by climate weather disasters, such as hurricanes or flooding, and 15 percent lived near a disastrous wildfire.

The Federal Emergency Management Agency (FEMA) declared eight statewide emergencies, covering 135 million people. Climate disasters killed more than 650 people in the United States alone.

Meanwhile, the fossil fuel energy system kept pumping out more and more greenhouse gases, with U.S. emissions rising 6.2 percent in 2021, driven by a 17 percent increase in coal-fired electricity.

The federal government's response? Instead of ending leasing of federal public lands for oil and gas drilling as promised a year earlier, the Biden administration issued more than 3,500 drilling permits and put a record number of acres—80 million—up for lease to drill in the Gulf of Mexico. "This administration seems to actually have a zeal for catering to the oil and gas industry," Jeremy Nichols of WildEarth Guardians told the *Washington Post*.

In 2022, while setting ambitious goals to transition to electric cars and allocating a record $370 billion to combat climate change, the federal government also opened public lands in the pristine Arctic to new oil and gas drilling. By its own estimate, burning those fossil fuels would release the carbon equivalent of two million gas-powered cars each year.

While continuing to be one of the largest contributors to climate change, the United States was also becoming one of the places hardest hit. Over the last fifty years, the country warmed 68 percent faster than the rest of the planet, according to a 2022 report by the United Nations. "The things Americans value most are at risk," the report warned.

The 21, desperate to stop this dangerous trend, wondered: would Judge Ann Aiken ever allow them to amend their complaint and move forward with their case?

PART IV

Do Young People Have a Constitutional Right to Stable Climate?

Progress in the States
2020–2023

August 2022 marked seven years since the filing of *Juliana v. United States* and a year and a half since the youth asked to amend their complaint, with no word from Judge Aiken. The federal district court continued to be backed up with cases from the pandemic. Judge Aiken was busy digesting lengthy briefs and absorbing new Supreme Court rulings. She also likely knew the importance of the decision and was honing her thoughts so her words would rise to the magnitude of the moment and stand up in an appeal.

Still, the young people and their legal team couldn't help but feel frustrated and impatient. "I'm sure Judge Aiken is doing the best she can under the circumstances," Julia said. "But no one can do enough right now in this emergency. It feels like we can't move fast enough."

While waiting for a ruling on the federal case, Our Children's Trust threw themselves into their state cases, which had been gaining subtle traction.

Something promising was tucked into an October 2020 ruling in Kelsey Juliana's Oregon state case. Though the court denied the youths' claims, Chief Justice Martha Walters wrote a powerful dissent, which is an on-the-record disagreement. In the dissent, she recognized the "ravages of climate change" and pointed out that "the judicial branch has an important constitutional role to play and should declare the governing law."

Just a year later, something similar played out in Washington State, where Aji was a plaintiff. That case was also dismissed before trial. But Chief Justice Steven González, joined by Justice G. Helen Whitener, offered another powerful dissent: "The court should not avoid its constitutional obligations that protect not only the rights of these youths but all future generations who will suffer from the consequences of climate change."

These dissenting opinions marked real progress. "It might seem like a loss, with one person in your favor and the rest against you," Julia said. "But dissenting opinions are how constitutional law evolves."

This is what happened with segregation. Only one judge dissented in the 1896 ruling in *Plessy v. Ferguson*, which legalized the segregation of Black and white people. But that singular dissent lay the groundwork for the 1954 ruling in *Brown v. Board of Education*, which made school segregation illegal. "Dissenting opinions are like these lights shining that path toward justice," Julia said. "Part of our work is to collect those dissents as we educate the judiciary on this whole new area of human rights law."

Georgetown University's Lisa Heinzerling also noticed this trend in the youths' climate cases. "A growing body of dissents are a marker of potential change in the law," she said. "It suggests that it's not just one judge, one outlier, that there are other people reading the law the same way."

In February 2022, an Alaska Supreme Court justice dramatically reversed himself. The court issued a 3-2 split decision against the youth plaintiffs in *Sagoonick v. State of Alaska*. But it would've been 4-1 except that Justice Peter Maassen, who had ruled against climate youth in a similar earlier case, had changed his thinking. His dissent, joined by Justice Susan Carney, read: "The law requires that the State, in pursuing its energy policy, recognize individual Alaskans' constitutional right to a livable climate. A declaratory judgment to that effect would be an admittedly small step in the daunting project of focusing governmental response to this existential crisis. But it is a step we can and should take."

Nathan, who was not involved in the Alaska case, took notice. "Judges don't change their minds very often," he said. "It was really powerful in showing the arc of how the country is changing."

Then, on June 14, 2022, something even more remarkable happened. The Montana Supreme Court ruled that the sixteen young plaintiffs in *Held v. State of Montana* could proceed to trial. It was a stunning victory for Our Children's Trust, which filed the case just two years earlier with a new group of local youth in collaboration with local law firms. The case was based on the Montana constitution, which specified that "a clean and healthful environment" is a right for "present and future generations." The youth asked the court to declare that Montana's fossil fuel energy policies and actions violate their state constitutional rights.

The Montana trial, heard by Judge Kathy Seeley in June 2023, would unfold similarly to a federal trial, but would focus specifically on Montana youth and their state government. The sixteen young climate plaintiffs would take the stand to share how summers and falls were getting ever more dangerous with extreme wildfires and heat; how they suffered from climate-change-induced asthma attacks and heat exhaustion; how droughts and wildfires affected their ranches and their hunting; and how they feared for their futures and their children's futures. Scientists and other experts would testify under oath about the horrors of climate change and the state's contributions to it. First-named plaintiff Rikki Held, who was 18 when the case was filed, said getting to trial was "like seeing the end of the tunnel or maybe the start of something big."

"There's a lot of reason for hope right now because the tide is turning," Julia said. "It's turning in favor of young people."

But *Held v. Montana* was a state case. The federal government was a much bigger contributor to climate change. To make a real difference, the 21 wanted to face the *federal* government in court. That could not happen until Judge Aiken ruled.

Green Light to Trial
June 2023

While the *Juliana* youth waited, Julia Olson, Our Children's Trust, and the Montana youth prepared for the first-ever constitutional climate trial and first-ever children's climate trial in U.S. history. The trial was scheduled to begin June 12, 2023, at the First Judicial District Court in Helena, Montana.

The lawyers and staff were "insanely busy," gathering all the images and graphics to display as visual aids and preparing the Montana youth and experts to testify. The lawyers tested questions based on the youths' depositions and experts' reports, but sometimes they had to rewrite the questions to elicit more pointed testimony. For weeks, everyone had been working around the clock with no days off, losing sleep and missing meals.

In the midst of the push to prepare, one of Julia's staff posed a difficult question: "What if Judge Aiken rules on *Juliana* while we're busy with the Montana trial?"

Julia shook her head. "She hasn't ruled in two years. She's not going to rule during our Montana trial." She thought a minute. "If anything, it will be in July."

A few weeks later, the president of her board of directors asked: "Julia, what are you going to do if Judge Aiken rules right before Montana?"

Julia was confident. "She's not going to do that."

Then, on Thursday, June 1, 2023, less than two weeks before opening statements in the Montana trial, Julia arose after a short night's sleep, grabbed some tea, hopped on her computer, and then took her first shower in a week. Still dripping, Julia noticed her phone was blowing up. A text from her *Juliana* co-counsel read, "Judge Aiken just ruled in our favor!"

While overwhelmed by the timing, Julia was also overjoyed. After nearly eight years, the 21 *Juliana* plaintiffs were once again cleared for trial against the U.S. government. Julia and her assistant immediately emailed and texted the 21 plaintiffs with the news.

Levi texted back with ten excited emojis.

Nathan, who had graduated from college and completed a graduate certificate in tribal law while waiting for the ruling, got the email announcement during his first week at a new job.

"Oh!" he said in surprise. He quickly typed out a statement for the press and then got back to work. Almost immediately, his phone dinged with a text from Avery. Over the years, they had developed a close, sibling-like relationship.

"I'M SO EXCITED!" she wrote.

"Yessssss!" Nathan texted back.

It wasn't until after work that Nathan had time to read the ruling. He found the nineteen-page opinion to be "beautiful." Judge Aiken focused narrowly on the question of whether the youth could amend their complaint to focus squarely on declaratory relief. In other words, could they move to trial if they only asked the court to declare whether the government's actions were unconstitutional? Would such a change address the Ninth Circuit's concern that the courts could not create and manage a plan to address climate change?

Judge Aiken argued simply that sticking to declaratory relief would offer the court a remedy that they could grant. In fact, it was the core duty of courts, she wrote, to declare rights. "It is a foundational doctrine that when government conduct catastrophically harms American citizens, the judiciary is constitutionally required to perform its independent role and determine whether the challenged conduct . . . is unconstitutional," she wrote.

This new focus on declaratory relief as a path to trial fed Nathan's "radical but grounded optimism."

"A trial would transform the world, truly," he said. At a federal trial, the public would hear how climate change was hurting young people all across the country. Julia would finally have a chance to make her powerful arguments on the merits of the case on the record before a judge. Experts would offer compelling testimony under oath. The legal team could prove, using the government's own reports, that climate change was endangering the youths' lives, liberty, and property. The court, America, and the whole world would see that the U.S. government knew the climate crisis would happen and continued to underwrite the fossil fuel system anyway.

The Associated Press immediately released an article on the ruling, which the *Oregonian*, *Seattle Times*, and *Washington Post* picked up within days. Nathan guessed that other news outlets were preoccupied with the upcoming trial in Montana and were waiting to see how the Biden administration would respond to Judge Aiken's ruling. Would the administration continue to follow in the footsteps of the Trump White House? Would it appeal to the Ninth Circuit again, grabbing *Juliana* from the district court and asking for another intervention before trial?

Our Children's Trust and its supporters implored the Biden

administration not to fight the trial. "Bring your best case, bring your best experts, fight us in court!" Julia implored.

With climate change ever worsening, the youths' team wanted things to move fast, so they quickly filed a motion for an expedited trial. The plaintiffs might need four or five months to update their expert reports with new research and data. They and the government would depose the witnesses again. But the legal team had been ready before, and they would be ready again.

"We are going to get to trial," attorney Phil Gregory told the 21 time and again. "When you get up there and testify, you will see the effect that your testimony has and the way that the judge is going to be able to craft something that will change things—perhaps forever."

"Declaratory relief would be a big deal," according to Georgetown law professor Lisa Heinzerling. "If the court ultimately declared that the federal government had violated the plaintiffs' constitutional rights by promoting and funding fossil fuels over a fifty-year period, that would put the government in the position of being a very long-standing and consequential constitutional rule breaker. The government would have to take that seriously."

Many questions remain: If the 21 got to trial and if they won declaratory relief, would the ruling hold? Would the government appeal after the trial? Would the U.S. Supreme Court give the plaintiffs a full hearing if *Juliana v. United States* got to them again? If they accepted an appeal, would the youth win? These are all unknowns.

But Julia and the 21 young people know this: you have to believe you can make change. "Hope," Nathan said, "is a choice."

"In this work, and in our world," Julia said, "we need to set our mind toward creating the reality we want and the future we want. If you can't see it happening, if you don't envision it, if you don't work hard for it, then you are guaranteeing that it's not going to happen. So, the way we approach this case, and this work, and all these moments, is to just keep believing that we will get there."

Julia's deepest belief and deepest hope is that *Juliana v. United States* will go down in history as the *Brown v. Board of Education* on climate, the case that changed everything.

And in the meantime, the case and its 21 young plaintiffs are already leaving behind a powerful legacy.

Inspired by *Juliana*
2015 to the Present

Legal experts who once dismissed *Juliana v. United States* now call it pathbreaking, groundbreaking, and a landmark. Lisa Heinzerling, the Georgetown law professor who was so skeptical of the case at the outset, now calls it a "massive" case that is an "exemplar" and "leading edge."

"It brings up so much of the injustice of climate change, the intergenerational justice," she said, "and the fact that sometimes children say things to us that are correct—and we have a hard time hearing them."

People are listening now. "When this chapter is added to U.S. history textbooks in 50 years, students will study the global strikes, sit-ins, and rallies, and they will study the *Juliana v. U.S.* case," Katie Eder, head of a national network of youth activists, wrote in a *Truthout* editorial. Indeed, *Juliana v. United States* is already taught in dozens of law schools, including Yale, Harvard, Cornell, Boston College, Temple, Tulane, the University of Michigan, the University of Utah, and the University of Wyoming.

"This case is a shining example of what law can be," said Rick Reibstein, who teaches environmental law at Boston University. "This case gives me hope that we will not continue to cooperate in our own destruction."

Juliana has also dramatically transformed the conversation about climate change in the United States and globally. For decades, the public blamed fossil fuel companies. After all, it is the burning of their products—oil, gas, and coal—that releases the gases that are warming the planet. No one had accused governments of *causing* the climate crisis. People merely asked governments to do more to stop it.

But the *Juliana* case has uncovered and illuminated hard evidence that the federal government, through multiple presidential administrations, has knowingly and systemically caused this crisis. Moreover, government officials are responsible, not because they're failing to do something about climate change, but because they are actively engaged in promoting a system that is wreaking havoc with the climate. "If the government would stop licensing, permitting, and subsidizing the fossil fuel industry, the whole landscape would change," Julia has said time and again. The public is beginning to realize that their governments are culpable and may be legally liable. "The *Juliana* case does the homework to show this jaw-dropping transgression of duty on the part of federal officials," said Professor Mary Wood.

Climate change is a global problem, and from the beginning, Julia's legal strategy has been global. Over the past decade, Our Children's Trust and youth across the world have filed cases similar to *Juliana* against their governments. Julia and her colleagues have helped 7-year-old Rabab Ali argue that Pakistan's support of dirty coal violates her constitutional rights. They've supported 9-year-old Ridhima Pandey's demand that India follow its own environmental laws. And they've assisted fifteen young Canadians and sixty-five young Mexicans in filing constitutional complaints against their respective governments. "The idea behind our campaign and strategy is to target the most important governments, because if some of the big ones transform fossil fuel energy systems to clean energy and decarbonize, then there is going to be a ripple effect around the world," Julia said. "Even a few important wins will lead to transformational change."

Back in 2016, when *Juliana* was still young, Daniel Esty, an expert in environmental law and policy at Yale University, told the *Washington Post* that *Juliana* could end up serving "as a source of inspiration to young people across the world who might, in their own countries and in their own legal context, decide that they should pursue court cases or other legal action against those who appear to be foot-dragging on the issue of climate change." Indeed, *Juliana*'s influence has spread worldwide, igniting a massive legal movement to protect kids' climate rights. The *Juliana* plaintiffs have inspired a tsunami of cases across the globe, led by eight youth in Australia, nine youth in Germany, nineteen young people in South Korea, and twenty-five youth in Colombia.

Juliana also played a part in inspiring Greta Thunberg and fifteen other youth to file a petition with the United Nations arguing that the countries of Argentina, Brazil, France, Germany, and Turkey violated their rights under the United Nations Convention on the Rights of the Child by failing to reduce fossil fuel emissions. Six Portuguese youth have also filed a complaint with the European Court of Human Rights against thirty-three countries, arguing that the countries have discriminated against them by failing to sufficiently act to curb climate change.

Every country's constitution and court systems are different, but change has begun. German courts have already ruled that climate protection is an enforceable human right. The Colombian supreme court also ruled for the youth, requiring the government to halt deforestation and protect the rainforest. While the rest of the cases make their way through the courts, more may be filed.

Work continues apace in the United States, as well. With the help of Our Children's Trust, young people are continuing to press forward with climate lawsuits brought against state governments. Youth have recently filed new cases in Virginia and Utah and are stepping forward to lead new cases in Oregon, Washington, Michigan, Wisconsin, New Mexico, Alaska, and Texas. "Litigation will only increase as the climate threat reaches more palpably into the present," said Georgetown's Lisa Heinzerling. "I do believe the day will come when courts throw off their rigid and simplistic view of their own impotence in the face of this threat . . ."

Momentum continues to build. The sixteen youth plaintiffs in *Held v. State of Montana* began to change minds, hearts, and the law when they testified during their two-week trial in Helena in June 2023. Fifth-generation Montanan and soccer player Grace Gibson-Snyder testified about wildfire smoke driving her from practices and games, about watching iconic glaciers melting over time, and her fears about her future. "I am a citizen," Grace reminded the court. "It's my belief that the role of government is to protect its people. . . . When [governments] are actively making choices that are shown to harm the people, that is a betrayal of the people, and it's undermining the role of government in our society. And that is something that needs to be changed."

Soon, fourteen young plaintiffs in *Navahine F. v. Hawai'i Department of Transportation* will have a trial in Honolulu on their challenge to their state's fossil-fuel-focused transportation system, which is the largest source of climate pollution in the state. When 15-year-old plaintiff Mesina R. heard their case was headed to trial, she ran through her house screaming, "We made it through! We made it through!"

"In this movement, we get a lot of pushback, a lot of nos, and so to get a yes this early in the case relights the . . . hope that I have in democracy for solving this crisis," she said.

As Nathan and the other *Juliana* plaintiffs prepare for their own trial, they continue to follow the Montana and Hawaii cases closely. Nathan noticed how Judge Aiken's first ruling was cited in those and other cases and predicted that "anything that comes out of any of these trials is going to be used in future trials."

There is a dawning realization among judges at every level that eventually, courts need to clarify what the law is on climate change, Nathan said. Governments need to know, "What does the Constitution obligate us to do?"

While the case grinds through the system, for the 21 young plaintiffs whose names grace *Juliana v. United States,* the eight years and counting has been quite a ride. The lawsuit has helped the plaintiffs find their paths in some surprising ways. Nathan, who Julia watched transform into a scholarly young professional, now fights for a green future in Alaska by supporting local food systems and local jobs. "The state needs an economy," Nathan said. "You can't just take someone's job away and expect them to stand with you."

Isaac, with his ability to connect and his enjoyment of other people, discovered that meeting with members of Congress energized him. "Even in the event that the lawsuit gets thrown out, I'm going to have such a foot inside of the policy part of it," he says. "I'm going to break the door open, hopefully, and actually create some big change that way."

Working on the lawsuit has solidified Sahara's identity. "A big part of how I see myself now is as someone who takes action and does something if I see something that isn't right," Sahara said. One day, Julia's son attended a climate walkout at his high school, where Sahara was a senior. Afterward, he told her, "Mom, all these people spoke but Sahara had this powerful speaking presence and was the most eloquent. It was incredible."

Sahara wants to keep inspiring other young activists. "I'm just a random teenager; a lot of us are just random teenagers," they said. "Just look at what random teenagers can do."

Pulsing below the surface of this lawsuit is something greater. "Young people are ready to use their art, their poetry, their passion, their music, to engage with the world and be leaders today because, sure, we're a future generation but we're here now and we're not going to wait to make a difference." Xiuhtezcatl said. "Whether we win the lawsuit or not, we are already making ripples in the world to show that young people have power."

The world needs that power. "We are the ones inheriting the world and all the issues and problems," Sahara added, "so we know what work needs to be done."

The 21 young people have also shown how to persevere against daunting odds. An elementary school student once asked plaintiff Kelsey Juliana: "How do you keep from getting discouraged and angry when you hear our government lying about the effects of fossil fuels on our climate and fighting your case with all they have?"

Kelsey smiled warmly and answered: "This work must be done out of love. Motivation and activism and advocacy cannot come from rage or anger or hopelessness. These feelings are unsustainable, short-lived, and detrimental for those harboring them . . . ," she said. "We cannot push society toward more positive, inclusive, sustainable directions without LOVE as the main driver of activism.

"Because you cannot burn out of love."

THE SCIENCE OF CLIMATE CHANGE

You probably already know the basic science of climate change. The burning of fossil fuels such as gas, oil, and coal emits gases into the atmosphere that form a kind a blanket around our planet trapping in heat. Because of their heat-trapping properties, these emissions are called greenhouse gases. With our current energy system, the greatest contributor to global warming is carbon dioxide (CO_2). But other gases such as methane (CH_4) and hydrofluorocarbons (HFCs) also add to the problem. This global warming triggers changes in our global and regional climates.

Some people confuse climate with weather. Weather refers to regional short-term conditions. Will it be sunny or cloudy this week? What are the daytime and nighttime temperatures for the next ten days? Is there snow, rain, fog, hail, or wind in the forecast?

Climate refers to these weather patterns over a long period of time, thirty years or more. Global climate describes the climate of the planet as a whole, especially its average annual temperature. The planet has already warmed 2 degrees Fahrenheit (1.1 degrees Celsius) since the 1800s due to the burning of fossil fuels. The Intergovernmental Panel on Climate Change predicts a total rise of 2.5 to 10 degrees Fahrenheit over the next century. The United States has historically been the biggest contributor of greenhouse gases, with a quarter of dangerous emissions coming from America's energy system.

Global warming disrupts typical regional climates. Your regional climate captures what your weather is like, generally, over the course of a year. For example, the Pacific Northwest tends to be cloudy and wet with moderate temperatures. During its typical dry and sunny summers, temperatures generally stay below 90 F. Hurricanes, tornadoes, and even thunderstorms are rare. In contrast, the desert Southwest has low rainfall annually. Daytime and nighttime temperatures vary widely, with daytime summer temperatures commonly over 100 degrees F.

Different types of extreme weather are found in different regional climates. The East Coast suffers the most hurricanes. The Great Plains are known as tornado alley. The Plains and the upper Midwest are frequently blanketed with winter blizzards while the Gulf Coast and California coast suffer few to none.

Anyone living in the same place for a long time can get a sense of that region's climate. At least that used to be true. The warming planet is triggering drastic changes in regional climates. Places where snowstorms were rare are experiencing blizzards and ice storms. Hurricanes are getting more frequent and more severe. Flooding happens in areas not vulnerable to them before. Worldwide, extreme storms are becoming so frequent that they seem like a chronic condition.

Here is how climate change is impacting our planet and our lives.

GLOBAL IMPACTS
Wetter Atmosphere

For every 1.8 degrees Fahrenheit (1 degree Celsius) of warming, the atmosphere holds 7 percent more moisture. This not only makes wetter regions wetter, but it also makes drier areas drier. Enhanced evaporation dries out soil, plants, and surface water. This makes rainless periods drier than they would be in cooler conditions.

Another danger is that water vapor is itself a greenhouse gas. In fact, water vapor triples the warming from other greenhouse gases.

Melting Glaciers and Ice Caps

Arctic ice is currently melting at a rate of 13 percent per decade. Ice reflects heat, while water absorbs heat. As a result, the Arctic is warming twice as fast as the rest of the planet, triggering further melting of the polar ice cap.

Rising Seas

Melting glaciers and sea ice, combined with the expansion of water when it warms has caused sea levels to rise an average of eight to nine inches since 1880. Oceans may rise more than seven feet by the end of the century. While islands and the largest coastal cities such as New York City, Miami, Mumbai, and Sydney are at risk, rising sea levels also greatly increase inland flooding.

Ocean Acidification

Oceans absorb 30 percent of the carbon dioxide emitted by the burning of fossil fuels. Carbon dioxide becomes acidic when mixed with water. This process has already increased ocean acidity by 30 percent. Acidification eats away at shellfish, mussels, clams, and coral, disrupting the entire ocean ecosystem.

REGIONAL DISRUPTIONS

Heat Waves

A warming planet is easy to notice when summer heat starts earlier and lasts longer. But the number of heat waves has also spiked. The United States suffered roughly twenty days of major heat in the early 1980s; now we sweat through about a hundred and fifty days each year. Climate change also triggers deadly heat domes, such as the one that hit the Pacific Northwest in June 2020, where masses of hot air sit over a region for long periods.

Strange Cold Snaps

It might seem counterintuitive that global warming could cause cold snaps, blizzards, and ice storms, but warming can disrupt ocean currents, air currents, and jet streams, sending tongues of frigid Arctic air into lower latitudes. Some scientists attribute the severe cold snap of winter 2021 in the South-Central United States to Arctic warming. Fluctuations of the winds that encircle the poles, called the polar vortex, contributed to record-low temperature in thousands of towns and cities in states such as Texas, Oklahoma, and Arkansas.

More and More Severe Hurricanes

Oceans cover 71 percent of the earth's surface. So, when the planet heats up, the oceans heat up, too. Warmer oceans fuel more frequent and more severe tropical storms and hurricanes. Attribution science has suggested that every decade since 1979, a tropical storm has had an 8 percent greater chance of becoming a Category 3 or greater hurricane. According to NASA, the intensity, frequency, and duration of North Atlantic hurricanes, as well as the frequency of the strongest (Category 4 and 5) hurricanes, have all increased since the early 1980s.

More and More Severe Flooding

Because of climate change, NASA predicts "more precipitation for the northern United States and less for the Southwest," with a trend toward "increased heavy precipitation" events even where total precipitation is decreasing. More rain and more condensed periods of rain trigger floods. Rising seas also increase sunny-day flooding, where higher tides seep further and further inland, swelling rivers and covering roads even when no rain has fallen.

Tornadoes

Humid air near the ground colliding with cool, dry air high up can trigger thunderstorms and tornadoes. Warming lengthens the time each year when regions, especially the South, have hot, moist air near the ground. Ocean waters can also stay warmer later into the year. When a cold front collides with humid ocean air, conditions are ripe for out-of-season thunderstorms and tornadoes.

Drought

The higher the temperature, the more water evaporates from soil and plants. With climate change, drier regions are also becoming drier. Megadroughts, lasting more than thirty years, become increasingly likely with a warming planet, according to NASA, endangering water supplies and crops and upping wildfire danger.

Wildfires

Lack of rain and snow for long periods of time causes drought. The drought and high temperatures brought on by warming dehydrate vegetation, turning it to tinder. Climate change causes more fires, larger and hotter fires, and fires that burn earlier and later each year. The average fire season in the American West has lengthened by two and half months since the 1970s.

CASCADING IMPACTS

Species Extinction

Changing regional climates affect huge numbers of plants and animals, who depend on stable temperatures and adequate food and water supplies. Some plants and animals adapt, shifting their ranges to meet their needs. But many can't adapt quickly enough and are going extinct at such a fast rate that scientists are calling this the Sixth Mass Extinction. Scientists predict 30 to 40 percent of species may become extinct in the next thirty years, including 40 percent of amphibians and a quarter of birds.

Crop Failures

While some crops may benefit from longer growing seasons, others suffer from rising temperatures and changing regional climates. For instance, scientists expect corn yields to drop by almost a quarter within the next decade. Droughts, deluges, and unexpected freezes can also wreak havoc on crops, endangering food supplies.

Pest Problems

Insects flourish in warmer temperatures. Increasing numbers of pests nurtured by climate change can invade and destroy forests, gobble up crops, and even carry dangerous diseases to humans. The range of biting insects, such as mosquitoes, is shifting upward in the Northern Hemisphere, bringing with them diseases such as malaria, dengue fever, and West Nile virus.

Respiratory Diseases

Increases in ground-level ozone, pollen, and wildfire smoke due to climate change trigger and aggravate many respiratory conditions such as asthma and allergies. In recent years, the pollen season in the United States has lengthened anywhere from eleven to twenty-seven days. Though wildfires may be more common in the West, smoke from bigger and more frequent blazes is spreading across the country, sparking asthma attacks all across the nation.

Compound Catastrophes

As disasters and diseases become more prevalent and more deadly, it becomes more likely that people will face multiple climate catastrophes at the same time. Power knocked out by a violent thunderstorm makes a heat wave more deadly. Crop failures make it more difficult to feed refugees from climate disasters, such as wildfires, hurricanes, and rising seas.

Tipping Points and the Unknown

Our climate system seems to be absorbing the extra energy trapped by greenhouse gases in a predictable way so far. But many scientists fear warming between 1 and 2 degrees Celsius will cause such extreme changes that we don't know what might happen. Melting permafrost may accelerate the release of greenhouse gases to a level where scientists have no reliable models and cannot predict future impacts.

IN SUM

Sustainability scientist Kimberly Nicholas of Lund University in Sweden describes the basics of climate science this way:

It's warming.

It's us.

We're sure.

It's bad.

But we can fix it.

The next section shows how.

WE CAN FIX IT: A PLAN TO END THE CLIMATE CRISIS

In the *Juliana* lawsuit, the young people asked the courts to require the federal government to create and act on a plan that would stabilize the climate.

Currently our atmosphere retains more solar energy than is released back into space, putting Earth out of balance. To return to balance, scientific consensus has set the safe maximum level of atmospheric carbon dioxide at 350 parts per million or lower. Parts per million reflects the ratio of carbon dioxide molecules in the atmosphere to all the other molecules found there. Scientists know from studying fossils and samples of old Arctic ice that for the last 800,000 years, aside from recent years, carbon dioxide has remained below 300 parts per million. We are now well over 410 parts per million and are adding about 2 ppm every year. "If humanity wishes to preserve a planet similar to that on which civilization developed and to which life on Earth is adapted, paleoclimate evidence and ongoing climate change suggest that CO_2 will need to be reduced from [current levels] to at most 350 ppm," NASA climate scientist James Hansen said.

The 21 did not tell the courts or the federal government how to get there. They only asked that the goal and the plan be based on science.

Experts have developed a number of approaches that would work. Several of these experts have agreed to testify on the kids' behalf. For example, Stanford professor of civil and environmental engineering Mark Z. Jacobson has created plans for 145 countries, including the United States, to use wind power, hydroelectric power, and solar power paired with batteries to meet all projected energy needs by the 2050s.

Another expert lined up to testify for the 21 is James H. Williams, a professor of energy systems management at the University of San Francisco, who directs an international group of research teams pulled together by the United Nations to figure out how to rid the atmosphere of dangerous levels of carbon dioxide. "We can limit the risks of climate change and build a clean energy system that meets all our needs," Williams said. "We know what needs to be done. The U.S. can still lead the way. It will not disrupt our economy or way of life. It is a big task but not a foolhardy one. What is foolhardy is to stand by while the world burns."

In May 2019, Williams and his colleagues shared plans for the United States to stop adding carbon dioxide to the atmosphere and in fact to begin drawing carbon out of the atmosphere by 2050. The plans ensure that the United States would do its part to reach 350 ppm by 2100, keeping global heating to 1 degree Celsius. "The amazing thing is, it is so possible," Julia said. "We have immense opportunity to create jobs and live in healthier communities if we just do it."

The scientists outlined six different scenarios in the report, *350 PPM Pathways for the United States*, which stated: "The main finding is that 350 ppm pathways that meet all current and forecast U.S. energy needs are technically feasible using existing technologies . . . [and] are economically viable."

The Pathways proposal, which would provide all the energy that the U.S. Department of Energy forecasts we will need, would require:

Electrifying: Rapidly switching much of our energy sources, especially for heating and transportation, from fossil fuels to electricity. Currently, electricity covers 20 percent of energy needs. The Pathways proposal would move us to 60 percent of energy coming from electricity. Virtually all cars and heating would be powered by electricity.

Producing cleaner electricity: Retiring existing coal plants, doubling electricity generated with solar and wind, and expanding production and use of biofuels.

Increasing energy efficiency: Producing furnaces, appliances, and vehicles that require less energy.

Capturing carbon: This includes both grabbing carbon before it is emitted from power plants and factories and capturing it as it floats freely in the air. The carbon could be buried or transformed into renewable fuel.

Trucks, trains, and airplanes are difficult to electrify, so the Pathways proposal calls for large-scale production of biodiesel and bio-jet fuel. These liquid and gaseous fuels would be made from crops or created from carbon captured from the air so they would be carbon neutral.

No new nuclear plants would be required, but the existing fleet would be maintained until the 2040s.

To be effective, the Pathways proposal requires immediate, large-scale action.

In the 2020s, we would need to begin rapid electrification of cars and buildings. Coal plants would close, and some new natural gas plants built to replace that energy. We'd halt new projects to transport fossil fuels, such as pipelines, while building out transmission lines to carry renewable energy. Construction of carbon capture would begin.

In the 2030s, all cars and heating would be electric. Sixty percent of energy would come from renewables, such as solar, wind, geothermal and hydropower. Biodiesel and bio-jet fuels would be produced at a large scale. Most factories would capture carbon. Fossil fuel plants that capture 100 percent of carbon would be allowed.

The 2040s would focus on rolling out large-scale carbon capture projects and production of carbon-neutral biofuels and synthetic fuels. Nuclear power plants would be decommissioned, replaced with new-generation technologies.

The Pathways proposal does not require people to conserve more energy, limit driving, or even eat differently. Individual efforts to be part of the solution would simply help the country meet targets faster.

In fact, the most noticeable impact to ordinary life would be bill-paying. Most families pay for gas for their cars, oil or gas to heat their homes, electricity for lights and appliances. In a carbon-free world, they would pay one bill, for clean electricity.

Building out the clean energy system will create a vast number of infrastructure jobs. By producing more of our energy domestically, the system would decrease our dependence on foreign oil and improve national security. Ending fossil fuel extraction also better preserves the environment and the species that depend on it.

The researchers estimated the upfront cost of building the infrastructure to be between 2 to 3 percent of gross domestic product (GDP). That is nothing compared to what our country has spent going to war. World War I cost the United States about 16 percent of GDP; World War II cost a whopping 40 percent of GDP. The War on Terrorism cost about 4 percent of GDP. Keeping our planet livable is much less expensive.

In the long term, these upfront costs will be recovered by savings from a more efficient, lower-cost, stable energy system.

Remarkably, the Pathways proposal does not count in their favor the economic and health benefits of stabilizing the climate. The plans are economically feasible even without adding in the benefits of thriving crops, cleaner air and water, a healthier population, and avoiding the loss of life and high costs of extreme disasters.

350 PPM Pathways is not the only plan to address the climate crisis—whole books have been written on the topic—but they demonstrate that a healthy atmosphere and stable climate for ourselves, our children, and our grandchildren is well within our reach. And the 21 young plaintiffs argue, persuasively, that it is their constitutional right.

MEET THE 21

Learn about each plaintiff and what they were up to when this book went to press.

Levi Draheim, the youngest plaintiff at age 8 at the start of the lawsuit, still lives near the beach in Florida. The teenage swimmer, sailor, and nature lover is homeschooling for high school and volunteering at a local zoo that focuses on conservation.

Animal lover **Avery McRae**, age 10 when the lawsuit was filed, is in high school in Eugene, Oregon, where she is active in the environmental club. She has a dog, two rabbits, and a number of chickens, and enjoys riding horses.

Zealand Bell, of Eugene, Oregon, the son of public-school teachers, was 11 years old when he joined the lawsuit. He has graduated high school and is heading to college.

Sahara Valentine, age 11 at the time the suit started, has graduated high school and is on their way to study environmental justice in college. They plan to keep speaking out about climate change.

Hazel Van Ummersen, 11 years old when the lawsuit was filed, graduated high school in Eugene, Oregon, and is headed to a small liberal arts college. She has earned a black belt in tae kwon do.

Jayden Foytlin from Rayne, Louisiana, was 12 when the lawsuit started. She has graduated from high school and is heading to college.

Age 13 when the lawsuit was filed, **Isaac Vergun**, of Beaverton, Oregon, is now a student at Howard University in Washington,

D.C. He has worked to get his hometown to divest from fossil fuels and is a member of Plant-for-the-Planet, which has a goal of planting a trillion trees to capture carbon. He hopes to continue his environmental work through policy and politics.

Miko Vergun, age 14 and living in Beaverton, Oregon, at the time of filing, is the co-founder of Youth Acting for Our Earth, which trains youth climate activists. She will soon graduate from Oregon State University.

Navajo citizen **Jaime Butler** of the Tangle People Clan, was lead plaintiff in an Our Children's Trust climate lawsuit in Arizona called *Butler v. Brewer* when she was 11. She joined the *Juliana* suit at age 14. Jaime finished high school and is working and pursuing her passion as an artist.

Nic Venner, from Lakewood, Colorado, was 14 at the beginning of the suit. Their early involvement was inspired by the Catholic principal of preserving God's creation for future generations. Nic graduated high school and is studying theoretical mathematics in college, while also working with several environmental nonprofits.

Nathan Baring, joined *Juliana* at age 15. He has since graduated from Gustavus Adolphus College, and works to support tribal capacity and locally focused food systems in Alaska. He may one day go to law school.

Working with Our Children's Trust, **Aji Piper** of Seattle, Washington, first sued the Washington State Department of Ecology asking them to make a rule capping greenhouse gas emissions. The youth won an early round in the lawsuit, but the rulemaking was weak. Aji joined *Juliana* at age 15 and later was the lead plaintiff in the state constitutional suit *Aji P. v. State of Washington*. Aji finished high school, trained as an electrician doing solar installations, and works as a chef for a renowned sustainable food restaurant in Seattle.

Xiuhtezcatl Martinez from Boulder, Colorado, was a co-founder of the nonprofit youth activism organization Earth Guardians and joined the federal suit at age 15. Lead plaintiff in Our Children's Trust's Colorado climate case, *Martinez v. Colorado,* Xiuhtezcatl is currently a hip-hop artist, activist, model, and entrepreneur.

Journey Zephier is the son and grandson of tribal chiefs. Part of the suit since age 15, Journey has also served as a youth leader of the Earth Guardians group, Rising Youth for a Sustainable Earth.

Vic Barrett, from White Plains, New York, was 16 at the start of the lawsuit. A graduate of the University of Wisconsin–Madison, Vic is an organizer for Powershift Network, which supports and connects diverse youth working for environmental justice.

Sophie Kivlehan, from Allentown, Pennsylvania, was age 16 at the start of the lawsuit. She graduated from Dickinson University with a degree in biochemistry and molecular biology and is working on cancer research.

Miriam Oommen, age 18 when the suit was filed, graduated from Seattle University and lives off the grid in the Oregon coast range. They continue to sing and write songs, teach music, participate in direct action, and serve on the Board of Directors for the Civil Liberties Defense Center.

Tia Hatton, the Nordic skier from Bend, Oregon, was 18 at the beginning of the lawsuit. After graduating from the University of Oregon with a degree in environmental science and nonprofit management, Tia worked for a variety of nonprofit conservation organizations. She intends to shift her focus to advocating for children.

Alex Loznak from Kellogg, Oregon, joined the suit at age 18. He graduated from Columbia University and now studies law at the University of Oregon.

Born in rural Quebec, **Jacob Lebel** was 18 and living on his family's farm in Roseburg, Oregon, when the suit was filed. He has fought the proposed Jordan Cove natural gas pipeline and the Pacific Connector Pipeline, writes widely about the environment, and aspires to help create sustainable communities worldwide. Jacob is still farming and recently began a tannery business.

Kelsey Cascadia Rose Juliana the first-named, lead plaintiff from Eugene, Oregon, was 19 at the beginning of the case. She has marched 1,600 miles from Nebraska to Washington, D.C., to raise awareness of the climate crisis and has also been a plaintiff in *Chernaik v. Brown*, the youth climate case in Oregon. She graduated from the University of Oregon and works with youth as an outdoor education teacher.

LEGAL LANGUAGE EXPLAINED

Affidavit: A written statement made under oath that can be used as evidence in court.

Amicus brief: Also known as "friend of the court" brief. A written document submitted to the court by a person or group not part of a lawsuit that offers information, arguments, or perspectives in support of one side.

Answer: A written response submitted to the court that formally agrees with (admits) or counters (denies) specific accusations and statements of fact in a plaintiff's complaint and lays out the defense and counterarguments.

Appeal: A request for review made to a higher court (an appeals court or supreme court).

Bench trial: A trial conducted before a judge without a jury.

Brief: A written document submitted to a court that explains one side's arguments citing relevant laws and rulings in similar cases.

Circuit Court of Appeals: Thirteen federal regional circuit courts of appeal oversee all the district or trial courts in the United States and determine whether or not the law was applied properly by trial courts.

Civil case: A non-criminal dispute between parties.

Complaint: The official written document submitted to a court that begins a lawsuit by laying out what the plaintiffs said happened, how that action broke the law, and what they want the court to do about it.

Decision: The court's determination of who won and lost a motion, trial, or appeal.

Declaration: A written statement submitted to a court that a person legally promises is true.

Declaratory relief: A court ruling that clarifies the rights the parties hold and whether or not they have been violated.

Defendant: The person, people, or groups sued in a lawsuit.

Depose: The process of interviewing potential witnesses under oath before a trial.

Deposition: An interview given under oath where lawyers question potential witnesses in a lawsuit to determine what they might testify to in a trial.

Discovery: A pretrial process required by courts in which parties in a lawsuit exchange information about the witnesses and evidence they plan to present at trial.

District: The geographic area covered by a federal district court. *Juliana v. United States* was filed in the District of Oregon, which serves the area corresponding to the state of Oregon. The district has courthouses in Portland, Eugene, Medford, and Pendleton.

District Court: Also known as a trial court or lower court. In the federal court system, district courts are where lawsuits are filed, and trials are held. There are ninety-four federal district courts in the United States.

Dissent: An opinion written by one or more judges or justices in disagreement with the majority ruling. Dissents may present other interpretations of the laws, with supporting arguments. Though they do not affect the outcome of a particular case, they can signal a shift in judicial thinking.

Due process: A requirement stated in the 5th and 14th amendments of the U.S. Constitution that government cannot deprive people of rights (such as life, liberty, and property) without procedures that apply fairly and equally to everyone. Substantive due process has come to mean that some rights (life, liberty, and property and other related fundamental rights such as the right to privacy) should usually be beyond the reach of governmental interference.

Federal courts: While state courts handle controversies about state law, federal courts handle cases related to U.S. federal laws, the U.S. Constitution, and disputes that occur among states. The federal court system has ninety-four district (trial) courts, thirteen circuit courts (which are the first level of appeal), and one U.S. Supreme Court, the final level of appeal. *Juliana v. United States* is a federal case.

Hearing: Any proceeding before a judge without a jury meant to resolve issues between the parties.

Injury: A specific harm suffered by a specific person caused by someone else.

Injunction: A court order that keeps someone from beginning or continuing an action that threatens the rights of another.

Injunctive relief: When a court orders a party to stop doing something or requires action from the party.

Interlocutory appeal: An appeal that happens *before a final ruling* from a trial court.

Intervenor: A person or group not originally involved in a lawsuit who wants to join the case as a plaintiff or defendant because they think they have a stake in the outcome of the case.

Judge: A person who runs lower court proceedings, including hearings and trials, either alone or as a part of a panel.

Justice: Title given to members of high courts such as the U.S. Supreme Court.

Lawsuit: A dispute brought before a court of law.

Magistrate judge: A judge who assists a district court judge. The magistrate may handle scheduling and pretrial hearings.

Mandamus (writ of mandamus, mandamus appeal): Request asking a higher court to order the judge of a lower court to do something or stop doing something on the grounds that the lower court has greatly exceeded its authority.

Motion for judgment on the pleadings: A written request to the court asking it to decide a case before going to trial. This motion asks the court to assume all the facts in the complaint are true and to rule based on the court's interpretation of the law. This motion is typically made before discovery.

Motion for summary judgment: A written request to the court asking it to decide a case before going to trial. This motion is properly made when all parties agree that the most important facts are undisputed. With facts agreed upon, the court can rule based on its interpretation of the law. This motion is typically made after discovery.

Motion to amend: A written request made to a court asking permission to make changes to the original complaint.

Motion to dismiss: A written request by a party in a lawsuit to have the lawsuit immediately ended because it has no basis in law or fact or does not belong in court.

Opinion: A judge's written explanation of their decision or ruling.

Oral argument: A court proceeding where a judge or panel of judges listen to presentations from lawyers about a case and ask questions.

Party: One of the people or groups involved in a lawsuit. The plaintiffs and the defendants are parties.

Petition: A formal request made in writing.

Plaintiff: A person who brings a case to court.

Pleadings: The written documents presented to the court at the beginning of a lawsuit by the plaintiff (complaint) and defendant (answer) in which they state their claims and defenses.

Precedent: A previous court decision that may help determine how judges should rule in a current controversy before the court.

Pretrial motion: A request asking the judge to decide on some or all of the issues in a case before it goes to trial.

Pro bono: This Latin term meaning "for the public good" refers to lawyers or experts working on cases without payment.

Public trust doctrine: A legal principle from the time of the Roman Empire, passed down to the United States through the King of England, that holds the government has an obligation to maintain and protect certain natural resources, like air and water, for public use for present and future generations.

Redress: To fix, or correct, at least part of an injury in a lawsuit.

Relief: What the plaintiffs want the court to do to resolve a dispute. This can include declaring a right, enforcing a right, or requiring the defendant to correct or compensate the plaintiff.

Remedy: What a court orders to resolve a dispute.

Ruling: A court's decision on a matter in a lawsuit, including a decision on a motion, a final ruling on a case, or a ruling on an appeal.

Separation of powers: American democracy divides the government into three branches with separate roles: legislative, which makes the laws; executive, which implements the laws; and judicial, which interprets and enforces the laws.

Settlement: A legally binding agreement between two parties in a lawsuit that resolves the dispute and ends the lawsuit.

Standing: Also known as standing to sue. To bring a case to trial, the party bringing the suit must prove to the court that they have a right to sue. In federal court, that means showing individual injury caused by the defendant and that the court can do something to at least partially remedy the injury.

State courts: State courts handle cases about their state laws and state constitutions.

Stay: A (usually temporary) pause in legal proceedings in a lawsuit.

Substantive due process: The constitutional principle that some rights (life, liberty, and property and other related fundamental rights such as the right to privacy) should be beyond the reach of governmental interference.

Testify: To give evidence under oath as part of a trial.

U.S. Supreme Court: The highest appeals court in the U.S. court system. The Supreme Court has nine justices, and their rulings become the law of the land.

Without prejudice: Indicates that a court's decision is neither final nor permanent and parties can file more motions. A case dismissed without prejudice can be refiled with problems corrected.

With prejudice: Indicates that a court's decision is final and permanent. A case dismissed with prejudice cannot be brought back to court.

DIG DEEPER, BE INSPIRED, GET INVOLVED

LEARN MORE ABOUT *JULIANA V. UNITED STATES*

Our Children's Trust
Get updates on *Juliana v. United States* and other youth-led climate lawsuits
www.ourchildrenstrust.org

Youth v Gov, a film by Christi Cooper (Vulcan Productions, 2020)
Documentary film follows the case from filing to the 2019 dismissal of the
case. Streaming on Netflix until April 2024
www.youthvgovfilm.com

No Ordinary Lawsuit
Podcast on the case available on iTunes.
www.noordinarylawsuit.org

*As the World Burns: The New Generation of Activists and the Landmark
Legal Fight Against Climate Change*, by Lee van der Voo (Timber Press, 2020)

LISTEN TO PLAINTIFFS' MUSIC

Miriam Oommen
Chicken Shit with Foraging and the Hedgehog String Band (2021)

Xiuhtezcatl Martinez
Generation Ryse with Earth Guardians (2014)
Break Free (2018)
Voice Runners with Tru (2020)
Runaway Tapes (2020)
XI XI with Jaiia Cerff (2021)

READ PLAINTIFF'S BOOKS

*We Rise: The Earth Guardians Guide to Building a Movement That Restores
the Planet* by Xiuhtezcatl Martinez (Rodale, 2017)
Imaginary Borders: Pocket Change Collective by Xiuhtezcatl Martinez
(Penguin Workshop, 2020)

GET INVOLVED: YOUTH CLIMATE ACTION GROUPS

Our Children's Trust
Join youth-led climate lawsuits in your state and learn about other ways to support these efforts
www.ourchildrenstrust.org/get-involved

Earth Guardians
Trains diverse young people to lead climate, environmental, and social justice movements.
www.earthguardians.org

Sunrise Movement
Youth in more than 400 hubs around the United States organize for a stable climate and good jobs.
www.sunrisemovement.org

Zero Hour
A diverse group of youth who lead climate actions with chapters all around the world.
www.thisiszerohour.org

Fridays for Future
Inspired by Greta Thunberg, this youth-led international organization leads climate strikes and other actions worldwide.
www.fridaysforfuture.org

Power Shift Network
A group of organizations working together to mobilize the collective power of young people to address climate change and ensure environmental justice for all people.
www.powershift.org

LEARN MORE ABOUT CLIMATE CHANGE

An Inconvenient Truth, a film by Davis Guggenheim (Paramount, 2006)

An Inconvenient Truth: The Planetary Emergency of Global Warming and What We Can Do About It by Al Gore (Rodale, 2006)

The Uninhabitable Earth: Life after Warming by David Wallace-Wells (Penguin, 2020)

They Knew: The U.S. Federal Government's Fifty-Year Role in Causing the Climate Crisis, by James Gustave Speth (MIT Press, 2021)
Gus Speth is an expert for the plaintiffs in *Juliana,* and this book is essentially the expert report he filed with the court.

Global Climate Change: Vital Signs of the Planet
NASA's website monitors where we are on climate change (current carbon parts per million, global temperature, sea-level rise) as well as how we got here, the impacts of climate change and possible solutions.
www.climate.nasa.gov

EPA's Climate Change Indicators in the United States.
Data on climate change gathered from 50 government sources.
www.epa.gov/climate-indicators

United Nations Climate Action
Extensive coverage of climate change news worldwide.
www.un.org/en/climatechange

United Nation's Intergovernmental Panel on Climate Change (IPCC)
Current and past scientific reports on climate change.
www.ipcc.ch

LEARN MORE ABOUT CLIMATE RECOVERY PLANS

350 PPM Pathways
Juliana expert witness James Williams and his team's plan for the U.S. reaching 350 ppm by 2100.
www.resources.unsdsn.org/350-ppm-pathways-for-the-united-states
www.ourchildrenstrust.org/350-ppm-pathways

100% Clean, Renewable Energy and Storage for Everything by Mark Z. Jacobson (Cambridge University Press, 2020)
A textbook on how to stabilize the climate using wind, water, and solar energy coupled with battery storage.

The Solutions Project
The nonprofit started by Jacobson, actor and activist Mark Ruffalo, and a financial executive to fund and publicize projects that move the world to 100 percent renewable energy.
www.thesolutionsproject.org

Drawdown: The Most Comprehensive Plan Ever Proposed to Reverse Global Warming, edited by Paul Hawken (Penguin, 2018)
New York Times–best-selling book that offers 100 solutions to the climate crisis.

Project Drawdown
The nonprofit behind the book offers a website with information on up-to-date solutions.
www.drawdown.org

WATCH INSPIRING YOUTH PLAINTIFF SPEECHES AND OTHER VIDEOS

Xiuhtezcatl Martinez addresses the U.N. General Assembly on Climate Change, June 29, 2015.
www.youtube.com/watch?v=27gtZ1oV4kw&ab_channel=UnitedNations

Kid Warrior, the Xiuhtezcatl Martinez Story
www.youtu.be/M_EK_9m1H88

"One Day," Our Children's Trust
A music video montage of the *Juliana* plaintiffs in action.
www.youtu.be/NaHDNTVMiek

"Juliana v. United States: Meet the Kids Suing Over Climate Change," *The Years Project*
www.youtu.be/sd5K1ms1tOc

"*Juliana v. United States:* The Climate Lawsuit," *60 Minutes Overtime,*
March 3, 2019.
www.youtu.be/Nm3EAPlT89I

"The Juliana Kids Use Legal Action to Fight Against Climate Change,"
NowThis
www.youtube.com/watch?v=AVPtbh_TwLU&ab_channel=NowThisNews

WATCH COURT HEARINGS AND YOUTH PRESS CONFERENCES

March 9, 2016
Video of press conference after first hearing with Magistrate Judge Coffin in Eugene, Oregon.
www.youtube.com/watch?v=GQPeaCGMpOM

December 11, 2017
Video of hearing at Ninth Circuit Court of Appeals in San Francisco.
www.youtu.be/j0aDihmHep0

READ YOUTH PLAINTIFF COURT DECLARATIONS

Jayden Foytlin
www.ourchildrenstrust.org/s/JaydenDeclaration.pdf

Aji Piper
www.ourchildrenstrust.org/s/DktEntry-21-8-Aji-Dec-ISO-Urgent-Motion-
for-Preliminary-Injunction.pdf

Journey Zephier
www.ourchildrenstrust.org/s/DktEntry-21-7-Journey-Dec-ISO-Urgent-
Motion-for-Preliminary-Injunction.pdf

Levi Draheim
www.ourchildrenstrust.org/s/DktEntry-21-5-Levi-Dec-ISO-Urgent-
Motion-for-Preliminary-Injunction.pdf

READ COURT DOCUMENTS

First amended complaint filed by youth in *Juliana v. United States.*
www.ourchildrenstrust.org/s/YouthAmendedComplaintAgainstUS-a9b4.pdf

Government's first motion to dismiss.
www.static1.squarespace.com/static/571d109b04426270152febe0/t/576195bd2f
e1316f09d2ef81/1466013119008/15.11.17.Fed+MTD+Memo.pdf

Judge Aiken's historic ruling denying motion to dismiss.
www.ourchildrenstrust.org/s/Order-MTDAiken.pdf

Youth motion for preliminary injunction on new fossil fuel projects.
www.ourchildrenstrust.org/s/DktEntry-21-1-Urgent-Motion-for-
Preliminary-Injunction.pdf

Ninth Circuit Court of Appeals dismisses case 2-1 with Judge Staton
dissenting.
www.ourchildrenstrust.org/s/20200117-JULIANA-OPINION.pdf

Youth's motion to amend original complaint.
www.static1.squarespace.com/static/571d109b04426270152febe0/t/611fc49c81
5ca70240c1f30e/1629471901242/Doc+462+Motion+for+Leave+to+Amend.pdf

More rulings and briefs can be found at Our Children's Trust:
www.ourchildrenstrust.org/court-orders-and-pleadings

TIMELINE

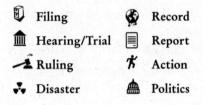

🗊 Filing   🌐 Record

🏛 Hearing/Trial   📄 Report

⚖ Ruling   🏃 Action

☢ Disaster   🏛 Politics

🗊 **May 4, 2011**
Our Children's Trust files first youth-led climate rights case *Alec L. v. Jackson*.

 June 5, 2014
D.C. Circuit Court of Appeals dismisses *Alec L. v Jackson/Alec L. v. McCarthy*.

🌐 **May 2015**
Alaska, where Nathan lives, has hottest May on record at 44.9 F, more than 7 degrees above average.

☢ **June–August 2015**
Five million acres—an area larger than Connecticut—burn in Alaska wildfire.

🗊 **August 12, 2015**
Our Children's Trust files *Juliana v. United States* in the U.S. District Court of Oregon.

☢ **August 15, 2015**
🌐 The Okanogan Complex Fire, which killed three firefighters, becomes the largest wildfire in Washington history. Aji suffers from the smoke.

🗊 **November 12, 2015**
Representatives of fossil fuel companies file motion to intervene, joining government as defendants in case.

🗊 **November 17, 2015**
U.S. government files motion to dismiss case in District Court of Oregon.

December 12, 2015
President Barack Obama joins the Paris Agreement for the United States to try to limit global warming to well below 2 degrees Celsius (3.6 degrees F).

 January 22–24, 2016
Crippling East Coast blizzard, affecting both Vic and Sophie, kills thirty-eight and breaks all-time snowfall records in Newark, NJ; Allentown and Harrisburg, PA; LaGuardia and JFK Airports, NY; and Baltimore, MD.

 March 9, 2016
In Eugene, District Court Magistrate Judge Thomas Coffin hears oral arguments on government defendants' motion to dismiss.

April 8, 2016
Judge Thomas Coffin recommends denial of the government's motions to dismiss.

 May 13–15, 2016
Break Free PNW camps on train tracks in Anacortes, Washington, to slow oil expansion. Miriam is arrested.

August 12, 2016
Catastrophic flooding in southern Louisiana kills thirteen people. Jayden's home and 146,000 more houses are damaged.

September 13, 2016
In Eugene, District Court Judge Ann Aiken hears oral arguments on defendants' motion to dismiss.

November 8, 2016
Donald Trump wins election for president.

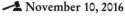 **November 10, 2016**
In historic ruling, Judge Ann Aiken upholds Judge Coffin's recommendation to deny motions to dismiss, stating, "I have no doubt that the right to a climate system capable of sustaining human life is fundamental . . ."

 January 13, 2017
Obama administration files seventy-page answer to the District Court of Oregon confirming many of the plaintiffs' allegations.

January 20, 2017
Donald Trump inaugurated.

March 7, 2017
Trump administration files for interlocutory appeal, asking Judge Aiken to allow them to appeal to the Ninth Circuit Court of Appeals and to stay proceedings.

April 29, 2017
People's Climate March in Washington, D.C, draws tens of thousands. *Juliana* plaintiffs speak.

May 1, 2017
Judge Coffin recommends denial of request for interlocutory appeal.

May 25, 2017
Fossil fuel intervenors file motion to withdraw from *Juliana v. United States*.

June 8, 2017
Judge Aiken agrees with Judge Coffin and denies request for interlocutory appeal.

June 9, 2017
Government files first request for writ of mandamus with the Ninth Circuit Court of Appeals.

August 30–September 12, 2017
Hurricane Irma kills 129 people and leaves millions without electricity or safe water. Levi evacuates.

October–November 2018
Ende Gelände protests block coal mining in Germany. Miriam participates in the civil action.

November 6–November 17, 2017
Parties to the Paris Agreement meet in Bonn, Germany. Miriam and Kelsey participate.

December 11, 2017
In San Francisco, Judges Sidney Thomas, Marsha Berzon, and Alex Kozinski of Ninth Circuit Court of Appeals hear oral arguments on the government's request for mandamus.

March 7, 2018
Ninth Circuit Court of Appeals denies government's first request for mandamus.

 April 12, 2018
Trial date set for October 29, 2018, in U.S District Court in Eugene, Judge Aiken presiding.

 May 9, 2018
Government files a motion in the District Court for protective order to shield it from requests for documents and a motion to stay the case.

 May 25, 2018
District Court Judge Coffin denies government's request for protective order and motion to stay.

 June 1, 2018
Government asks District Court Judge Aiken to review requests for protective order and motion to stay.

 June 29, 2018
District Court Judge Aiken denies requests for protective order and motion to stay.

 July 5, 2018
Government files second request for writ of mandamus with the Ninth District Court of Appeals.

 July 17, 2018
Government files for emergency stay of discovery with the United States Supreme Court.

 July 18, 2018
Judge Ann Aiken holds oral arguments on government motion of judgment on the pleadings and motion for summary judgment.

 July 20, 2018
Ninth Circuit Court denies second government request for mandamus.

 July 23, 2018
Youth plaintiffs reply to government's first petition to U.S. Supreme Court to stay case.

July 30, 2018
In Justice Anthony Kennedy's last ruling before retirement, U.S. Supreme Court denies government request to stay case.

August 2018
Swedish teenager Greta Thunberg begins School Strike for Climate by skipping school and sitting on the Swedish Parliament steps, kicking off Fridays for Future, a global movement.

October 5, 2018
Government files another motion in district court for emergency order to stay discovery.

October 8, 2018
Intergovernmental Panel on Climate Change (IPCC) releases report confirming that the Earth has warmed 1 degree Celsius since pre-industrial times.

October 12, 2018
Government files third writ of mandamus with the Ninth District Court of Appeals.

October 15, 2018
Judge Aiken rules on motion for judgment on the pleadings and summary of judgment. The case will go to trial, but without Trump as a defendant.

October 7–16, 2018
In the fourth-strongest storm ever to hit the U.S., Hurricane Michael, a Category 5, makes landfall in the Florida panhandle, killing more than sixteen people. Levi evacuates again. His school is destroyed.

October 18, 2018
Government applies to U.S. Supreme Court to stay case.

October 19, 2018
Chief Justice John Roberts of U.S. Supreme Court grants the government's request for temporary stay of the case.

October 22, 2018
Youth plaintiffs respond to request to stay case.

October 24, 2018

Judge Aiken cancels October 29 trial date while awaiting Supreme Court ruling.

 October 29, 2018

Plaintiffs lead rally at the Eugene courthouse on the canceled trial date. High school and college students from all over Oregon march in support.

 November 2, 2018

U.S. Supreme Court denies government request to stay case.

 November 21, 2018

Judge Aiken certifies case for interlocutory appeal with the Ninth Circuit Court of Appeals.

 November 23, 2018

Fourth National Climate Assessment catalogs impacts of rapid climate change.

 November 24, 2018

U.S.G.S. study shows surprising amount of fossil fuel production comes from federal lands.

 December 26, 2018

Ninth Circuit Court of Appeals denies government's third writ of mandamus.

December 26, 2018

Ninth Circuit Court of Appeals accepts government request for interlocutory appeal 2–1 with Judge Friedland dissenting.

 February 7, 2019

Youth file urgent motion for preliminary injunction on new fossil fuel projects to the Ninth Circuit Court of Appeals.

March 1, 2019

More than 30,000 youth sign amicus brief in support of *Juliana* plaintiffs.

June 4, 2019

Judges Mary Murguia, Andrew Hurwitz, and Josephine Staton of the Ninth Circuit Court of Appeals hear oral arguments in Portland on plaintiff's request for preliminary injunction and the government's interlocutory appeal. Rally follows.

August–September 2019
IPCC report says average global land temperatures have likely risen as much as 1.2 degrees Celsius (2.2 Fahrenheit).

September 20–27, 2019
In the largest protests of their kind in history, six million people around the world participate in marches protesting climate change.

November 4, 2019
Miriam and other activists from Portland Rising Tides protest the Trans Mountain Pipeline by preventing *Patagonia,* a ship carrying parts for the expansion, from docking.

January 17, 2020
Ninth Circuit Court of Appeals dismisses *Juliana v. United States* 2-1 with Judge Staton dissenting.

March 2020
Covid-19 shutdowns begin in the United States. In-person trials cease, and nonessential cases are put on the back burner.

September–October 2020
Historic wildfires ravage Oregon, pushing air quality to dangerous levels, destroying more than 4,000 homes and threatening Sahara, Isaac, Miko, Kelsey and Miriam.

November 4, 2020
Under President Trump's orders, the United States officially pulls out of the Paris Agreement.

November 7, 2020
Joe Biden wins presidential election

January 20, 2021
Joe Biden is sworn in as the 46th president of the United States

February 10, 2021
The full Ninth Circuit Court of Appeals declines to review the panel's dismissal.

February 19, 2021
The United States officially rejoins the Paris Agreement.

March 9, 2021

Plaintiffs file motion to amend the original complaint asking for declaratory relief.

 May 13, 2021

Judge Ann Aiken orders settlement discussions in *Juliana* case.

 June–July 2021

Oregon and Washington plaintiffs struggle through an extreme heat wave that sweeps through the Pacific Northwest, killing 580 people. July breaks the record for the hottest month on Earth.

🏛 **June 25, 2021**

Judge Aiken hears oral arguments by telephone on plaintiffs' request for a motion to amend the complaint.

☢ **July–October 2021**
💀 The Dixie Fire is the largest single fire in California history and the second-largest single fire in the history of the United States.

💀 **August 16, 2021**

For the first time ever, the government declares a water shortage in the Colorado River.

☢ **August 26–September 4, 2021**
💀 Hurricane Ida, tied as the strongest recorded cyclone on record to hit Louisiana, deluges the East Coast with rain, triggering the first-ever flash-flood warning in New York City. Newark, New Jersey, had its wettest day in history.

 November 1, 2021

Juliana plaintiffs end settlement talks with Biden administration.

🏛 **November 13, 2021**

Nations meeting in Glasgow to discuss Paris Agreement commit to reducing greenhouse gases by only 30 percent by 2030 and decide not to phase out coal. Pledges, which are not likely to be met, leave the world on track to warm 2.5 degrees Celsius (4.5 F).

⚖ **December 27, 2021**

Montana Supreme Court schedules trial for *Held v. State of Montana*. It will be the first youth-led constitutional climate rights trial in the United States.

January 2021–January 2022
Biden administration issues more than 3,500 drilling permits and puts a record number of acres—80 million—up for leasing to drill in the Gulf of Mexico.

February 28, 2022
IPCC report warns half of the human population will face life-threatening climate conditions by 2100.

August 16, 2022
President Biden signs a law projected to reduce carbon emission by 40 percent by 2030 but that also expands oil and gas drilling on public lands.

June 1, 2023
District Court Judge Ann Aiken rules that the 21 can amend their complaint to focus on declaratory judgment, putting *Juliana v. United States* back on a path to trial.

June 12–20, 2023
Montana Judge Kathy Seeley presides over *Held v. State of Montana*, the first youth-led climate rights trial in a courthouse in Helena, Montana.

Fall 2023 or Spring 2024
Hawaii Judge Jeffrey Crabtree presides over *Navahine F. v. Hawai'i Department of Transportation,* the second youth-led climate rights trial and the first to challenge a state's transportation system, in a courthouse in Honolulu.

Today
Juliana v. United States is still pending.

As a writer fascinated by unfolding stories that will likely go down in history, my research is a mix of distilling and quoting recent primary and secondary sources, conducting interviews with people about the recent past and their current thoughts, and observing and noting incidents as they happen.

To write this book, I relied heavily on the excellent reporting done for national and local news outlets. I also relied on videos, transcripts, and written opinions of court proceedings and rulings. In most cases, I worked from video recordings and materials received directly from courts or lawyers rather than published versions. In general, I have chosen short, nontechnical excerpts that illuminate important ideas or dynamics that took place. These are all credited in the notes below.

The bulk of the story of *Juliana v. United States* comes from interviews with five key youth plaintiffs and their lawyers about their recollections of what happened and how they felt about it. They reconstructed important moments for me, sharing details to the best of their ability. Where recollections differed, I did my best to focus on areas of agreement. Quotations from these unpublished interviews were lightly edited and fact-checked with interviewees for clarity and accuracy in April–July 2022. If a passage or quotation is not otherwise footnoted it comes from the following interviews:

Nathan Baring: May 19, 2021; March 6, 2022, June 2023

Sharon Baring, Nathan's mom: May 19, 2021

Levi Draheim: May 5, 2021, May 6, 2021

Leigh-Ann Draheim, Levi's mom: May 6, 2021

Philip Gregory: September 28, 2021; March 8, 2022; March 22, 2022

Julia Olson: November 17, 2020; September 21, 2021; March 26, 30, 2022; August 5, 2022, June 2023.

Miriam Oommen: June 28, 2021; July 1, 2021

Sahara Valentine: July 1, 2021; July 6, 2021; March 10, 2022

Isaac Vergun: April 8, 15, 16, 20, 2021

I reached out to government lawyers who worked on the case requesting interviews, with the following results:

Sean C. Duffy, trial attorney for U.S. Justice Department who represented both the Obama and Biden administrations in *Juliana v. United States,* refused a request for an interview. "*Juliana v. United States* [is] an active case and I do not have Department approval to comment on active cases," he wrote.

Jeffrey C. Clark, former President Trump's Assistant Attorney General of the Environment and Natural Resources Division who argued the case for the administration, could not be reached for comment. He has been subpoenaed by the U.S. House Select committee investigating the January 6 insurrection at the U.S. Capitol. The Senate Committee on the Judiciary found that Jeffrey Clark was involved in efforts to interrupt the peaceful transfer of presidential power.

Eric Grant, Deputy Assistant Attorney General in the Environment and Natural Resources Division of the U.S. Department of Justice under former president Trump, did not reply to requests for an interview.

As a result, the government's perspective comes from court filing and arguments made in court and the few comments reported in the media, which are noted below.

Source Notes

There is no better gift:
"Celebrating the Constitution: Chief Justice John G. Roberts tells *Scholastic News* why kids should care about the U.S. Constitution," *Scholastic News* 4, vol. 69, no. 2 (September 11, 2006): 5.

Industry lawyers on the case include: Quin Sorenson, Sidley Austin LLP; Roger Martella, Jr., Sidley Austin LLP; Benjamin Tannen, Sidley Austin LLP; Frank Volpe, Sidley Austin LLP; Marie Eckert, Miller Nash Graham & Dunn LLP; Suzanne Lacampagne, Miller Nash Graham & Dunn LLP.

U.S. Department of Justice lawyers on the case include: Eric Grant, Deputy Assistant Attorney General, U.S. Department of Justice, Environment & Natural Resources Division; Jeffrey Clark, Assistant Attorney General, U.S. Department of Justice, Environment & Natural Resources Division; Sean Duffy, U.S. Department of Justice, Environment & Natural Resources Division; Marissa Piropato, U.S. Department of Justice, Environment & Natural Resources Division; Clare Boronow, U.S. Department of Justice, Environment & Natural Resources Division; Frank Singer, U.S. Department of Justice, Environment & Natural Resources Division; Erika Norman, U.S. Department of Justice, Environment & Natural Resources Division; Andrew C. Mergen, U.S. Department of Justice, Environment & Natural Resources Division; Sommer H. Engels, U.S. Department of Justice, Environment & Natural Resources Division; Robert J. Lundman, U.S. Department of Justice, Environment & Natural Resources Division; Noel J. Francisco, Solicitor General, U.S. Department of Justice; Jeffrey H. Wood, Acting Assistant Attorney General, U.S. Department of Justice; Jeffrey B. Wall, Deputy Solicitor General, U.S. Department of Justice; Edwin S. Kneedler, Deputy Solicitor General, U.S. Department of Justice; Jonathan Y. Ellis, Assistant to the Solicitor General, U.S. Department of Justice; Christopher G. Michel, Assistant to the Solicitor General, U.S. Department of Justice.

PART I

Prologue

Unless otherwise noted, this material comes from the "Declaration of Jayden F. in Support of Plaintiffs' Opposition to Defendants' Motion to Dismiss," *Juliana v. United States*, September 7, 2016; *As the World Burns*; *Youth v Gov*; and from fact-checking with Jayden in spring 2022.

"Wake up!": Lee van der Voo, *As the World Burns: The next generation of activists and the landmark legal fight against climate change* (Portland, Oregon: Timber Press, 2020), 69.

"It's coming from": *Youth v Gov*, directed by Christi Cooper, (Barrelmaker and Vulcan Productions, 2020); www.netflix.com/title/81586492.

Oh my god: van der Voo, *As the World Burns*, 70.

"It's like a pool," Cooper, *Youth v Gov*.

More than 20 inches: Mary Elizabeth Griggs, "Why Is Louisiana Flooding So Badly, and How Can We Prepare for It Next Time?" *Popular Science*, August 19, 2016. In fact, gauges measured 21.86 to 31.39 inches falling in 48 hours.

thousand-year flood: Matthew Teague, "Louisiana left stunned by damage from '1,000-year' flood," *The Guardian*, August 16, 2016.

eight five-hundred-year floods and five more thousand-year floods: Dara Lind, "The '500-year' flood, explained," Vox, August 28, 2017.

Fearing electrocution: van der Voo, *As the World Burns*, 70.

In fact, as Jayden and the people: Bureau of Ocean Energy Management, "Gulf of Mexico Lease Sale Yields $18 Million In High Bids on 138,240 Acres in Western Planning Area," news release, August 24, 2016. The auction covered 24 million acres; Virginia is approximately 27 million acres.

1:
A Lawsuit Is Born

Unless otherwise noted, this material comes from author interviews with lawyers Julia Olson and Philip Gregory and Professor Mary Wood.

Why aren't we doing more: Ambar Espinoza, "Episode Two: Origin Stories," December 23, 2018, in *No Ordinary Lawsuit*, produced by Our Children's Trust, podcast, MP3 audio. Fact-checking with Julia Olson.

"It just hit me like a rock": Julia Olson, "Climate Change on Trial: An Earth Day Conversation with Julia Olson, Lead Attorney for Landmark Children's Climate Lawsuit," UCLA Law School lecture, November 27, 2020.

"There are moments": Author interview with lawyer Julia Olson and fact-checking.

"until we can have the federal government": Olson, "Climate Change on Trial."

2:
An Audacious Plan

This material comes from interviews with lawyers Julia Olson and Philip Gregory and Professor Mary Wood, from "Episode Two: Origin Stories," of the podcast *No Ordinary Lawsuit* and from the author's hike up Spencer Butte.

"We're going to file": van der Voo, *As the World Burns,* 140.

Kids Versus Global Warming: Robin Young, "16-year-old Sues Government Over Global Warming," Here & Now, NPR, June 21, 2011.

"There's this amazing girl": Olson, interview.

"Yes, I want to do that": Olson, interview.

17-year-old Akilah and other youth plaintiffs: Our Children's Trust, "Legal Proceedings in All 50 States," OurChildrensTrust.org, accessed April 2022; www.ourchildrenstrust.org/other-proceedings-in-all-50-states.

"I didn't just want": Olson, "Climate Change on Trial," 40:29.

"She looks you in the eye": Author interview with Phil Gregory, March 8, 2022.

3:
First Attempts

Unless otherwise noted, this material comes from interviews with Mary Wood and Julia Olson.

"In bringing: Amended Complaint for Declaratory Judgment and Equitable Relief, *Chernaik v. State of Oregon,* May 16, 2011.

Alec L. v. McCarthy: The case was first filed in federal court in California as *Alec L. v. Jackson.*

"Young people will be affected": Our Children's Trust, "Youth Sue the Government to Preserve the Future and Halt Climate Change," news release, May 4, 2011.

In federal court, in 2014: Judgment of United States Court of Appeals for the District of Columbia Circuit, *Alec L. v. McCarthy,* June 5, 2014.

The United States was responsible for a quarter: Hannah Ritchie, "Who has contributed most to global CO2 emissions?" *Our World Data,* October 1, 2019; Adam Aton, "Fossil Fuel Extraction on Public Lands Produces One Quarter of U.S. Emissions," *Scientific American,* November 27, 2018.

"In order to protect": Julia Olson, "Remarks for 2022 Katharine & George Alexander Prize Award Ceremony," Santa Clara University School of Law, Santa Clara, California, March 29, 2022.

4:
Life

Unless otherwise noted, this material and quotations comes from author interviews with youth plaintiff Sahara Valentine, July 1 and 6, 2021, and March 10, 2022, and from fact-checking with her.

"I want to be part": Olson, interview.

"I was so impressed": Olson, interview.

Pollen seasons: Harvard T.H. Chan School of Public Health, "Pollen seasons are getting longer, driven by climate change"; www.hsph.harvard.edu/news/hsph-in-the-news/pollen-seasons-are-getting-longer-driven-by-climate-change/.

Worse, more-frequent: Bill Gabbert, "Review of the 2015 wildfire season in the Northwest," *Wildfire Today,* February 14, 2016. In fact, the first half of 2015 was the warmest first six months of any year in Oregon and Washington since recordkeeping began in 1895 and 2015 was the worse fire season in history.

Avery rode: Ciara O'Rourke, "The 11-Year-Old Suing Trump Over Climate Change," *The Atlantic,* February 9, 2017.

5:
Liberty

Unless otherwise noted, this material comes from author interviews with youth plaintiff Nathan Baring and his mom, Sharon Baring, May 9, 2021.

"beautiful diversity of our country"; *"geography of America the beautiful":* Olson, remarks, Alexander Prize.

Alaska, he learned, was warming: Patricia Cochran, "Alaska," Third National Climate Assessment, May 6; 2014. www.nca2014.globalchange.gov/report/regions/alaska.

Ice that used: Known as the Ice–Albedo Feedback.

This rapid climate change: Cochran, Third Climate Assessment.

"If you have eyes": Julia Rosen, "Is it our constitutional right to live in a world safe from climate change?" *The Los Angeles Times,* June 3, 2019.

Permafrost in Alaska: Ronald P. Daanen, "Permafrost and Periglacial Hazards," Alaska Department of Natural Resources Geological and Geophysical Surveys; www.dggs.alaska.gov/hazards/permafrost.html#:~:text=Permafrost%20in%20Alaska,of%20the%20Arctic%20Coastal%20Plain.

40 percent of the world's permafrost: S.E. Chadburn, E.J. Burke et al., "An observation-based constraint on permafrost loss as a function of global warming," *Nature Climate Change* 7, 340-344 (2017).

At least a quarter of the state's jobs: Resource Development Council for Alaska, "Alaska's Oil & Gas Industry"; www.akrdc.org/oil-and-gas. Statistics from 2017–2020.

99 percent: Krishna Ramanujan, "More than 99.9% of studies agree: Humans caused climate change," *Cornell (University) Chronicle,* October 19, 2021.

6:
Life, Liberty, Property

Unless otherwise noted, this material and quotations comes from author interviews with youth plaintiff Levi Draheim and his mother Leigh-Ann Draheim, and "Declaration of Levi D. in Support of Plaintiffs' Urgent Motion Under Circuit Rule 27-3 (b) for Preliminary Injunction," *Juliana v. United States,* February 7, 2019.

he'd seen maps and *Would he ever be able:* Declaration of Levi D., map, 4–5.

"the barrier island" and *"I know that there is":* Declaration of Levi D., 15.

He mentioned that Our Children's Trust: Author interviews with Leigh-Ann Draheim, spring 2021.

"What happens if we lose?": Leigh-Ann Draheim, interview.

Julia explained . . . in a year: Leigh-Ann Draheim, interview; Olson, fact-check.

"absolutely the longest time ever": Author interviews with Levi Draheim, spring 2021.

"I wanted to be able": Levi Draheim, interviews.

"We're just a bunch of": Levi Draheim, interviews.

"We expected": Leigh-Ann Draheim, interviews.

7:
Oregon Youth Plaintiffs Meet

Unless otherwise noted, this material comes from author interviews and fact-checking with Isaac Vergun and the author's visit to the Friendly Street Market.

Julia originally wanted: Olson, interview.

whose five islands: COP23, "The Marshall Islands," www.cop23.com.fj/marshallislands/

Rising seas had already toppled: Curt Storlazzi, "The Impact of Sea-Level Rise and Climate Change on Department of Defense Installations on Atolls in the Pacific Ocean," U.S. Geological Survey RC-2334, February 2018.

"That'd be super devastating": Miko Vergun, Corvallis Climate Action Alliance's Healthy Planet = Healthy People Campaign, remarks, September 25, 2020.

African Americans suffered from: MaryAnn De Pietro, "What to know about asthma in African Americans," *Medical News Today,* March 29, 2021.

While an average of: Asthma and Allergy

Foundation of America, "Asthma Facts and Figures"; www.aafa.org/asthma-facts/. Accessed April 2022.

After all, people of color: Tracy Fernandez Rysavy and André Floyd, "People of Color Are on the Front Lines of the Climate Crisis," *Green American,* Spring 2016.

8:
Building A Case

Unless otherwise noted, this material comes from interviews with youth plaintiffs Isaac Vergun and Nathan Baring, lawyers Julia Olson and Phil Gregory, and First Amended Complaint for Declaratory and Injunctive Relief, *Juliana v. United States,* September 10, 2015.

"Good lawyers are good storytellers": Isaac Vergun recollection of Julia Olson's comments, fact-checked with Olson.

Sahara and Isaac had asthma to lengthening droughts and wildfire seasons: First Amended Complaint for Declaratory and Injunctive Relief, *Juliana v. United States,* September 10, 2015, 6–33.

"We all had to become experts": Author interview with Phil Gregory.

The team also had to present evidence: First Amended Complaint for Declaratory and Injunctive Relief, *Juliana v. United States,* September 10, 2015, 6-33.

The young people were particularly: Gregory, interview.

the level that science showed: Roberto Molar-Candanosa, "2015 State of the

Climate: Carbon Dioxide," climate. gov, August 2, 2016, and MN350, "The origins of 350 and the history of atmospheric CO2," MN350.org, accessed May 2022.

9:
Case Filed

Description of filing day comes from author interviews and fact-checking with youth plaintiff Isaac Vergun, a photo and video from the filing day, and the author's visit to the offices of Our Children's Trust and to the Wayne L. Morse Courthouse, both in Eugene, Oregon, February 11, 2022.

To electronically file the complaint: Aine Pennello, "Kids Sue President Obama over Climate Change," Shift by MSNBC, video, August 12, 2015.

"It passed over my head": Sahara Valentine, interview.

"Me being a super hyperactive kid": Levi Draheim, interview.

"I was like, 'Oh, shit": Nathan Baring, interview.

"provocative": Richard Frank, "And a Child Shall Sue Them: Ambitious New Climate Lawsuit Filed Against Obama Administration," Legal Planet, August 17, 2015.

"first-of-its-kind": Tony Dokoupil, "'Future generations' sue Obama administration over climate change," MSNBC, August 12, 2015.

"a landmark": Robert Hunziker, "Children Fight Governmental Climate Policies," CounterPunch, August 17, 2015; www.counterpunch.

org/2015/08/17/children-fight-governmental-climate-policies/.

"At first glance": Eric Holthaus, "Children Sue Over Climate Change," Slate.com., November 16, 2015.

"Whether this case gains": Holthaus, *"Children Sue."*

"I thought it was not only a little crazy": Lisa Heinzerling, "A Meditation on *Juliana v. United States,"* Environmental Law & Policy Program Lecture Series, University of Michigan Law School, Ann Arbor, Michigan, January 30, 2020.

a budget of $350,000: ProPublica, "Our Childrens (sic) Trust," *Nonprofit Explorer,* for fiscal year 2015; www. projects.propublica.org/nonprofits/ organizations/273094382.

10,000 lawyers and budget of $27 billion: U.S. Department of Justice, "U.S. Department of Justice Overview"; 4. www.justice.gov/about/ fy15-budget-and-performance.

"When you sue a government": Gregory, interview.

10:
Strange Bedfellows

Just weeks earlier and *"the biggest":* Coral Davenport and Gardiner Harris, "Obama to Unveil Tougher Environmental Plan with His Legacy in Mind," *New York Times,* August 2, 2015.

And he banned: Robert Rapier, "President Obama's Energy Report Card," *Forbes,* December 12, 2016.

who had received: Alex Glorioso, "Oil & Gas: Background," *OpenSecrets,* March 2016;

www.opensecrets.org/industries/background.php?cycle=2022&ind=E01.

"We've opened" and *"60 percent in the next":* Tim McDonnell, "Here's Every State of the Union Climate Promise Made by Obama," *The New Republic,* January 12, 2016.

By 2016: Sonali Prasad et al., "Obama's dirty secret: the fossil fuel projects the US littered around the world," *The Guardian,* December 1, 2016.

"In my opinion, this lawsuit": Exhibit A, Declaration of Dr. James E. Hansen in Support of Plaintiffs' Complaint for Declaratory and Injunctive Relief, *Juliana v. United States,* August 12, 2015.

"this lawsuit": John Schwartz, "Young People Are Suing the Trump Administration over Climate Change. She's Their Lawyer," *New York Times,* October 23, 2018.

People told Julia it was hopeless: Olson, "Climate Change on Trial."

three industry groups: The American Petroleum Institute, American Fuel and Petrochemical Manufacturers, and the National Association of Manufacturers.

"a direct threat" to *"of the economy":* Memorandum in Support of Motion to Intervene, *Juliana v. United States,* November 12, 2015, 3.

"It was really weird": Miko Vergun speech to Corvallis Climate Action Alliance's Heathy Planet = Healthy People Campaign, September 25, 2020, and fact-checking.

"I started realizing": Sharon Baring, interview.

Paris Agreement limitations: Robert Watson et al., "The Truth Behind the Paris Agreement Climate Pledges," Universal Ecological Fund, November 2019 and UNEP Copenhagen Climate Centre, "The Heat Is On," October 26, 2021.

Ban on crude oil: Kate Aronoff, "Obama's Climate Legacy and the Lie of Energy Independence," *The New Republic,* February 19, 2020.

"[We]'ll have": Coco McPherson, "Why Young Americans Are Suing Obama Over Climate Change," *Rolling Stone,* March 12, 2016.

"Cases like this,": Ciara O'Rouke, "Meet the Oregon Attorney Suing President Trump over Climate Change," *Portland Monthly,* August 14, 2017.

"The planet": John D. Sutter, "Meet the mom litigating the 'biggest case on the planet,'" CNN, September 13, 2016.

11:
Meet the Plaintiffs

Unless otherwise noted, this material comes from recollection of Nathan Baring, Levi Draheim, Leigh-Ann Draheim, Sahara Valentine, Isaac Vergun, and Miriam Oommen. Quotes attributed to them are from author interviews with them. The description of the courthouse comes from the plaintiffs' recollections and the author's visit there.

"I'm trusting" to *"I will never know":* Sharon Baring, interview.

"What if the other": van der Voo, *As the World Burns,* 83.

Julia scooted out to *"seen anything like it":* Olson, interview.

"All Eyes"; "The most important": Andrea Germanos, "All Eyes on Oregon Courtroom Where It's 'Small Children vs Big Oil,'" Common Dreams, March 9, 2016.

Avery, who was staying: John D. Sutter, "Climate kids take on the feds," CNN, March 9, 2016.

"[The kids] wore" to *"versus the feds":* Sutter, "Climate kids."

12:
All Rise

The material and quotations come from Kristi L. Anderson, Official Federal Reporter, "Reporter's Transcript of Proceedings, Eugene, Oregon, Wednesday, March 9, 2016," *Juliana v. United States,* March 9, 2016, 4–5, 7, 11–12, 18, 20–21, 31–32, 52–53, 66, 68, 75 and recollections of Nathan Baring, Levi Draheim, Sahara Valentine, Isaac Vergun, and Miriam Oommen. Quotes attributed to them are from author interviews with them. The description of the courthouse comes from the plaintiffs' recollection, the author's visit there, and photos of the judge and the courtroom.

There's often a moment to *all access to it*: Olson, interview.

"keep the courthouse": Olson, interview.

"People should be": Coco McPherson, "Why Young Americans Are Suing Obama Over Climate Change," *Rolling Stone,* March 12, 2016.

13:
The Court of Public Opinion

Unless otherwise noted, this material comes from a video of the press conference: 350Eugene, "Our Children's Trust Press Conference at Federal Court," video, March 9, 2016; www.youtube.com/watch?v=GQ-PeaCGMpOM&ab_channel=350Eugene.

"Federal Court Judge" to *"probability of success*: Matthew Berger and Dawn Reeves, "Judge Appears Skeptical of Youth Plaintiffs' Standing in Novel Climate Case," InsideEPA, March 9, 2016.

14:
Youth: 1, Government/Oil Companies: 0

About a month: Olson, interview.

"This decision marks"; "Judge Coffin": Our Children's Trust, "Federal Court Affirms Constitutional Rights of Kids and Denies Motions of Government and Fossil Fuel Industry in Youth's Landmark Climate Change Case," news release, April 8, 2016.

Xiuhtezcatl and Vic rowdy video: Our Children's Trust, "Youth Plaintiffs Respond to Federal Court Ruling in Their Favor," Wednesday, April 13, 2016; www.vimeo.com/162705977.

"unprecedented" to *"alleged harm":* Order and Findings & Recommendations, *Juliana v. United States,* April 8, 2016, 1, 5–6, 10, 11-12.

"global warming may": James Conca, "Federal Court Rules on Climate Change in Favor of Today's Children," *Forbes,* April 10, 2016,.

"Major Victory" to *"subsidize pollution":* John D. Sutter, "'Major Victory' for Kids Suing Obama," CNN, April 11, 2016.

15:
On the Other Side of the Law

Unless otherwise noted, this material and quotations comes from youth plaintiff Miriam Oommen's recollections shared in interviews with the author and Nick Turner, "Break Free: Student Protesters in Anacortes," *The Spectator,* May 18, 2016.

In May 2016, plaintiff Miriam Oommen opened an email: Author interviews with youth plaintiff Miriam Oommen and lawyer Julia Olson.

"There's a very important": Olson, interview.

16:
A Thousand-Year Flood

Unless otherwise noted, this material and all quotations come from "Declaration of Jayden F. in Support of Plaintiffs' Opposition to Defendants' Motion to Dismiss," *Juliana v. United States,* September 7, 2016, 2–7, 11; and interviews with Julia Olson.

"I was like": Valentine, interview.

she granted an interview to *"rest of you aren't crying":* Sutter, "Meet the mom."

17:
All Together Now

Unless otherwise noted, this material comes from the recollections of Nathan Baring, Levi Draheim, Leigh-Ann Draheim, Sahara Valentine, Isaac Vergun, Miriam Oommen and Julia Olson. Quotes attributed to them are from author interviews with them.

"A couple of quick reminders" to *"Aji!":* Cooper, *Youth v Gov.*

neurodivergent: van der Voo, *As the World Burns,* 51, and Olson, fact-checking.

I want to be free, lyrics by Ronny Hickel, reprinted with permission.

18:
Second Hearing

Unless otherwise noted, this material comes from the recollections of Nathan Baring, Levi Draheim, Leigh-Ann Draheim, Sahara Valentine, Isaac Vergun, Miriam Oommen and Julia Olson. Quotes attributed to them are from author interviews and fact-checking with them; and Kristi L. Anderson, "Reporter's Transcript of Proceedings," September 13, 2016, *Juliana v. United States,* 4–5, 8, 13, 27, 39–43, 50–51, 64, 80.

We slash and we burn: lyrics by Xiuhtezcatl Martinez, printed with permission.

"All right" and *"a bow tie":* Cooper, *Youth v Gov.*

Really? to *more drilling:* van der Voo, *As the World Burns,* p. 71 and fact-checking with Jayden.

"I don't want to see": John D. Sutter, "Saving the Planet for Future Generations," CNN, September 13, 2016.

At a press to *"a huge change":* Our Children's Trust: "Victoria [sic] - Our Children's Trust press conference following hearing before Judge Aiken," video, September 13, 2016; www.youtu.be/YTKbBjuwrTY.

19:
They Knew

This material comes from interviews with Phil Gregory; Lee van der Voo, *As the World Burns*, 143–145; Cooper, *Youth v Gov;* the author's review of photos of the presidential libraries; and First Amended Complaint for Declaratory and Injunctive Relief, *Juliana v. United States,* September 10, 2015, 51–52.

"Every president" to *"in over 20 years":* Steve Croft, "Lawsuit Could Put Climate Change on Trial," *60 Minutes Overtime,* March 3, 2019.

20:
Climate-Denier-in-Chief
Unless otherwise noted, this material comes from interviews with youth plaintiffs Isaac Vergun and Miriam Oommen.

Democrats fielded: David Roberts, "Hillary Clinton's Climate Policies Explained," Vox, July 29, 2016.

Trump who posted to *"fat dose of global warming":* Dylan Matthews, "Donald Trump has tweeted climate change skepticism 115 times. Here's all of it," Vox, June 1, 2017.

"Every president": O'Rouke, "Meet the Oregon."

21:
A Constitutional Right to a Stable Climate

Julia was grinning to *"ordered society . . ."* Cooper, *Youth v Gov.*

Julia was moved: Molodanof, "Hope is a Song," 221.

Avery and Sahara grabbed to *"long way to go":* Valentine, interview.

"Exercising" to *"nor progress":* Judge Ann Aiken, Opinion and Order, *Juliana v. United States,* September 10, 2016, 32.

Isaac's mom to *overjoyed ; "I felt like":* Vergun, interview.

That night to *cheering:* Levi Draheim, interview.

"After about ten": Nathan Baring, interview.

Time magazine reported: Justin Worland, "These Kids Are Suing the Federal Government to Demand Climate Action. They Just Won an Important Victory," *Time,* November 10, 2016.

"This is huge": Lauren Duca, "Kids Just Won the Right to Sue the Government over Global Warming," *Teen Vogue,* November 12, 2016.

"a remarkable opinion": Ted Scheinman, "Can a Surprise Lawsuit in Oregon Save American Climate Policy?" Pacific Standard, November 11, 2016.

"Unprecedented" to *"future generations":* Eric Holthaus, "The Kids Suing the Government Over Climate Change Are Our Best Hope Now," Slate.com, November 14, 2016.

"Most courts are:" Andrea Powell, "Meet the kids trying to put the government on trial for its climate policies," Pacific Standard, October 29, 2018.

"I think the fact": Chelsea Harvey, "Trump could face the 'biggest trial of the century'—over climate change," *Washington Post,* December 1, 2016.

"I will confess": Ann Carlson comments during Olson, "Climate Change on Trial."

PART II

22:
Obama Responds

"I'd very much like": Abby Rabinowitz, "The Plucky Millennials Racing to Save the World from Donald Trump," *The New Republic,* November 15, 2016.

So the lawyer approached: Gregory, interview.

"Settle this": Ted Scheinman, "Can a Surprise Lawsuit in Oregon Save American Climate Policy?" Pacific Standard, November 11, 2016.

Carbon dioxide emissions to *from 1850 to 2012:* John C. Cruden and Sean C. Duffy, "Federal Defendants Answer to the First Amended Complaint for Declaratory and Injunctive Relief (EFC No. 7)," *Juliana v. United States,* January 13, 2017, as quoted in Magistrate Judge Coffin, "Findings and Recommendations," *Juliana v. United States,* May 1, 2017.

"The Obama administration": Gregory, interview.

23:
The Changing of the Guard

Unless otherwise noted, this material comes from Kristi Anderson, "Reporter's Transcript of Proceedings, Eugene, Oregon, Tuesday, February 7, 2017," *Juliana v. United States,* February 7, 2017, 4, 7–8, 22, 29, 55–56.

removed all mentions and *systematically overturning:* Coral Davenport, "With

Trump in Charge, Climate Change References Purged from Website," *New York Times,* January 20, 2017.

Julia and her team to *government balked:* Gregory and Olson, interviews.

They turned up the heat to *on government policies and actions:* Gregory, interview.

ExxonMobil knew the risks: Natasha Geiling, "Fossil fuel groups try to flee landmark climate lawsuit before it goes to trial," ThinkProgress.org, May 26, 2017.

"a rare move": Abby Smith, "Kids' Lawsuit Over Climate Change Faces Big Test in Federal Court," Bloomberg Law, December 8, 2017.

24:
Three Plaintiffs Struggle

Unless otherwise noted, this material including quotes comes from Neela Banerkee, "Fighting Climate Change Can Be a Lonely Battle in Oil Country, Especially for a Kid," *Times-Picayune,* June 13, 2017.

Louisiana's largest industries: World Atlas, *"The Biggest Industries in Louisiana";* www.worldatlas.com/articles/the-biggest-industries-in-louisiana.html.

In the recent election: Ballotpedia, *"Presidential election in Louisiana, 201,";* www.ballotpedia.org/Presidential_election_in_Louisiana,_2016.

people gossiped about her: van der Voo, *As the World Burns,* 68.

"You're being brainwashed": van der Voo, *As the World Burns,* 71.

That spring, Miriam to nerve-wracking: Oommen, interview.

Levi's speeches: phone videos shared by Leigh-Ann Draheim.

25:
Marching Ahead

Unless otherwise noted, this material comes from Neela Banerkee, "Fighting Climate Change Can Be a Lonely Battle in Oil Country, Especially for a Kid," *Times-Picayune,* June 13, 2017.

Levi and Al Gore material: Phone videos shared by Leigh-Ann Draheim.

Isaac meets with Congress: Isaac Vergun, interview.

The march: Isaac and Levi Draheim, interviews.

"would put the cart" to *"micromanage":* Magistrate Judge Thomas Coffin, Findings & Recommendations, *Juliana v. United States,* May 1, 2017, 8–10, 15.

"Fossil Fuel Groups": Natasha Geiling, "Fossil Fuel Groups," ThinkProgress, May 26, 2017.

"We are confident": Joe Palazzolo, "Oil Lobbyists Ask to Leave Oregon Climate Change Suit," *The Wall Street Journal,* May 26, 2017.

"We didn't want them": Olson, interview.

"Defendants' motion" to *"DENIED":* Judge Ann Aiken, ORDER, *Juliana v. United States,* June 8, 2017, 4.

26:
Evacuate, Evacuate!

"It's actually a petition" to *"It's hard to express:* Our Children's Trust, "Year End Meeting," November 17, 2021.

The governor of Florida ordered: Jeremy Berke, "Nearly 7 million people told to evacuate in Florida and Georgia as Hurricane Irma approaches with 125-mph winds," Business Insider, September 9, 2017.

"We need to get" to *"It was a close call";* *"They had to realize":* Levi and Leigh-Ann Draheim, interviews.

Scientists strongly linked: Anne Sneed, "Was the Extreme 2017 Hurricane Season Driven by Climate Change?" *Scientific American,* October 26, 2017.

pay for four years: Stephen Leahy, "Hidden Costs of Climate Change Running Hundreds of Billions a Year," *National Geographic,* September 27, 2017; and Michael Schramm, "Bernie Sanders issues bill to make 4-year colleges tuition-free," *USA Today,* May 19, 2015; and The Universal Ecological Fund, "The Economic Case for Climate Action," September 2017.

27:
Desperate to Do More

Unless otherwise noted, this material comes from interviews with Miriam Oommen.

Birdsong lyrics by Miriam Oommen. Reprinted with permission.

"Peaceful, nonviolent," Olson, interview.

"vitally important": Cotchett Pitre & McCarthy LLP, "Ninth Circuit to Hear CPM Client's Oral Argument Regarding Climate Change in *Juliana v. United States,"* November 16, 2017.

28:

The Cost of Speaking Up

Unless otherwise noted, hearing material comes from "Transcript of Proceedings," *United States of America v. United States District Court of Oregon* and *Juliana,* et al., December 11, 2017, 3–5, 7, 14–19, 24, 30–33, 45–48 and interviews with Julia Olson, Isaac Vergun, Miriam Oommen, Nathan Baring, and author review of photographs of the courthouse.

Nathan had to choose to *"all this":* Baring, interview.

Other plaintiffs to *"be a lot":* Valentine, interview.

"The little climate case that could": Andrew Freeman, "Youth climate trial reaches federal appeals court, as judges signal it's going to trial," Mashable, December 11, 2017.

Juliana was now on a national—even international: Gregory, interview.

"To prepare for the oral argument" to *felt ready:* Olson, interview.

Julia wanted to *proceed as scheduled:* Gregory, interview.

"Prominent Appeals Court Judge": Matt Zapotosky, "Prominent appeals court judge accused of sexual misconduct," *Washington Post,* December 8, 2017.

"founded on the principles": Federalist Society, "Our Purpose," accessed October 12, 2021; www.fedsoc.org/ about-us.

When Judge Kozinski reached the door: Olson, interview.

But by now they were aware: Smith, "Kids' Lawsuit."

"If the government prevails": Joel Stronberg, *"Juliana v. US:* For Children of All Ages," Resilience.org, December 14, 2017.

The kids didn't know: Leigh-Ann Draheim, interview.

29:

A Dizzying Flurry of Motions

Unless otherwise noted, this material comes from interviews with Isaac Vergun and Nathan Baring.

"Oh my god, finally!": Climate Countdown, "Our Children's Trust Receives Decisions from Ninth Circuit," Video, March 7, 2018.

"Teenagers Defeat": Kartikay Mehrotra, "Teenagers Defeat Trump's Move to Kill Climate Change Lawsuit," Bloomberg, March 7, 2018.

The ruling of the three-judge panel to *"course of litigation":* Chief Judge Thomas, "Order," *United States of America v. United States District Court of Oregon* and *Juliana,* et al., March 7, 2018, 5, 9.

"pulled out all the stops": Julia Rosen, "Is it our constitutional right to live in a world safe from climate change?" *The Los Angeles Times,* June 3, 2019.

30:
The Highest Court in the Land

Unless otherwise noted, quotations come from interviews with Sahara Valentine, Isaac Vergun, and Miriam Oommen.

On July 17, 2018, as Julia was about to *"foot in the door with the Supreme Court":* Olson, interview.

A bit of a Supreme Court geek: Olson, "Climate Change on Trial."

Julia and her team suggested to *"nor progress":* "Response Brief of Respondents *Juliana*, et al., to Application for a Stay Pending Disposition by the United States Court of Appeals for the Ninth Circuit of a Petition for a Writ of Mandamus to the United States District Court for the District Court of Oregon and Any Further Proceedings in This Court and Request for an Administrative Stay," *Juliana v. United States*, July 23, 2018, 19.

"dead on arrival": Chelsea Harvey, "Trump could Face the 'biggest trial of the century'—over climate change," *Washington Post*, December 1, 2016.

31:
The Arc Is Long

"Julia backpacked" to *"October 29, 2018, still stood":* Olson, interview.

"Relieved, happy, excited": Valentine, interview.

"It boosted": Isaac Vergun, interview.

Julia couldn't deny: John Schwartz, "Young People Are Suing the Trump Administration over Climate Change.

She's Their Lawyer." *New York Times*, October 23, 2018.

Supreme court ruling language: U.S. Supreme Court, "Order in Pending Case United States, et al. v. USDC OR," July 30, 2018.

"The Supreme Court has shown": Lisa Heinzerling interview, March 2022.

32:
Preparing for Trial

Many trial scenes in movies: Lucy Lang, "Lawyer Breaks Down Courtroom Scenes from Film & TV," *Technique Critique*, Season One, Episode 7.

"Perhaps because the government": Gregory, interview.

"It was crunch time": Olson, "Climate Change on Trial Q&A."

The legal team to *tell their story in court*: Olson, interview.

"The most important rule": John Schwartz, "Young People Are Suing the Trump Administration over Climate Change. She's their Lawyer," *New York Times*, October 23, 2018.

"Look": Gregory, interview.

Sahara, just 13 to *they whispered*: Valentine, interview.

Greta Thunberg story: Jonathan Watts, "Greta Thunberg, schoolgirl climate change warrior: 'Some people can let things go. I can't,'" *The Guardian*, March 11, 2019.

A typical week: Gregory, interview.

"a tremendous amount of knowledge": Ambar Espinoza, "Episode Three:

Government Knew," February 14, 2019, in *No Ordinary Lawsuit,* produced by Our Children's Trust, podcast, MP3 audio.

The current level of dependence: "Declaration of Joseph E. Stiglitz, PhD, in Support of Plaintiffs' Urgent Motions Under Circuit Rule 27-3(b) for Preliminary Injunction," *Juliana v. United States,* February 7, 2019, 5 and "Urgent Motion," 6.

"Wow" to *They got very little sleep:* Olson, interview.

While the federal government: Cooper, *Youth v Gov.*

Julia, Phil and the rest to *And on and on:* Gregory, interview.

"I had a good impression": Kartikay Mehrotra, "Ambitious Climate Suit Pitting Teens Against Trump Faces Test," Bloomberg, December 11, 2017.

"We couldn't get the government" to *"snow measurements have you taken in Bend":* Gregory, interview.

"They asked Miko" to *harassment of the witnesses:* Cooper, *Youth v Gov.*

"The nature of the questioning" to *"judge their story":* Gregory, interview.

"It would be hard to imagine": Chelsea Harvey, "Trump could face the 'biggest trial of the century'—over climate change," *Washington Post,* December 1, 2016.

33:
The Home Front

"This redundant motion" to *"The fact that their":* Our Children's Trust Press Release, "Trump Administration's Desperation Grows as *Juliana v. United States* Trial Approaches," October 5, 2018.

not taken a direct hit: NOAA, "Hurricane Michael upgraded to a Category 5 at time of U.S. landfall," April 19, 2019.

While the family prepared: The United Nations Intergovernmental Panel on Climate Change, "Special Report: Global Warming to 1.5 degree C," October 8, 2018.

Draheim family experience of Hurricane Irma: Levi and Leigh-Ann Draheim, interviews.

"Climate change was feeling way more real": Isaac Vergun, interview.

A giant oak tree: Cooper, *Youth v Gov.*

Miko visit to Marshall Islands including quotations except as noted below: Aletta Brady, "Miko Vergun," Our Climate Voices, April 2, 2019.

"What happens when the water comes up?" to *"We die":* Horus Alas and Kaia Hubbard, "Tackling 'Eco-Anxiety' by Group Action," *U.S. News & World Report,* August 11, 2021.

"We're going to trial": Miko Vergun, "Keynote Address, Living Future Unconference," May 2, 2018.

34:
Countdown to Trial

Unless otherwise noted, this material comes from interviews with Isaac Vergun, Nathan Baring, Levi Draheim, Miriam Oommen, and Sahara Valentine.

Aji, from Seattle: "Declaration of Aji P. in Support of the Plaintiffs' Urgent

Motion under Circuit Rule 27-3(b) for Preliminary Injunction," February 7, 2019, 2.

"There's a fierce urgency": McKayla Haack, "Missoula community members take part in nationwide rally," NBC Montana, October 29, 2018.

"I can't comprehend that": Andrea Powell, "Meet the kids trying to put the government on trial for its climate policies," Pacific Standard, October 29, 2018.

"The most powerful": Our Children's Trust, "Trump Administration Attempts to Delay *Juliana v. United States* Trial by Pleading with the Ninth Circuit for the *Third* Time," news release, October 12, 2018.

Continued prepping to *"prepare our reply":* Gregory, interview.

"a light pause" to *reply brief early on Monday*: Olson and Gregory, interviews.

"Beyond the legal defects": Jeffrey H. Wood, "Keynote Speech 26th Fall Conference of the American Bar Association's Environment, Energy, and Resources Section, Remarks as Prepared for Delivery," October 19, 2018.

contributed more to global: Mengpin Ge, Johannes Friedrich and Thomas Damass, "6 Graphs Explain the World's Top 10 Emitters," World Resources Institute, November 25, 2014.

"Our world is burning": Garrett Epps, "The Government Is Trying to Silence 21 Kids Hurt by Climate Change," *The Atlantic,* October 24, 2018.

35:
VACATED

Unless otherwise noted, this material comes from interviews with Isaac Vergun, Nathan Baring, Levi Draheim, Leigh-Ann Draheim, Miriam Oommen, Sahara Valentine, and Julia Olson.

"Scheduling order": "Scheduling Order by Judge Ann L. Aiken U.S. District Court, District of Oregon, Notice of Electronic Filing, *Juliana v. United States of America,* et al., Case number 6:15-cv-01517-AA," October 24, 2018.

"The Trump administration" to *"fossil fuel energy system":* Ambar Espinoza, "Update #1: *Juliana v. United States* Case Halted on the Eve of Trial," October 23, 2018, in *No Ordinary Lawsuit,* produced by Our Children's Trust, podcast, MP3 audio.

"clumsy"; "fumbly and huffy": van der Voo, *As the World Burns,* 95.

36:
Rather Be in Court

Unless otherwise noted, this material comes from interviews with Isaac Vergun, Nathan Baring, Levi Draheim, Miriam Oommen, and Sahara Valentine.

Aji opened with: Cooper, *Youth v Gov.*

"These young plaintiffs" to *"do the right thing":* Ambar Espinoza, "Update #2: Their Day Outside Court," October 31, 2018, in *No Ordinary Lawsuit,* produced by Our Children's Trust, podcast, MP3 audio.

"I am a kid": John D. Sutter, "Feds are 'trying to silence' the kids suing the Trump administration over global warming," CNN, October 30, 2018.

"I have personally had to evacuate": Rachel McDonald, "Climate Kids Rally for a Trial at Eugene Federal Courthouse," KLCC, October 29, 2018.

"The wildfires around my farm": Espinoza, "Update #2."

"I still believe our justice system": Ambar Espinoza, "Episode Two: Origin Stories," December 23, 2018, in *No Ordinary Lawsuit,* produced by Our Children's Trust, podcast, MP3 audio.

"The power of the people" to *"our day in court":* Lorraine Chow, "Pending Youth Climate Case Inspires Nationwide Movement," EcoWatch, October 29, 2018.

37:
Too Little, Too Late

Unless otherwise noted, this material and quotations come from interviews with Levi Draheim, Miriam Oommen, Nathan Baring, Isaac Vergun, Sahara Valentine, Phil Gregory, and Julia Olson.

"I want to trust": Jacob Pinter, "Young Activists Can Sue Government Over Climate Change, Supreme Court Says," National Public Radio, November 3, 2018.

"The Supreme Court order": Jacob Pinter, "Young Activists Can Sue Government Over Climate Change, Supreme Court Says," National Public Radio, November 3, 2018.

"Just wondering": Ambar Espinoza, "Mini Episode: A Whirlwind Trip to the Nation's Media Capital," in *No Ordinary Lawsuit,* produced by Our Children's Trust, podcast, MP3 audio.

"I feel wiped": Ambar Espinoza, "Mini Episode: A Whirlwind Trip to the Nation's Media Capital," in *No Ordinary Lawsuit,* produced by Our Children's Trust, podcast, MP3 audio.

It lifted restrictions on drilling: National Geographic, "EXPLAINER: A running list of how President Trump is changing environmental policy," Accessed October 28, 2021; www.nationalgeographic.com/science/article/how-trump-is-changing-science-environment.

"We're all in a bus": Mark Kaufman, "Why the Trump administration is terrified of these children," Yahoo News, October 31, 2018.

"Bullied into": Heinzerling, *interview.*

"a dare" to *"You want the case":* van der Voo, *As the World Burns,* 161.

"presents growing challenges" to *"well-being":* Fourth National Climate Assessment, Volume II: Impacts, Risks, and Adaptation in the United States, November 23, 2018, 36, 48.

The U.S. Geological Survey found: M.D. Merrill, B.M. Sleeter, P.A. Freeman, J. Liu, P.D. Warwick, and B.C. Reed, "Federal lands greenhouse emissions and sequestration in the United States—Estimates for 2005–14: U.S. Geological Survey Scientific Investigations Report 2018–5131," 2018, 31 and Alex Thompson, "New federal report says public lands are a significant source of US greenhouse gas emissions," The Wilderness Society, November 24, 2018.

"I know we're in oil country" to *while he was in office:* Valerie Richardson,

"Obama Takes Credit for the U.S. Oil and Gas Boom," *The Washington Times,* November 28, 2018.

38:

This Has to STOP

Unless otherwise noted, this material comes from interviews with Phil Gregory, Sahara Valentine, and Nathan Baring.

Citing the federal government's to *"increasing [greenhouse gas] emissions":* "Urgent Motion Under Circuit Rule 27-3(b) for Preliminary Injunction," *Juliana v. United States,* February 7, 2019, 1–2 and "Declaration of Peter A. Erickson in Support of Plaintiffs' Urgent Motion Under Circuit Rule 27-3(B) for Preliminary Injunction," *Juliana v. United States,* February 7, 13–14.

"Plaintiffs made every": "Urgent Motion," 3.

"I think the aggressiveness": Joel Stronberg, *"Juliana v. US:* Plaintiffs Ask the Appeals Court to Enjoin the Federal Government," Resilience, February 13, 2019.

"Plaintiffs' request": Abby Smith, "Weighing Kids' Climate Lawsuit, Judges to Probe Courts' Role," Bloomberg Law, June 3, 2019.

"the United States is expanding oil": "Declaration of Peter A. Erickson in Support of Plaintiffs' Urgent Motion Under Circuit Rule 27-3(B) for Preliminary Injunction," *Juliana v. United States,* February 7, 2019, 11–12 and "Urgent Motion," 7.

"What we do today": "Declaration of Eric Rignot, PhD, in Support of Plaintiffs' Urgent Motion Under Circuit Rule 27-3(B) for Preliminary Injunction," *Juliana v. United States,* February 7, 2019, 6, 8 and "Urgent Motion," 10.

"Continuing U.S. emissions": "Urgent Motion," 19.

"I am so frustrated": "Declaration of Levi D. in Support of the Plaintiffs' Urgent Motion Under Circuit Rule 27-3(b) for Preliminary Injunction," *Juliana v. United States,* February 7, 2019, 6.

"This was a very hard": "Declaration of Levi D.," 14.

"If we had started" to *"We're not":* "Declaration of Aji P. in Support of Plaintiffs' Urgent Motion Under Circuit Rule 27-3(B) For Preliminary Injunction," *Juliana v. United States,* February 7, 2019, 2–6.

"Children are people": "Brief of Amicus Curiae Zero Hour on Behalf of Approximately 32,340 Children and Young People in Support of the Plaintiffs-Appellees," *Juliana v. United States,* March 1, 2019, 5.

"Due to climate change"; "I want to be able to live"; "As the ones": "Brief of Amicus Curiae Zero Hour," Appendix B, 19–20, 22, 32.

39:

Backlash

Once Julia learned to *work cut out for her:* Olson, interview.

"A lot of people": Olivia Molodanof and Jessica Durney, "Hope is a Song in a Weary Throat: An interview with Julia Olson," *Hastings Environmental*

Journal, Volume 24, No. 2, January 1, 2018.

The CBS program to *"is the law":* Steve Kroft, "The climate change lawsuit that could stop the U.S. government from supporting fossil fuels," CBS News/*60 Minutes,* March 3, 2019.

"Youth Climate Strike Sparks" to *"borderline abusive":* Valerie Richardson, "Youth Climate Strike sparks debate on use of students as props," *The Washington Times,* March 13, 2019.

"They're not listening" to *"get out of the way":* Xiuhtezcatl Martinez, *Amanpour and Company,* PBS, September 27, 2019.

"On Climate"; "Letting children lead": Paul H. Tice, "On Climate, the Kids Are All Wrong; And a band of ignorant brats shall lead them: Some things have hardly changed since 1212," *The Wall Street Journal,* March 12, 2019.

Social media criticism: Interviews with Isaac Vergun, Miriam Oommen, and Leigh-Ann Draheim.

"I just scream": van der Voo, *As the World Burns,* 218–219.

40:

Bigger Than Ever

Unless otherwise noted, this material comes from interviews with Isaac Vergun, Sahara Valentine, Levi Draheim, Leigh-Ann Draheim, Julia Olson, and Nathan Baring.

"A trio of federal": Smith, "Weighing Kids' Climate."

"In my heart": John Schwartz, "Judges

Give Both Sides a Grilling in Youth Climate Case Against the Government," *New York Times,* June 4, 2019.

"If the Constitution": Julia Rosen, "Is it our constitutional right to live in a world safe from climate change?" *The Los Angeles Times,* June 3, 2019.

Leonardo DiCaprio tweet: @ LeoDiCaprio, June 4, 2019; www.twitter.com/leodicaprio/ status/1135970089738616834.

"As the Juliana plaintiffs argue": Renee N. Salas, Wendy Jacobs, and Frederica Perera, "The Case of *Juliana v. U.S.*— Children and the Health Burdens of Climate Change," *New England Journal of Medicine,* May 30, 2019.

41:

"Do We Get to Act?"

This material comes from "Reporter's Transcript of Proceedings," *Juliana v. United States,* June 4, 2019, 6–8, 12, 15, 16, 18, 19, 27–30, 32–33, 36, 51; author's viewing of video of proceedings; and interviews with Julia Olson, Miriam Oommen, Isaac Vergun, Levi Draheim, and Sahara Valentine.

42:

Let the Youth Be Heard!

Unless otherwise noted, this material comes from interviews with Miriam Oommen, Leigh-Ann Draheim, Nathan Baring, Sahara Valentine, and author viewing of the rally.

"I think eventually": CBS/AP, "Does climate change violate children's right to life, liberty and property? A U.S.

court may decide," CBSnews.com, June 5, 2019.

"the only way they lose"; "I don't think": Smith, "Weighing Kids' Climate."

"The panel": Abby Smith, "Kids' Climate Claims 'Compelling' But Court Queries Own Role," Bloomberg Law, June 4, 2019.

"If they rule in favor": Geoff Dembicki, "Inside the Courtroom Where Teens Are Suing the Government Over the Climate Crisis," Vice, June 4, 2019.

"There's no real telling": Rosen, "Is it our constitutional right."

43:
Demanding Action

Hearing description and testimony: House Foreign Affairs Committee, "Voices Leading the Next Generation on the Global Climate Crisis," YouTube video, September 18, 2019.

"not considered safe" and *"poses significant risks to natural and human systems"*: IPCC, "Global Warming of 1.5 degrees C," Technical Summary, p. 44.

"I find myself" to *"in the streets"*: Our Children's Trust, "BREAKING: The press conference featuring Juliana plaintiffs and Greta Thunberg is underway at the U.S. Supreme Court," Facebook video, September 18, 2019.

As Nathan listened, Baring, interview.

44:
STRIKE!

South Eugene walkout: Valentine, interview.

For hours: Sarah Kaplan, Lauren Lumpkin, and Brady Dennis, "'We will make them hear us': Millions of youths around the world strike for action," Washington Post, September 20, 2019.

"You had a future"; "Our streets flood"; "Adults are like": Somini Sengupta, "Protesting Climate Change, Young People Take to Streets in Global Strike," New York Times, September 21, 2019.

Act as if: Scott Neuman and Bill Chappell, "Young People Lead Millions to Protest Global Inaction on Climate Change," NPR, September 20, 2019.

Size of strike: Eliza Barclay and Brian Resnick, "How big was the global climate strike?" Vox, September 22, 2019.

45:
No Other Choice

Unless otherwise noted, this material comes from interviews with Miriam Oommen.

"Part of why"; "Trump": Lee van der Voo, "Young climate activists chain selves to Washington pier amid pipeline delivery," The Guardian, November 5, 2019.

"I might actually": van der Voo, As the World Burns, 250.

46:
The Ninth Circuit Rules

Unless otherwise noted, this material comes from "Opinion, United States Court of Appeals for the Ninth District," Juliana v. United States, January 17, 2020, 11, 14, 15, 26, 31–34, 36, 43, 49, 64, and interviews with Nathan

Baring, Julia Olson, Sahara Valentine, Leigh-Ann Draheim, Miriam Oommen, and Levi Draheim.

"Court Quashes": John Schwartz, "Court Quashes Youth Climate Change Case Against Government," *New York Times,* January 17, 2020.

"Court Tosses": Peter Wade, "Court Tosses Landmark Climate Change Case Brought on Behalf of Youth," *Rolling Stone,* January 17, 2020.

"Appeals Court": Ryan J. Farrick, "Appeals Court Kills 'Climate Kids' Lawsuit," Legal Reader, January 17, 2020.

"Hey, everyone"; "I don't understand: Cooper, *Youth v Gov.*

Julia shared the plaintiffs' outrage: John D. Sutter, "Meet the mom litigating the 'biggest case on the planet," CNN, September 13, 2016.

"This is far from over"; "I know that": Brady Dennis, "Federal appeals court tosses landmark youth climate lawsuit against U.S. government," *Washington Post,* January 17, 2020.

"The idea that": John Schwartz, "Court Quashes Youth Climate Change Case Against Government," *New York Times,* January 17, 2020.

"This is a very serious blow": Gillian Flaccus, "US court dismisses suit by youths over climate change," Yahoo! News, January 17, 2020.

"For now"; "pleased with the outcome": John Schwartz, "Court Quashes Youth Climate Change Case Against Government," *New York Times,* January 17, 2020.

"I would hold": "Opinion, United States Court of Appeals," 64 and Cooper, *Youth v Gov.*

"If the situation"; "The courts are still coming": Madeleine Carlisle, "A Federal Court Threw Out a High-Profile Climate Lawsuit. Here's What It Might Mean for the Future of Climate Litigation," *Time,* January 19, 2020.

PART III

47:
Pandemic

Unless otherwise noted, this material comes from interviews with Sahara Valentine, Nathan Baring, Miriam Oommen, Isaac Vergun, and Levi Draheim.

A few days before to *went into lockdown*: Derrick Bryson Taylor, "A Timeline of the Coronavirus Pandemic," *New York Times,* March 17, 2021.

The world continued to warm: Chris Mooney and John Muyskens, "2°C: Beyond the Limit: Dangerous new hot zones are spreading around the world," *Washington Post,* September 11, 2019.

Seas that had already risen: Ocean Portal Team, "Sea-Level Rise," Smithsonian Ocean; www.ocean.si.edu/through-time/ancient-seas/sea-level-rise.

Megadroughts threatened: NASA, "NASA Study Finds Carbon Emissions Could Dramatically Increase Risk of U.S. Megadroughts," NASA, February 12, 2015.

Ninety-nine percent: Global Coral Reef Monitoring Network, *"Status of Coral Reefs of the World: 2020,"*

October 5, 2021; www.unep.org/ resources/status-coral-reefs-world-2020.

One third of Earth's: Cristian Román-Palacios and John J. Wiens, "Recent responses to climate change reveal the drivers of species extinction and survival," PNAS, February 10, 2020.

"I worry perpetually": Olson, "Climate Change on Trial."

In the previous to 4,000 houses: Zach Urness, "Oregon's 2020 wildfire season brought a new level of destruction. It could be just the beginning," *Salem Statesman Journal,* October 30, 2020.

"It's not hard for Democratic": Kate Aronoff, "Obama's Climate Legacy and the Lie of Energy Independence," *The New Republic,* February 19, 2020.

In fact, youth represented: John Ryan, "13 kids sue Washington state for life, liberty and a livable climate," KUOW/ NPR, February 20, 2018.

And at a time when the U.S.: Umair Irfan, "Democrats have made a puzzling decision to drop their demand to end fossil fuel subsidies," Vox, August 19, 2020.

48:
A New Administration

On the campaign trail: Juliet Eilperin and Dino Grandoni, "Biden vowed to ban new drilling on public lands. It won't be easy." *Washington Post,* November 19, 2020.

He bragged: Dino Grandoni, "The Energy 202: 'Look at my record, child,' Biden responds to environmental activist," *Washington Post,* October 29, 2019.

Trump falsely claimed: Michael Kranish, "New details emerge of Oval Office confrontation three days before Jan. 6," *Washington Post,* June 14, 2022.

Before leaving office, the Trump; "Biden vowed"; Eilperin and Grandoni.

On his first day: Jean Chemnick, "Here Are All the Climate Actions Biden Took on Day One," Scientific American's *E&E News,* January 21, 2021.

The year 2020 tied: Copernicus Climate Change Service, "2020 warmest year on record for Europe; globally, 2020 ties with 2016 for warmest year recorded," January 8, 2012.

Even with President Biden's: Juliet Eilperin and Annie Linskey, "How Biden aims to amp up the government's fight against climate change," *Washington Post,* November 11, 2020.

49:
What *Could* the Court Do?

"If I told my clients": Ellen M. Gilmer, "Young Climate Plaintiffs Seek Second Chance in Federal Court," Bloomberg Law, March 3, 2020.

"The general rule": Ellen M. Gilmer, "Youth Climate Plaintiffs Face Continued Legal Risks After Defeat," Bloomberg Law, January 23, 2020.

"This is the most conservative": Ellen M. Gilmer, "Young Climate Litigants Push High Court Fight Some Call Reckless," Bloomberg Law, February 11, 2021.

"I have an ethical obligation": Gilmer, "Young Climate Plaintiffs."

And Nathan worried: Baring, interview.

"It's really, really normal": Our Children's Trust, "Motion to Amend Recap Meeting," Zoom, July 1, 2021.

"the first step": Julia Olson, "Remarks for 2022 Katharine & George Alexander Prize Award Ceremony," Santa Clara University School of Law, March 29, 2022.

"It tells the": Olson, interview.

"As the Constitution directs": Nathan Baring, *"Juliana v. United States* still seeking its day in court," *Register-Guard*, March 11, 2021.

This case is "never say die": Steve Curwood, "Youth Plaintiffs Try Again," Living on Earth, May 28, 2021.

To Isaac to "end of everything": Isaac Vergun, interview.

50:
Settlement?

Miriam had to *"does anything"*: Oommen, interview.

"It's an incredible," Baring, interview.

They wanted a seat at the table: Gregory, interview.

"in the room where it happened": Lin-Manuel Miranda, "The Room Where It Happens," *Hamilton*, 2015.

Dan Farber: Sebastien Malo, "No Room for Novelty in Climate Kids and Biden Admin Negotiation Expert Say," Reuters, May 15, 2021.

51:
"What's It to You?"

Unless otherwise noted, this material comes from Eleanor G. Knapp,

"Reporter's Transcript of Proceedings Eugene, Oregon, Friday June 25, 2021," *Juliana v. United States,* June 25, 2021, 3–4, 6, 24, 28, 30, 33, 35, 38, 42, 47–50, 52.

As the date to *into her oral argument*: Gregory, interview.

"Dangerous temperatures": National Weather Service Alert, June 25, 2021.

With projected temperatures: Jason Samenow, "Pacific Northwest faces one of its most severe heat waves in history," *Washington Post*, June 24, 2021.

Indeed, much of the west to *"Long duration heat waves are DEADLY"*: Sarah Kaplan, "Record-setting heat blasts the West," *Washington Post,* June 17, 2021.

That's because: Camilo Mora, Chelsie W.W. Counsell, Coral R. Bielecki, Leo V. Louis, "Twenty-Seven Ways a Heat Wave Can Kill You," *Circulation: Cardiovascular Quality and Outcomes,* Volume 10, Issue 111, November 2017.

If the world continued to *could triple*: Sarah Kaplan, "Record Setting Heat Blasts the West," *Washington Post*, June 17, 2021.

The morning of the hearing to *dialed in*: Gregory, interview.

"Plaintiff must have": Justice Kavanaugh, "Opinion of the Court," 594 U.S. *Transunion LLC v. Ramirez*, June 25, 2021, 7.

The 21 completely: Valentine, interview.

They just continued to say: Our Children's Trust, "Motion to Amend Recap Meeting," Zoom, July 1, 2021.

The government continued to *people of the United States:* Olson, interview.

Georgetown law to *"could have done":* Heinzerling, interview.

52:

Things Heat Up

July broke: National Oceanic and Atmospheric Administration, "It's official: July was Earth's hottest month on record," NOAA, August 13, 2021.

The heat wave packed to *"life and death":* Sarah Kaplan, "Climate change has gotten deadly. It will get worse." *Washington Post,* July 3, 2021.

With water temperatures: Sarah Kaplan, "How climate change helped make Hurricane Ida one of Louisiana's worst," *Washington Post,* August 30, 2021.

"The schools are not open": Tim Craig, Ashley Cusick, Holly Bailey and Emmanuel Felton, "Southeast Louisiana residents desperate for food, power, water and help in Ida's aftermath," *Washington Post,* August 31, 2021.

As much as four inches: Jeff Halverson and Jason Samenow, "Here's what made the New York City flooding so devastating," *Washington Post,* September 2, 2021.

"It was terrible" to *"current threat":* David R. Baker, Shannon D. Harrington, and Skylar Woodhouse, "Hurricane Ida Aftermath Delivers Deadly Lesson on Climate Change," Bloomberg, September 2, 2021.

Parched forests erupted: David Simeral, "U.S. Drought Monitor, West," July 3, 2021.

Some wildfires were so large: Matthew Cappucci, "Extreme fire behavior has erupted in the West. Here's what that means." *Washington Post,* July 20, 2021.

"It's important for [everyone]": Paulina Firozi, Marisa Iati, and María Luisa Paúl, "Caldor Fire explodes, leveling parts of a California town and forcing thousands to evacuate," *Washington Post,* August 18, 2021.

For the first time ever: Karin Brulliard and Joshua Partlow, "First-ever water shortage declared on the Colorado River, triggering water cuts for some states in the West," *Washington Post,* August 16, 2021.

"Climate change has loaded": Sarah Kaplan, "Climate change has gotten deadly. It will get worse." *Washington Post,* July 3, 2021.

"Nearly 1 in 3 Americans": Sarah Kaplan and Andrew Ba Tran, "Nearly 1 in 3 Americans experienced a weather disaster this summer," *Washington Post,* September 4, 2021.

Without drastic: United Nations Framework Convention on Climate Change, "Conference of the Parties serving as the meeting of the Parties to the Paris Agreement, Third session, Glasgow, 31 October to 12 November 2021 Advance Report," September 17, 2021.

A child born in 2021 to *deadly heat waves*: Wim Thiery et al., "Intergenerational Inequities in Exposure to Climate Extremes," *Science,* September 2021, and Sarah Kaplan, "Today's kids will live through three times as many climate disasters as their grandparents, study said," *Washington Post,* September 26, 2021.

The grim reality: Kaplan, "Today's kids will."

As the nations negotiated to *Australia and Japan:* Kasha Patel, "During climate negotiations at COP26, extreme weather was rampant around the world," *Washington Post,* November 13, 2021.

"Try harder"; "The difference"; "Warming beyond": Brady Dennis and Sarah Kaplan, "At COP26, nations speed climate action but leave world still headed for dangerous warming," *Washington Post,* November 13, 2021

The final Glasgow Climate Pact to *wildlife and ecosystems:* Emma Ross-Thomas, "Does the Glasgow Pact Really Matter?" Bloomberg Green, November 13, 2021.

The United States, unwilling: Jennifer Hijazi, "U.N. Environment Rights Bolster Case for Global Climate Litigation," Bloomberg Law, October 19, 2021.

"After the first thing": Baring, interview.

"It was very obvious": Valentine, interview.

"While I am unable to share": Our Children's Trust, "No Settlement in *Juliana v. U.S.*," email to supporters, November 1, 2021.

53:
Two Years of Climate Chaos

"I urge President Biden": Our Children's Trust, "Sen. Merkley and Rep. Jones Lead Letters to President Biden and

165+ Orgs Join Letter to DOJ in Support of Children's Rights to a Safe Climate and *Juliana v. U.S.* plaintiffs," news release, November 18, 2021.

Towns from Pennsylvania to *in U.S. history:* Washington Post staff, "The record-breaking tornadoes that swept the United States, by the numbers," *Washington Post,* December 13, 2021.

In drought-plagued Colorado: Jason Samenow, Jacob Feuerstein, and Becky Bolinger, "How extreme climate conditions fueled unprecedented Colorado fire," *Washington Post,* December 31, 2021.

December also brought "icemageddon": David Hambling, "Why did Alaskan officials coin the term 'icemageddon'?" *The Guardian,* January 15, 2022, and Baring, interview.

Alaska Fish and Game: Ned Rozell, "Midwinter rain on snow is a game changer," University of Alaska Fairbanks news release, January 13, 2022.

"unprecedented": Jason Samenow, Jacob Feuerstein, and Becky Bolinger, "How extreme climate conditions fueled unprecedented Colorado fire," *Washington Post,* December 31, 2021.

"extraordinary": Zach Levitt and Bonnie Berkowitz, "Cold, heat, fires, hurricanes and tornadoes: The year in weather disasters," *Washington Post,* December 17, 2021.

"unsettling": Sarah Kaplan and Brady Dennis, "2021 brought a wave of extreme weather disasters. Scientists say worse lies ahead," *Washington Post,* December 17, 2021.

And they pointed: Sarah Kaplan and John Muyskens, "The past seven years have been the hottest in recorded history, new data shows," *Washington Post,* January 13, 2022.

In 2021, more than 90 to *in the United States alone:* Sarah Kaplan and Andrew Ba Tran, "More than 40 percent of Americans live in counties hit by climate disasters in 2021," *Washington Post,* January 5, 2022.

Meanwhile, the fossil fuel energy system kept pumping: Brady Dennis and Maxine Joselow, "U.S. emissions surged in 2021, putting the nation further off track from its climate targets," *Washington Post,* January 10, 2022.

Instead of ending leasing to *"oil and gas industry":* Anna Phillips, "Biden outpaces Trump in issuing drilling permits on public lands," *Washington Post,* January 27, 2022.

allocating a record: Ari Natter, "Here's What's in Democrats' $370 Billion Climate Spending Deal," Bloomberg, July 28, 2022.

the country warmed to *"most are at risk":* Brad Plummer and Raymond Zhong, "Draft Report Offers Starkest View Yet of U.S. Climate Threats," *New York Times,* November 8, 2022.

54:
Progress in the States

August 2022 marked to *"can't move fast enough":* Olson, interview

"ravages of climate change" to *"the judicial branch":* E.J Walters, "Dissent to Order," *Chernaik v. Brown,* Oregon Supreme Court, October 22, 2020, 181 and 177.

"The court should not" C.J. González, "Dissent to Order," *Aji P. v. State of Washington,* Supreme Court of Washington Order, October 6, 2021, 5.

"It might seem like a loss" ; *"Dissenting opinions":* Our Children's Trust, "Year End Meeting," Zoom, November 17, 2021.

Only one judge dissented: Plessy v. Ferguson, 163 U.S. 537 (1896).

"A growing body," Heinzerling, interview.

dramatically reversed himself: Olson and Baring interviews.

"The law requires,": Justice Peter Maassen, "Opinion," Supreme Court of the State of Alaska, *Sagoonick v. State of Alaska,* January 28, 2022, 68.

"Judges don't change": Baring, interview.

"a clean" ; *"present and future":* Article IX, Section 1, The Constitution of the State of Montana and Kathy Seely, District Court Judge, "Order on Motion to Dismiss," *Held v. State of Montana,* August 4, 2021.

"like seeing the end": Our Children's Trust, *"Held v. State of Montana,* Countdown to First Children's Climate Trial in U.S. History!," OCT webinar, February 7, 2022.

Then, on June 14 to *"in favor of young people":* Olson, interview.

55:
Green Light to Trial

"insanely busy" to *ten excited emojis:* Olson, interview.

"It is a foundational": Judge Ann Aiken, *Juliana v. United States,* Opinion and Order, June 1, 2023, 18.

This new focus to *Nathan, who had:* Baring and Olson, interviews.

"We are going to get to trial": Ambar Espinoza, "Mini Episode: A Whirlwind Trip to the Nation's Media Capital," in *No Ordinary Lawsuit,* produced by Our Children's Trust, podcast, MP3 audio.

"Declaratory relief": Heinzerling, interview.

"Hope is a choice": Baring, interview.

"In this work" to *changed everything:* Olson, interview.

56:
Inspired by *Juliana*

"massive"; "exemplar"; "leading edge"; "It brings up": Heinzerling, interview.

"When this chapter": Katie Eder, "This Tuesday a U.S. Federal Court May Decide the Fate of the Climate," Truthout, June 1, 2019.

Indeed, Juliana v. United States: Declaration of Julia A. Olson in Support of Answer of Real Parties in Interest to Petition for a Writ of Mandamus and Emergency Motion Under Circuit Rule, 27-3, November 19, 2018, 16a.

"This case is a shining example": Rick Reibstein, "Can Our Children Trust Us with Their Future," *American Bar Association,* accessed October 28, 2021.

"If the government would stop": Our Children's Trust, "Year End Meeting," Zoom, November 17, 2021.

"The Juliana case does": Ambar Espinoza, "Episode One: Against All Odds," November 16, 2018, in *No Ordinary Lawsuit,* produced by Our Children's Trust, podcast, MP3 audio.

Cases in Pakistan, India, Canada, and Mexico: Our Children's Trust, "Active Global Cases," accessed May 2022; www.ourchildrenstrust.org/active-global-cases.

"The idea behind": Molodanof, "Hope is a Song," 216–217.

"as a source of inspiration": Chelsea Harvey, "Trump could face the 'biggest trial of the century'—over climate change," *Washington Post,* December 1, 2016.

Cases in Australia, Germany, South Korea, and Colombia: Our Children's Trust, "Other Global Actions," accessed May 2022; www.ourchildrenstrust.org/other-global-actions.

Greta Thunberg and fifteen: Miranda Bryant, "Young climate activists vow to keep fighting despite UN setback," *The Guardian,* October 20, 2021, and Miranda Bryant, "Youth activists petition UN to declare 'systemwide climate emergency,'" *The Guardian,* November 10, 2012.

Six Portuguese youth: Umberto Bacchi, "Portuguese youth sue European states over 'life-threatening' climate change," Reuters, September 3, 2020.

"*Litigation will only increase*": Lisa Heinzerling, "A Meditation on *Juliana v. United States*," Environmental Law & Policy Program Lecture Series, University of Michigan Law School, Ann Arbor, Michigan, January 30, 2020.

"*I am a citizen*": Author's notes from video of court proceedings, *Held v. State of Montana*, June 12, 2023.

"*We made it*" to "*solving this crisis*": Ku'uwehi Hiraishi, "Hawaii teens lead second youth climate change trial in US history," Hawaii Public Radio, April 10, 2023.

"*anything that comes*"; "*what does the Constitution*": Baring, interview.

"*The state needs*": Baring, interview.

"*Even in the event*": Isaac Vergun, interview.

"*A big part*"; "*I'm just*": Valentine, interview.

"*Mom, all these people*": Olson, interview.

"*Young people are ready*": Bill Maher, *Real Time with Bill Maher*, "Interview with Xiuhtezcatl Martinez," YouTube, June 24, 2016.

"*Whether we win*": Skavlan, "Xiuhtezcatl Martinez interview:- Young People have power! Our voices are powerful I SVT/NRK/Skavlan," YouTube, November 20, 2016.

"*We are the ones inheriting*": Valentine, interview.

"*This work must be done*" to "*burn out of love*": Americans Who Tell the Truth, *Kelsey Juliana: Biography*.

THE SCIENCE OF CLIMATE CHANGE

The burning of: Julia Rosen, "The Science of Climate Change Explained: Facts, Evidence and Proof," *New York Times,* April 19, 2021.

But other gases: David Doniger, "Methane and HFCs: Milestones on the Pathway to Safer Climate," NRDC, September 27, 2017.

Some people confuse climate: NASA staff, "What's the difference between climate and weather?" NASA.gov, February 1, 2005.

The planet has already warmed: Rosen, "The Science."

The Intergovernmental Panel on Climate Change predicts: NASA staff, "The Effects of Climate Change," NASA.gov, accessed May 26, 2022; www.climate.nasa. gov/effects/#:~:text=The%20 Intergovernmental%20Panel%20on%20 Climate,Fahrenheit%20over%20the%20 next%20century.

The United States has historically: Simon Evans, "Analysis: Which countries are historically responsible for climate change?" Carbon Brief.org, October 5, 2021.

Global warming disrupts: NOAA staff, "Climate Zones," NOAA, accessed May 26, 2022; www.weather.gov/jetstream/climates.

In contrast: CLIMAS: Climate Assessment for the Southwest; www. climas.arizona.edu/sw-climate/ sw-temperature, accessed May 30, 2022.

Different types of extreme weather:

"Teacher-Friendly Guide to the Earth Science of the Northeastern US," *Paleontological Research Institution* and *National Science Foundation*, accessed May 26, 2022; www.geology.teacherfriendlyguide.org/index.php/81-southwestern/climate-sw/629-climate-present-sw.

The Plains and the upper Midwest: UCAR staff, "Blizzards," UCAR, accessed May 26, 2022. www.scied.ucar.edu/learning- ..zone/storms/blizzards#:~:text=In%20the%20United%20States%2C%20blizzards,Coast%20and%20the%20California%20coast.

Anyone living in the same place: UCAR staff, "Climate Change: Regional Impacts," *UCAR,* accessed May 26, 2022; www.scied.ucar.edu/learning-zone/climate-change-impacts/regional#:~:text=Changes%20in%20Earth's%20climate%20have,impacts%20on%20people%20and%20ecosystems.

GLOBAL IMPACTS

Unless otherwise noted, the global impact and regional disruptions material comes from NASA's climate change website, especially the section on the effects found at www.climate.nasa.gov/effects/.

Clausius-Clapeyron equation: Ashleigh Massam, "The Physics of Precipitation in a Warming Climate," JBArisk.com, April 16, 2020.

This not only makes wetter regions: Melissa Denchak and Jeff Turrentine, "Global Climate Change: What You Need to Know," NRDC, September 21, 2021.

Another danger is that water vapor: Alan Buis, "The Atmosphere: Keeping a Weather Eye on Earth's Climate Instabilities," NASA, October 30, 2019.

Rising Seas: Rebecca Lindsey, "Climate Change: Global Sea Level," climate.gov, April 19, 2022.

Oceans absorb: Denchak and Turrentine, "Global Climate Change"; www.nrdc.org/stories/global-climate-change-what-you-need-know#effects.

REGIONAL DISTRUPTIONS

The United States suffered: EPA, "Climate Change Indicators: Heat Waves"; www.epa.gov/climate-indicators/climate-change-indicators-heat-waves, accessed May 30, 2022.

Climate change also triggers: Hallie Golden, "The 'heat dome' explained: why the pacific north-west is experiencing record temperatures," *The Guardian,* June 29, 2021.

Some scientists attribute: Zach Levitt and Bonnie Berkowitz, "Cold, heat, fires, hurricanes and tornadoes: The year in weather disasters," *Washington Post,* December 17, 2021.

Oceans cover: Water Science School, "How Much Water is There on Earth?" USGS, November 13, 2019.

Attribution science has suggested: Henry Fountain, "Climate Change Is Making Hurricanes Stronger, Researchers Find," *New York Times,* May 18, 2020.

Because of climate change: Levitt and

Berkowitz, "Cold, heat, fires, hurricanes and tornadoes."

Humid air near the ground: National Geographic Staff, "Tornadoes, explained," *National Geographic,* August 28, 2019.

Megadroughts, lasting more: Ben Brumfield, "Risk of American 'megadroughts' for decades, NASA warns," CNN, March 4, 2015; www.cnn.com/2015/02/14/us/nasa-study-western-megadrought/index.html.

Lack of rain and snow: EPA staff, "Climate Change Indicators: Wildfires," EPA.gov, accessed May 26, 2022.

The average fire season: Winston Choi-Schagrin and Elena Shao, "Why Does the American West Have So Many Wildfires?" *New York Times,* August 1, 2022.

CASCADING IMPACTS

Changing regional climates: Laura Ferguson, "The Extinction Crisis," *Tufts Now,* May 21, 2019.

While some crops may benefit: Ellen Gray, "Global Climate Change Impact on Crops Expected Within 10 Years, NASA Study Finds," NASA.gov, November 2, 2021.

Insects flourish: Esther Ngumbi, "How changes in weather patterns could lead to more insect invasions," University of Illinois Department of Entomology, February 26, 2020.

The range of biting insects: Rob Jordan, "How does climate change affect disease?" *Stanford Earth Matters Magazine,* March 15, 2019.

Climate change causes and aggravates: AAFA staff, "Climate and Health," AAFA, accessed May 26, 2022; www.aafa.org/climate-and-health/.

Though wildfires may be: Kasha Patel, "Wildfire smoke harms more people in the Eastern U.S. than West, study shows," *Washington Post,* October 20, 2021.

As disasters and disease: Jeff Berardelli, "Climate change will bring multiple disasters at once, study finds," CBS News, November 19, 2018.

Tipping points: Renee Cho, "How Close Are We to Climate Tipping Points?" *State of the Planet: News from the Columbia Climate School,* November 11, 2021.

It's warming: Kimberly Nicholas, *Under the Sky We Make,* G.P. Putnam's Sons, 2021.

WE CAN FIX IT: A PLAN TO END CLIMATE CHANGE

Unless otherwise noted, this material comes from Ben Haley, Ryan Jones, Gabe Kwok, Jeremy Hargreaves, Jamil Farbes, and James H. Williams, "350 PPM Pathways for the United States: U.S. Deep Decarbonization Pathways Project," *Evolved Energy Research,* May 8, 2019.

For the last 800,000: Rebecca Lindsey, "Climate Change: Atmospheric Carbon Dioxide," Climate.gov, August 14, 2020.

"If humanity wishes to preserve": MN350 Staff, "Why 350?" MN350, accessed May 26, 2022; www.mn350.org/understanding350/.

"We can limit the risks": Our Children's Trust, "Groundbreaking Report Shows United States Can lead the Way Toward Climate Recovery Without Economic Hardship," Our Children's Trust Press Release, May 9, 2019.

"The amazing thing is": Olson, "Climate Change on Trial."

That is nothing compared: Norwich University Online, "The Cost of U.S. Wars Then and Now Infographic," Norwich University Online, October 20, 2020.

So Many Thanks

My deepest gratitude goes to the 21 youth plaintiffs for their important work. I am so, so sorry that you have had to devote so much of your young lives to fixing a problem not of your making. You have shaken me up and inspired me and so many others.

Special thanks to the five plaintiffs—Nathan Baring, Levi Draheim, Miriam Oommen, Sahara Valentine, and Isaac Vergun—who so generously shared their struggles, joys, and insights in many long and lively interviews. This book would not be possible without your generosity.

Julia Olson, you are a visionary, an intellectual powerhouse, and a kind and generous person. It has been an honor to write about your life's work and a beautiful thing to see the care with which you amplify the voices of young people. Thank you for making time while managing multiple major lawsuits to share your experiences and insights for this book. Many thanks, too, to Phil Gregory and Professor Mary Wood for helping me bring the behind-the-scenes to life. Speaking of behind the scenes, Erin Barnhart and Susan Carey have been incredibly helpful in facilitating interviews and with the massive fact-checking effort. Thank you so much!

I am deeply appreciative to Professor Lisa Heinzerling for sharing a thoughtful analysis of the case and for reviewing the manuscript for accuracy.

Huge thanks to young adult writing assistant Claire Alongi who shared this whole journey with me and buoyed me with her excitement, supported me with her research, and commented on multiple drafts. I also appreciate the background research done by Jennifer Ladwig and Kira Mesch and the astute comments offered by young adult readers Isabel Fogel and Natalie Swope.

I deeply appreciate the amazingly insightful and helpful critique offered by Chloe Ackerman, Eileen Bobek, Addie Boswell, Anne Broyles, Cathy Camper, Ruth Feldman, Robin Herrera, Heidi Kaufman, Barbara Kerley, Deb Miller Landau, Sara Ryan, Kaarin Smith, and Emily Whitman. Thanks to Amber Keyser for helping me find my way through the darkness of writing a climate crisis book and to Dani Swope for helping me get unstuck.

To editor extraordinaire, Virginia Duncan, thank you for your passion for this project and your wisdom in helping me shape it. Thank you to the whole Greenwillow and HarperCollins crew, including Tim Smith, Chris Fortunato, and Barbara Rounds-Smith for their thorough copyedit and proofread, and to Paul Zakris for the lovely design. I am so grateful to have such a supportive home for my work. To my agent Fiona Kenshole, thank you for your unbridled enthusiasm for this book and for all the ways you support my creative spirit.

Special shout-out to Izzi Rusch, who traveled to Eugene, Oregon, in 2016, at age 13, to support the young plaintiffs during their first hearing. Your excitement about the lawsuit planted the seed of this book. And finally, to my family, Craig, Cobi, and Izzi Rusch, and to all the Swopes for all the encouragement and joy. Our environment affects our lives, and you create the supportive environment that makes this work possible. Thank you.